The
Virtues
of the
Vicious

The
Virtues
of the
Vicious

 Jacob Riis,
Stephen Crane,
and the
Spectacle
of the Slum

KEITH GANDAL

New York • *Oxford*
Oxford University Press
1997

Oxford University Press

Oxford   New York
Athens   Auckland   Bangkok   Bogota   Bombay
Buenos Aires   Calcutta   Cape Town   Dar es Salaam
Delhi   Florence   Hong Kong   Istanbul   Karachi
Kuala Lumpur   Madras   Madrid   Melbourne
Mexico City   Nairobi   Paris   Singapore
Taipei   Tokyo   Toronto   Warsaw

and associated companies in
Berlin   Ibadan

Published by Oxford University Press, Inc.
198 Madison Avenue, New York, New York 10016

Oxford is a registered trademark of Oxford University Press

Library of Congress Cataloging-in-Publication Data
Gandal, Keith.
The virtues of the vicious : Jacob Riis, Stephen Crane and the
spectacle of the slum / by Keith Gandal.
p.   cm.
Includes bibliographical references and index.
ISBN 0-19-511063-3
1. Crane, Stephen, 1871–1900. Maggie, a girl of the streets.
2. Riis, Jacob A. (Jacob August), 1849–1914. How the other half
lives.   3. American prose literature—19th century—History and
criticism.   4. Didactic literature, American—History and criticism.
5. Riis, Jacob A. (Jacob August), 1849–1914—Influence.   6. Slums—
New York (State)—New York—Historiography.   7. City and town life
in literature.   8. Social ethics in literature.   9. Slums in
literature.   10. Spectacular, The.   I. Title.
PS1449.C85M334   1997
813'.4—DC20   96-44306

1   3   5   7   9   8   6   4   2
Printed in the United States of America
on acid-free paper

for
Genevieve, my wife

Acknowledgments

This book has been ten years in its genesis, and specifically for its first incarnation as my dissertation at Berkeley, I am indebted to Walter Benn Michaels and Tony Kaes who gave me dexterous intellectual guidance and to Scott Busby and Stephen Kotkin for their friendly readership. I am also grateful to Michel Foucault. Though he did not live to see a page of this, I recognize the impact that my time spent studying with him had on the conception of the project.

Long-term projects such as this one do not come to fruition without financial backing. I would like to thank the U.S. Department of Education, Amherst College, and the English Department at the University of California at Berkeley for fellowship support in the writing of the manuscript. I would also like to thank Mount Saint Mary's College for grant support in the revision of the book.

In regard to the realization of the final shape of *The Virtues of the Vicious*, I am grateful to my editor at Oxford University Press, T. Susan Chang, and to Peter Dorsey at Mount Saint Mary's for their expert editorial advice. Liz Maguire, Elda Rotor, and Rahul Mehta, also at Oxford, deserve my thanks for their help in bringing this book into existence. I would also like to thank Judy Ott for her administrative support and my wife Genevieve, not only for intangibles, which are indicated by the dedication, but for her very practical assistance with the design of the cover.

Acknowledgments can give the impression that a book was always an eventuality, but this book exists today partly because of the people who had faith in it. In this group, I would like to mention John Wilkins, whose consistent encouragement has been a marvel. I would also like to mention the members of the English Department of Mount Saint Mary's who have taken me into their community, in particular Robert Ducharme, William Heath, and William Craft.

In this regard of faith, and in a host of others, I would like most of all to thank Eric Sundquist, who saw this project through from the first inklings to its final form.

Contents

Introduction   3

Part I   The New Ethnography of the Slum

1   Riis and Charity Writing   27

2   Crane and Slum Fiction   39

Part II   Slum Spectacle

3   The Touristic Ethic and Photography   61

4   "In Search of Excitement":
The Ethics of Entertainment   74

Part III   Slum Psychology

5   Self-Esteem and the Tough   91

6   Psychological Moralities of the Slum   115

Afterword   130

Notes   139

References   193

Index   201

The

Virtues

of the

Vicious

Introduction

During the 1820s and 1830s, Joseph Tuckerman, a minister at large in Boston, wrote a series of reports on poverty; among his topics were the permanently poor of his city. In describing this group, he spoke of low wages and material destitution, but he also insisted on a distinction between "the impotent poor," "who are virtuous and estimable," and those "who are greatly debased and vicious." Of the first class, "some of them are truly virtuous; and all of them, in an important sense, are respectable. They have, perhaps, been inefficient, and not as provident as they should have been for a time of weakness, or of sickness, or of old age." The second class is made up of the "idle, intemperate, and improvident," "who are broken in constitution and health by the viciousness of their lives." They are "daily extending disease through their bodies, and corruption and misery through their minds, by the indulgence of their vitiated and lawless appetite for ardent spirits."[1]

Tuckerman went on to "illustrate" both types of permanent poverty with "examples." He talked about "sick" and "aged" people, and "a venerable woman, now in heaven . . . who for years had the sole care of a deranged daughter." He mentioned "beggars who employ every mode of imposture to obtain their objects," and "families which avail themselves even of the food that is obtained by begging to obtain the means of living in intoxication and riot and all possible debasement."[2]

Almost 150 years later, in 1977, after the famous New York City blackout that brought widespread looting, *Time* magazine attempted, in a cover story, to depict "the American Underclass": those "people who are seen to be stuck more or less

3

permanently at the bottom." In addition to giving an economic portrait of the ghettos, the article described the bulk of the people of the slums as "socially alien" and psychologically destitute. The members of the underclass "are victims and victimizers in the culture of the street hustle, the quick fix, the rip-off and, not least, violent crime. Their bleak environment nurtures values that are often radically at odds with those of the majority—even the majority of the poor." What distinguishes the American underclass, "this subculture," even from other poor populations "is the weakness of family structure, the presence of competing street values, and the lack of hope amidst affluence all around." "The underclass [is] a nucleus of psychological [as well as] material destitution," the article asserted. "Jobs, of course, are the most obvious need of the underclass—not only economically, but also psychologically and culturally. . . . [W]ork is more than a source of income. It is also a source of status and self-esteem." "A lot of youngsters, especially blacks, have a negative self-image," a social service expert was quoted as saying. "We try to make them believe in self-esteem and in getting a new and positive image of themselves."[3]

The *Time* article included quotations from ghetto dwellers: "[Y]ou're looking at a weird dude," says an "ex-junkie" turned "panhandler," and from a drug-dealing "mother of seven," we learn that in street jargon a dose of heroin is called a "spoon." The article was also peppered with numerous, mostly color photos, including pictures of "an elderly woman . . . atop a trash can," "a glue-sniffer," and "a jobless man . . . through a shattered tenement window."[4]

These accounts do not address the same material and economic conditions, and though they both take as their subject the permanent poor of the city, they do not describe populations of the same ethnic, racial, and behavioral makeup.[5] Nonetheless, they suggest dramatically different styles of representing the urban poor.

A century and a half ago we had the traditional moral version of poverty, with its careful distinctions between virtue and viciousness and its talk of character, appetites and temptation, corruption and degradation. This rendition of the poor has not disappeared, but it has been largely displaced by a language that uses anthropological and psychological terms. In our own time, there is, in regards to the slum, regularly talk of a separate culture, competing values, and low self-esteem, mixed in with Protestant moral notions of work, family structure, and hope.

These accounts differ as to what makes the poor person other: they disagree as to what the subjective experience of urban poverty is.[6] For Tuckerman, that experience is one of moral corruption and degradation; for *Time*, what makes the slum dweller other is his inculcation in separate values and his development of low self-esteem, as well as his alienation from traditional morals. The problem for Tuckerman is to inculcate morality in a group that has largely been deprived of that instruction; today the subjective problem is more complicated. The underclass must be weaned from its separate values and returned to the mainstream, as well as bolstered in self-esteem. Middle-class reformers have a moral *and* psychological agenda.

And this conceptual shift has been accompanied by a no less dramatic revolution in the modes of representing the poor: most obviously the introduction of photographs, but also the inclusion of the slang of the slums. This change is a matter of sensibility as much as technology. The pictorial representation of the slums cannot be reduced to the invention of the camera: the technological means existed for decades before slum snapshots appeared in a book in America (they appeared in an English publication almost twenty years earlier)[7] and, of course, charity writers could avail themselves of drawings (as did a landmark study that was published forty years after Tuckerman filed his reports.)[8] Tuckerman included numerous examples of particular poor people to illustrate his claims, but he apparently did not find it necessary or appropriate to illustrate his text with pictures of poor people or their own words. Where Tuckerman speaks abstractly of "intoxication" and "ardent spirits," *Time* talks in a concrete and colloquial manner about glue-sniffing and "spoons" of heroin. The *Time* article, with its visual and vernacular reporting, its color photos and linguistic snatches of local color, reflects an aesthetic and touristic interest in the urban poor as a spectacle that charity writers of 150 years earlier did not share—and would have found lurid and immoral.[9]

It is not surprising to us that our current vernacular and visual reporting on the slums would have been considered morally scandalous by charity writers of a century and a half ago. Though our society maintains the same basic morality, we are inclined to say, its strictures have been reasonably relaxed. We would likely say much the same about psychology. We tend to see psychology as gently opposed to traditional morality; historically speaking, we would say, it has been in the business of mitigating morality's harsh imperatives. Freud says it pretty clearly: psychoanalysis sets out to lower the ethical demands of the cultural superego.[10]

But in fact, psychology does something different from this as well. It does not simply lower ethical demands; it changes them. Psychology is not an amoral knowledge. The ethical demand of Protestant morality was (and is) to assert one's character or conscience against temptation and the onslaught of the passions. The ethical demand of today's psychology, in this particular case of the underclass, is to develop one's self-esteem or individuality despite the hostile constraints of one's environment. To focus the difference, consider that in traditional morality, the passions are to be controlled by will. Self-esteem, on the other hand, cannot be generated by will. (This is why the generation of self-esteem is such a tricky operation: according to the social service expert quoted in *Time*, it seems to involve the imagination, not the will.) The difference approaches a direct reversal: self-esteem—or at least "self-love" or "pride"—was traditionally one of the passions that needed to be regulated by will or conscience; today, our ethical problem is not to keep it in bounds but to nurture it.

Along the same lines, our new slumming aesthetic implies that there is nothing wrong with teasing other "passions," such as shock, horror, or curiosity. We want a life full of feeling, especially pleasure. This modern aesthetic also implies that there is nothing wrong with treating the poor as spectacles rather than with the traditional Christian brotherhood and moral severity. To put a premium on self-esteem, to enjoy photographs of drunkards or descriptions of heroin use: these imply a different ethical relation to others and to oneself.

The change from Tuckerman's reporting to today's—in both form and content—indicates and has been made possible by the rise of an alternative morality. Today we live in a culture with two moralities, one of which is not generally recognized as such. Its nonrecognition, in fact, is fundamental to its functioning. The relation between these moralities is by no means monolithic; it is manifold. At times they can reinforce each other, as in *Time*'s social prescription: according to the article, moral and psychological improvement will go hand in hand; with a job, the individual will at once become solvent, mentally healthier, and more responsible and family-oriented.

But these moralities are generally in tension, sometimes in open combat. *Time*'s neat equation of the moral and the psychological, in fact, involves some sleight of hand. In this "culture of the street hustle, the quick fix, the rip-off and . . . violent crime," are the "victimizers" psychologically destitute, along with the "victims"?[11] Though *Time* glosses over this issue,[12] plenty of other contemporary accounts indicate that the victimizers may have low morals but possess high self-esteem. A 1989 *San Francisco Chronicle* piece, for example, reports that "a lot of youngsters join a gang because . . . it helps their self-esteem."[13] What the oversight of the *Time* article indicates is that self-esteem—or psychological health—has the status of a value in our society. This idea is familiar. What is not so familiar is that self-esteem is a value that at times is at odds with those of traditional morality. For it is a value that we are eager to bring into the pantheon of traditional Protestant morals; we do not usually recognize it as possessing a separate ethical valence.

Moral Transformation in American Life
and the Representation of the Slum

Much has been written about the decline of morality in American life, and cultural historians and social commentators have generally traced its beginning to the rapid industrialization and urbanization of the last half of the nineteenth century. A traditional, disciplinary, morally based social order begins to break apart and is eventually supplanted by another sort of society. Our modern order has been alternatively characterized as consumerist, capitalist, bureaucratic, technocratic, corporate, narcissistic, and therapeutic, but our most respected and popular scholars agree that there is a moral void at the center of a society that relentlessly attends to our social, psychological, and economic ordering.[14] Jackson Lears, for instance, characterizes our present-day "therapeutic world view" as "self-absorbed nihilism" and a "nonmorality."[15] Certainly scholars have described various new ethics in American life as they discuss the decline of traditional morality: new sexual mores have replaced the old ethics of chastity and fidelity, a new consumer ethic of immediate gratification has undermined the work ethic, and so on.[16] But the general consensus seems to be that there has been a net loss in morality.

I find this characterization problematic, and the problem stems from the fact that these scholars take up only part of the subject of morality, only the tip of the iceberg. These authors describe changes first in actual behaviors and second in codes of conduct, but following Michel Foucault, one can say that morality involves a third aspect—an aspect which they seem to neglect and which perhaps leads them to construe "the void within," to borrow a phrase from Christopher Lasch.[17]

This third aspect to the history of morals is the relation one ought to have with oneself and others, beginning with the determination of what it is in oneself that is ethically important and ought to be attended to, what Foucault calls "the ethical substance."[18] In Protestant morality, that part of the self that was important was one's character and passions. If spiritual transcendence is rare in the modern consumer and therapeutic order and is only a small part of the contemporary discourse on the poor, it is because the new ethics does not call for this kind of relation to oneself, in which one transcends one's passions in favor of the spiritual. The valuable part of oneself has been redefined as something like individuality, feelings, or self-esteem, which need to be discovered and developed—despite social constraints.

My aim is to analyze the changes in the upper- and middle-class representation of the poor and to show within this literature, not an absolute decline in morality, but the decline of Protestant morality and the rise of an alternative ethics.[19] My field of operation will be very small. I will examine the documentary and imaginative literature of the slums at the end of the nineteenth century, the transitional period when it first seems to be taking on the features of its current forms. I will subsequently focus my attention on Jacob Riis and Stephen Crane, not because the same argument could not be developed by examining a wide range of writers but because they are well-known enough to be of intrinsic interest; because their styles are such that their representations remain interesting even at close reading; because both of their first books on the subject were shocking at the time and in some obvious and important ways unlike any other books that had come before; and because they represent two distinct discursive cases of the ethical transformation that I am attempting to describe.[20] I have chosen to focus on both a documentary and a fiction writer not because I will explore the relationship between their genres but, rather, because the exploration of each of these figures, usually examined primarily in the limited context of his own genre, sheds light on the other and changes, I think, our view of both.[21] And that both of my subjects are men is also no coincidence but, rather, as we shall see, a result of the masculine nature of the turn-of-the-century interest in the slums.

These new practices of slum representation began to come into their own about a hundred years ago, during the era of intense industrialization and urbanization as well as "the new immigration" which this technological revolution made possible: the great immigration from southern and southeastern Europe, which saw the largest number of newcomers to the United States in its history. New York City in 1890, for example, had a total population of 1,515,301, of which 43 percent was foreign-born and 1,219,218 were of foreign parentage.[22] In the course of the 1890s, the slum emerged as a spectacle in the popular arts of representation: the urban poor were discovered as a fresh topic by police reporters, novelists, photographers, true-crime writers, muckrakers, and social reformers, some of whom were expressly challenging traditional moral descriptions as well as moralistic analyses that attributed poverty to individual vice.

At the beginning of the decade, photojournalist Jacob Riis published dramatic snapshots of the New York slums in the first book in America on the subject to contain pictures.[23] Although *How the Other Half Lives* (1890) mostly focused on environmental causes of poverty and crime, it was also one of the first books to present ethnographic[24] and psychological details that challenged traditional moralistic accounts, to talk about the separate "ways" of slum dwellers—which were not necessarily immoral in their difference—and to speak of the importance of "individuality" or self-esteem in addition to "moral character" (in the reformation of the poor).

In the course of the decade, numerous documentary accounts and more than a score of novels or books of stories and sketches about slum life appeared. Probably the most dramatic renditions of its otherness were authored by Stephen Crane, who pushed both ethnographic and psychological analysis a good deal further than Riis. It was not only youthful bravado that led Crane to warn some of his readers in an inscription to his first novel, *Maggie: A Girl of the Streets* (1893), that they would be "greatly shocked by this book."[25] Crane's surprising representations of the slums, especially in *Maggie*, suggested social causes for individual vice and misery, but this is not what made the book a scandal. In addition, these representations of the slums included the profane local vernacular, demonstrated not only different customs but a radically different ethics in the Bowery, and indicated a human interiority that centered around something like "self-esteem" and had nothing at all to do with moral character.

Both Riis and Crane have reputations as crusaders for social justice and as fearlessly honest writers; they are credited with overturning harsh, moralistic conventions in the depiction of the poor and low life, coming to grips with uncomfortable realities, and contributing to a fundamental discovery of the Progressive Era, namely, the importance of environmental or social factors in individual behavior. Riis is generally seen to represent a kind of humanitarian moral position because he holds onto traditional values at the same time that he is sympathetic about the difficulties that poverty creates for meeting these ethical demands.[26] Meanwhile,

Crane is seen either as some sort of existentialist or ethicist (that is to say, a more realistic moralist, like Riis) or as a purely amoral realist or even a determinist—and a critic of morality in general.[27]

On closer analysis, however, none of these accounts are sufficient. Some of Riis's critics downplay the importance of "his racial and ethnic stereotypes" and his use of "picturesque detail"[28] and characterize his career as an enlightened moral and social crusade; this is pretty easy to do because Riis is famous for helping to bring about dramatic social reforms, such as slum clearances and building codes.[29] But Riis not only softens or humanizes traditional morality; he also represents a number of direct and scandalous, though often unwitting, challenges to it: with his shameless photographs and his dogged pursuit of exotic sights at the expense of both slum privacy and cleanliness, with his praise of pride and his shocking faith in the tough or gang member, with his rejection of disciplinary institutions such as the juvenile asylum, and with his advocacy of an aesthetic tenement architecture, he unknowingly asserts an alternative ethics.

Crane is doing likewise, but he knows what he is doing. He believes that the traditional moral concept of will is fantastical; on the other hand, he understands that amoral realism is equally impossible. One may be honest, but for Crane this does not mean one can report the facts; it only means that one can report one's vision of things: as he puts it, "a man is born into the world with his own pair of eyes and he is not at all responsible for his vision—he is merely responsible for his quality of personal honesty."[30] The simple fact is, Crane uses unmistakably moral language in his fiction and elsewhere—words such as "soul," "ethics," and "cowardice"—and not only ironically. We tend to imagine that he must be either some sort of streamlined moralist or else amoral; what other possibilities are there?[31] But there *is* a third possibility, and it is that he is partaking of an entirely other type of morality: a morality in which the ethical equipment and the ethical process are not the same as they are in traditional Protestant morality or, for that matter, in Christian or even classical ethics. For starters, Crane's work contains no concept of will, conscience, moral character, eternal soul, or reason as a higher faculty or supreme arbitrator. When Crane uses the word "soul" at certain points in *Maggie*, he is not referring to the Christian soul or the Protestant conscience or even the existentialist will. He means something else, something like deep feelings or emotion, intimate feelings about others and oneself, including self-esteem.

It is not that Riis challenges and supplements moral conceptions about the poor with psychological insights, while Crane tosses out morality in favor of psychology; it is not that Riis expects less of the poor morally, while Crane expects nothing at all. No doubt Riis expects less in the way of Protestant moral rectitude, but at the same time he asserts new moral expectations and imagines political strategies to help effect them. He wants to see the pride of the poor person preserved and nurtured (within bounds); he thinks that this is good and is in fact something the city should see to in its social institutions. Crane also seems to have

novel ethical expectations, expectations that are similar to Riis's. He faults the
Bowery for its "lack of ambition" or its willingness to "be knocked flat and accept
the licking";[32] his heroes, meanwhile, have managed to preserve a sense of self in
the face of a tyrannical environment, against which they are thus able to fight.

I am claiming, in short, that it is possible to read in Jacob Riis's *How the Other
Half Lives* and in Stephen Crane's *Maggie* the decline of the nineteenth-century
mental philosophy of "moral character" and the rise of a modern psychology of
"self-esteem," the decline of the nineteenth-century styles of sentimentalism and
moralism and the rise of a modern aesthetic of excitement or spectacle. Riis's
study and Crane's novel represent some of the first volleys fired in what Warren
Susman calls "one of the fundamental conflicts of twentieth-century America": a
"profound clash between different moral orders," "between two cultures—an
older culture, often loosely labeled Puritan-republican, producer-capitalist culture,
and a newly emerging culture of abundance" or consumption.[33]

The Slum and the Quest for Masculinity

The literature on the poor is a particularly ripe field for observing the development
of our modern, hybrid ethics because the issue of the poor was a traditional moral
hot spot for the middle class. The poor were a locus, a linchpin for middle-class
morals; the poor provided an ethical counterexample en masse, on a macroscopic
level. Not only were they instructive, and not only did they provide the foil for
middle-class moral identity; they were a field for intervention and domination in
the name of morality.

And beginning in the 1890s, I want to suggest, they started also to serve as a re-
source for the ethical revitalization of a middle-class culture that had begun to
doubt itself, its faith in automatic material progress, and its moral discourse—and
that had begun to react against its "stifling atmosphere of bourgeois materialism"[34]
and Victorian morality. Progressive social reform of the slums has rightly been
seen as a part of a general late-nineteenth-century activism in response to the political corruption and social ravages of a new industrial society.[35] But the outpour-
ing of interest in the slums in the 1890s was also part of a new and diverse quest for
intense experience in response to a perceived "feminization"[36] and "overcivilization"[37] of American life. It was part of a popular and national search for what John
Higham has called "fresh sources of energy" and "emotional kicks."[38] Theodore
Roosevelt is often seen to have articulated this anxious quest in a famous speech
of 1899 called "The Strenuous Life," in which he rejected "the soft spirit of the
cloistered life" and "the base spirit of gain" in favor of "a life of strife . . . and
hard and dangerous endeavor."[39] "We are well aware of the aggressive nationalism
that sprang up after 1890," Higham wrote in his well-known 1965 essay, "The Re-
orientation of American Culture in the 1890s," and he drew attention to what were
then often unnoticed but "analogous ferments in other spheres: a boom in sports

and recreation; a revitalized interest in untamed nature; a quickening of popular music; an unsettling of the condition of women."[40] To this list should be added a fascination with the slums.

Riis and Crane—and the interest in the raw experience of the slums—should be associated with the various movements of the 1880s and 1890s that Ann Douglas has classed together as an anti-Victorian and "militant crusade for masculinity"[41] and that Jackson Lears has recently identified as a pervasive antimodernist "recoil from an 'overcivilized' modern existence to more intense forms of physical or spiritual experience supposedly embodied in medieval or Oriental cultures."[42] The turn-of-the-century interest in the slums is of course partly an interest in social reform, but only partly.

Crane was never a moral or social reformer, and even Riis did not originally enter the slums for the purposes of reform. Crane began to frequent the Bowery as an adolescent because, as he told people, it was the only interesting place in New York.[43] Crane came from a family with a minister father and temperance-speaker mother, and from an early age, he found middle-class culture dull and oppressive and considered "American religion 'mildewed.'"[44] He was smoking cigarettes and drinking beer before the age of seven,[45] and later, as a young man, he dropped out of college and moved to the Bowery. The slums would turn out to be Crane's first stop in a short life of adventure-seeking that also took him out west, to Mexico, and to two wars (as a correspondent).

Crane's attitude toward settled, domestic life would always remain ambivalent at best, even after he set up his own markedly nontraditional home as an expatriate living in an English manor out of wedlock with a woman who had been the former owner of a nightclub in Florida. After only a year in England with the woman he referred to as his wife, he was anxious to get out and so excited to get to the new Spanish-American War that his friend Joseph Conrad noted that "HE WAS READY TO SWIM THE OCEAN."[46] In the same spirit, when the war ended, instead of returning home, he sneaked into Cuba and went into hiding. As J. C. Levenson commented, Crane "actually lived what his average countrymen collectively dreamed."[47]

His writing is also decidedly masculine and fiercely antisentimental. He dismissed the Victorian novels of his contemporaries as "pink valentines."[48] Crane became famous as the author of *The Red Badge of Courage* (1895) and is still, of course, best known as a war writer, and his Western fiction is arguably the third focus of his career:[49] as R. W. Stallman has observed, "his men are essentially men without women."[50] Moreover, a strong strain of misogyny infects in his prose. Crane was part of the beginning, as Van Wyck Brooks observed, of the cave-man propensity in modern American letters.[51]

Riis, meanwhile, entered Mulberry Street as a police reporter at what he "called the heroic age of police reporting,"[52] and it was his job to "gather . . . and handle . . . all the news that means trouble to some one: the murders, fires, suicides, robberies." What Riis initially found compelling about the slums is "the fact that [on the police beat] it is all a great human drama. . . . The reporter who is behind the scenes sees the tumult of the passions, and not rarely a human heroism that redeems the rest."[53] Riis's writing about the reform of the slums is often itself presented in the heroic mode: he has a book called *The Battle with the Slum* (originally titled *A Ten Years' War*), and his autobiography includes the story of his victorious attempt to get rid of the police lodging houses, in one of which, as a new immigrant, he is robbed and his dog killed.[54] His eventual popularity as a slum writer has much to do with the fact, as the *Indianapolis News* reported, that he "knew how to put scientific and sociological truths in such a way as to make one think he was reading romance. Jacob Riis's career was a romantic one, for he had the romantic temperament."[55] Roosevelt himself eulogized the Danish immigrant Riis as the "man who came nearest to being the ideal American citizen," and he specifically gave the social reformer his seal of manly approval with the claim that Riis's "goodness was free from the least taint of priggishness or self-righteousness";[56] he was not to be confused with the clergymen and female friendly visitors who had previously dominated urban reform work.[57]

Though most of Riis's career and oeuvre was focused on the slums, he sometimes ventured outside of them as an author, and it is his love of adventure and manly heroism that could be said to unify his entire body of writing.[58] His autobiography, *The Making of an American* (1901), presents his own immigration to America in unmistakably romantic terms: he leaves his native land and goes into exile because the father of the young woman he loves forbids her to marry a carpenter; he is determined to make something of himself and win her hand, and eventually he does. "So I went out into the world to seek my fortune," Riis writes, and "when next we met . . . , we knelt to be made man and wife."[59]

Riis's biography of his friend and hero Roosevelt is largely a celebration of masculine daring, and it covers not only Roosevelt's "courageous" stint as president of the Police Board of New York City, fighting political corruption (alongside Riis), but also his "manly" exploits as a hunter out west and of course as the leader of the Rough Riders on San Juan Hill.[60] Riis also wrote *Hero Tales of the Far North* (1910), a historical adventure book for children that likewise champions martial bravery. The first story is about "a knight errant of the sea who fought for the love of it as well as of the flag" and whose "enterprises were often of a hair-raising kind."[61]

It should be added that Riis's ethos of masculine adventure involved an appreciation, in his slum writing and elsewhere, of a male lustiness which friendly visitors and other guardians of Victorian decency would hardly have condoned—and which no doubt insured Riis against any priggishness. He takes obvious enjoyment in recounting street flirtations in *How the Other Half Lives*, as well as his knight errant's trick of mixing military reconnaissance with "girl-watching" in *Hero Tales*.[62]

Thus Crane and Riis participate, either personally or vicariously, in what might be identified as three major foci of the turn-of-the-century popular American movement for strenuousness: war, the West, and the slums. And with the addition of the slums to these older, now rediscovered zones of American manhood,[63] the panoply of supermasculine figures that included the soldier (and his new counterpart the war correspondent, which Crane helped to popularize), the cowboy, the hunter, and the Indian was augmented with the tireless (and never priggish or selfrighteous) social reformer, the dogged city reporter, the hard-living bohemian writer, and, as we shall see, the dubious figure of the ultraviolent tough as well.

It might well be said that our current psychological ethics could not have developed in the way that it has without this masculinist crisis of modernity and, in particular, this specific and complex confrontation and exchange between the middle class and the urban, largely immigrant poor. The mainstream reform of Riis as well as the bohemian rebellion of Crane can be seen, again like Lears's "antimodernism," as "complex blend[s] of accommodation and protest" of "new and secular cultural modes."[64] In the turn-of-the-century slums, Riis and Crane perceived not just vice that needed to be shunned and stamped out, as the middle class was used to thinking, but alternative customs and exotic sights that provided excitement and enjoyment—and also, especially in the case of Crane, a sort of moral inspiration. The slums had previously appeared to the middle class as an ethical morass that was short on moral character and needed to be kept at a distance and reformed. Riis and Crane unearth there a new territory for adventure which is exciting partly because it is dangerous and strange and partly because the slum presents a more advanced culture of consumption,[65] one whose vulgar styles of spectacle and speech these writers incorporate into their own. And they also discover in the slums a heterodox model of self-esteem—the violent, swaggering tough, with whom they are both deeply fascinated.

This new "psychological ethics" was not the creation of the poor that middleclass observers discovered in their slumming expeditions; nor was it an invention of the middle class that was then saddled on the poor in order to control them. The middle class found new ways to observe, perceive, and intervene in the lives of the urban poor, but these modes of observation, perception, and intervention were responses not only to middle-class worries about the slums but also to middle-class anxieties about itself. And not only did they transform the middle-class notion of the poor; they also helped to alter the middle-class conception of itself.

Catching "the Slum When off Its Guard"

Riis and Crane were able to reconceive the slums no doubt because they had new evidence about the poor that previous writers lacked:[66] but this new evidence in turn resulted from the new—and adventurous—tactics of observation and contacts with the poor that they undertook to establish. Clergymen and mostly female charity workers (or friendly visitors) generally made daylight visits and were out of the bad parts of town by nightfall; they also preserved the proper distance of authority and, at times, formality. Riis and Crane, emboldened by an ethos of adventure, dispensed with these restrictions, found new vantage points from which to view the slums, and cultivated unofficial contacts with the urban poor.[67]

The urban poor knew who their official observers were and knew how to play the charity, religion, and police games. In a "mission church" in *Maggie*, Crane imagines that "many of the sinners were impatient over the pictured depths of their degradation. They were waiting for soup-tickets."[68] But they know how to stand around patiently and reverently enough. A striking feature of the poor people in Charles Loring Brace's 1872 book, *The Dangerous Classes of New York*, is that nearly all of them speak his moral language; they attest to anxiety about their vices and so on, even when they seem to him very superficially concerned. Presumably, Brace has not put words in their mouths; rather, his subjects are very aware of who they are talking to. They suspect (to use the words of one of his street urchins) a "pious dodge"[69] and behave themselves accordingly.

Meanwhile, Riis and Crane did not merely snoop around after dark, Riis with a new dry-plate camera and flash that allowed him to photograph candid scenes, both indoors and at night (he did not need to set up lighting).[70] Riis's camera was a kind of passport to the interior of the slums; it was often more powerful at opening doors than the police were. He carried what must have been to many of the locals a curious and quasi-magical device; he found that people generally like to have their pictures taken, even criminals wanted by the police. As a photographer, he was not relating to the poor as a reformer, a clergyman, a charity worker, or a policeman, and they did not treat him as any of these. "Photography was a license to go wherever I wanted and do what I wanted to do," the photographer Dianne Arbus claimed,[71] and the same was true for Riis. Occasionally Riis was chased out of a neighborhood for "pok[ing] his nose" and his camera in the private business of the slum dwellers, but more often they were eager to have their picture taken:[72] a tramp gladly posed for Riis (for a quarter), and one gang of toughs went so far as to demonstrate, on camera, how they went about committing a robbery. The poor could relax, have fun, show off for Riis, whereas they would be guarded with a policeman or a charity worker, who had come to change their lives.

Crane perhaps did Riis one better in his insinuation into the life of the Lower East Side: he hung out in a bohemian community of art students and artists and eventually moved in. The poor became his neighbors, and at least in one case, recorded in his "Experiment in Misery" (1894), Crane did undercover work: he dressed up as a bum, spent a night in a flophouse, and ate at cheap dives. Both of these writers overstepped the old limits of slum observation.

And their new evidence amounted to dramatic anomalies in the old paradigm. For Riis, the old moral paradigm merely needed some adjustment, some cutting out here, some pasting in there; for Crane, the old paradigm needed to be tossed out and replaced.[73] In both cases, though, they were making new generalizations

"A Black-and-Tan Dive in 'Africa'" (*taken at night*) *from* How the Other Half Lives, *by Jacob Riis* (*photo courtesy of the Museum of the City of New York*)

from their evidence—with the help of the current psychology,[74] criminology, philosophy,[75] literature,[76] and all other intellectual concepts at their disposal.[77] They were not arriving at realities, though they certainly had a good deal more evidence: they were constructing new paradigms.

And given the evidence they came up with and the intellectual tools they had access to, it is no coincidence that they should come up with ideas that bear more than a family resemblance to each other—any more than it is a coincidence that they were both haunting the slums in the middle of the night, when writers never found it seemly or appropriate to do so before. To say that Riis was a newspaperman and Crane was a slummer and later a bohemian (and also an urban journalist) is only to begin to specify the conditions that allowed them to be doing what they were doing in the first place. The new sensational journalism of the mass-market dailies, the unprecedented fad for "slumming parties,"[78] the growing bohemian population in Manhattan, and thus in some way the fact that Riis and Crane felt they could frequent the slums, take pictures of toughs, and listen to their profane vernacular without endangering their immortal souls or at least earning the hatred of their middle-class peers: whichever of these one chooses to focus on, it is clear that a rather large breach in the old middle-class moral regime was opening up and that Riis and Crane were stepping into it—and tearing it further.

Consider the gap opened up by the bohemian community in New York. Already in 1858, the *New York Times* noted, with regret and trepidation, "that the tribe [of Bohemians] has become so numerous among us as to form a distinct and recognizable class." "It would be better to cultivate a familiarity with any kind of coarse and honest art, or any sort of regular employment," warned the paper, "than to become refined and artistic only to fall into the company of the Bohemians. . . . [T]he Bohemian cannot be called a useful member of society."[79] But he or she did not have to be very useful. Nineteenth-century patterns of urbanization, industrialization, and immigration had created a city sharply divided, geographically, between rich and poor; this meant middle-class fugitives from their own social stratum could live together in the slums rather cheaply. Crane lived one winter mostly on cheap potato salad purchased in a nearby grocery. Artists could afford to offend middle-class sensibilities—as Crane conscientiously did with *Maggie*—because they could afford not to sell their work.

Or consider the breach in traditional morals opened up by the large daily newspaper. Made possible by specific technological advances, including photography, and also by the urbanization and immigration that created a huge city audience, the daily developed new forms of reporting to attract a large share of the reading market. In essence, a general pursuit of the picturesque in the slums (not limited to crime reporting and political muckraking)[80] was institutionalized in the city newspaper in the course of the 1880s, and in the 1890s the large dailies responded to the craze for the strenuous life most obviously with the introduction of the modern sports page and a jingoistic reporting of the Spanish-American War:[81] and these innovations had much to do with turning journalism into a big business.

According to Alan Trachtenberg, the large daily newspapers developed a new conception of news itself: the notion of the "human interest" story. Joseph Pulitzer, who bought the New York *World* in 1883 and increased its worth thirty-fold in the next decade,[82] instructed his reporters to focus on "what is original, distinctive, dramatic, romantic . . . odd, apt to be talked about."[83] When an editor at another paper condemned the *World*'s new style as vulgar—morally suspect—Pulitzer replied, "I want to talk to a nation, not to a select committee."[84] Other newspapers soon followed Pulitzer's lead. And "the nether side of New York" or "the other half" was discovered and exploited as a particularly rich source of this sort of exotic news.[85] When Riis took a job with the New York *Tribune* and the Associated Press Bureau (and thus indirectly for the New York *World*, *Mail and Express*, and *Morning Journal*), he was taking on a new mission and a new perspective.[86]

It was the habit of picturesque journalism that pushed the eventual social investigator of *How the Other Half Lives* to explore and record things that previous charity writers considered irrelevant. His journalistic interest in sightseeing—developed as a police reporter—increased his purview of the slums. Previous charity workers had not, for instance, considered it necessary to stalk the tenements at three in the morning, as Riis does: he wanted to catch "the slum when off its guard."[87] It was the insertion of the "search for excitement" into the crusade for moral and social reform, the generalizing of the police reporter's jurisdiction to what might be called the "social beat," the mixed agenda of spectacle with charity and surveillance, that created Riis's urban tourism. Either way one looks at it, the crucial condition is that the newspaper was encouraging such a mixture of formerly separate activities.

This is not a book about aesthetics or ethics; rather, it is necessarily about both. The new styles of urban representation were themselves evidence of the ethical transformation they were helping to popularize; conversely, these aesthetics would be unthinkable without a shift in morals. Aesthetics had long been an ethical issue within a morality that was concerned with the control of the passions: high art or beauty appealed to the loftier intellectual faculties; low art catered to the passions. Of all discursive fields, that on the subject of the poor must be considered one of the most traditionally serious and solemn, if also sentimental. It was originally the domain of clergymen; the gravity of the subject matter required a correspondingly grave tone. The discourse was tightly laced, and there were basically three notes to hit: moral condemnation of vice, civic concern about order, and brotherly sympathy for physical deprivation. Riis and Crane often present the slums in a different, more exciting tenor: as a fascinating entertainment to be consumed. Riis's photographs and his depiction of exotic sights and strange habits would have been a scandal before the 1880s and the development of the large daily newspaper. Crane's inclusion of gutter language and alternative slum values still was.[88]

Scholarly Context

This book is an attempt to characterize the meaning of the written and photographic outburst about the slums at the turn of the century—through attention to both documentary and fiction and through an analysis of ethics. Late-nineteenth-century literary realism is today no longer interpreted as a neutral act of mimesis (in which the realist attempts to describe the social changes of industrialization and immigration) or a critical act of protest (in which the realist decries the drastic social conditions of urban capitalism).[89] Realism is now situated as a cultural practice within capitalism; it is seen to be complicit with the forces of both the newer consumer culture and the older Protestant, disciplinary society. As Amy Kaplan explains, "[R]ealism is now related primarily to the rise of *consumer culture* in the late nineteenth century, in which the process of commodification makes all forms of the quotidian perform in what Guy Debord has called the 'society of the spectacle.' . . . Realism is similarly related to the *culture of surveillance*, in which the realist participates in the panoptic forces which both control and produce the real world by seeing it without being seen in turn."[90] (The Panopticon is Jeremy Bentham's circular penitentiary, with a central observation tower that allows a guard to look into all the separate cells; Foucault discusses it as a model for what he calls discipline, in *Discipline and Punish* [1977].)[91] But there tends to be a problem with these newer accounts as well; they are too global or abstract. Kaplan reasonably objects that "by treating realism as an expression of consumer culture or a form of social incorporation, these studies tend to overlook the profound social disturbances that inform realistic narratives."[92]

One very important disturbance, I would add, is the very tension between "the rise of consumer culture" and "the culture of surveillence" or discipline.[93] Once these "cultures"—and the ethics that go along with them—are investigated at close range, it becomes clear that they are often dramatically incompatible. To put it briefly, the traditional middle-class strategies of discipline and surveillance are sometimes supplemented, but also sometimes undercut, by the new politics of spectacle and consumption. A fundamental discursive battle is being waged in realist literature, both in content and in style: it seems to me that Riis's work is wildly self-contradictory, morally schizophrenic, while Crane's work is a profound ethical assault on the morality that underlies disciplinary society. I do not want us to miss the trees for the forest: this book is interested in cultural or ethical conflict, in discursive breaks, in fault lines between practices of power, and I think the juxtaposition of the documentary writer and photographer Riis and the novelist Crane turns out to highlight these tensions, which are often missed.

Mark Seltzer, for example, seems to me reductive when he deduces the realist and naturalist novel from the general phenomenon of disciplinary society, calling this novel "one final institutionalization of the panoptic technology." Seltzer notes in *Henry James and the Art of Power* (1984) that the "realist and naturalist novel . . . appears on the scene at the same time that the disciplinary society takes power," and he finds that it "supplements the increasing 'disciplining' of modern Western society since the eighteenth century." The realist novel's omniscient narration, and its attention to vice, criminality, and deviation, Seltzer construes as a "covert policing action" and as an "aesthetic duplication and formalizing of social practices of normalization."[94] Specifically in regard to Riis and Crane, Seltzer finds in "Statistical Persons" (1987) that their

> realist project of making visible is perfectly in line with the techniques of a certain social disciplining—the opening up of the everyday ordinariness of every body to, and the fabrication of individuals under, the perfect eye of something like the police. . . . [T]he realist vision of the urban underworld involves a disciplinary relation between seeing (seeing and being seen) and the exercising of power. The realist investment in seeing entails a policing of the real.[95]

Following this sort of reasoning, Crane's slum tales and Riis's *How the Other Half Lives* might indeed be construed as model panoptic texts. After all, it might be asked, doesn't Crane, in "An Experiment in Misery," infiltrate the pauper population in disguise, gain the trust of his subjects, and thereby discover undercover methods of surveillance? And aren't his character sketches of Bowery toughs, gang members, and beggars similar to police accounts of the same? Likewise, it might be asked, doesn't Riis engage in a virtual around-the-clock oversight of the immigrant population (sometimes taking to the streets with his flash camera in the middle of the night to catch people off guard)? Isn't his camera the equivalent of a mobile observation tower, and aren't his photographs—of toughs, of illicit beer dives, of tenement sweatshops—somewhat akin to police mug shots? Is it any co-incidence that Riis called his first flash photography excursion a "raiding party," that his initial team of assistants included a Health Department Bureau official, that he was occasionally accompanied on his later photographic outings by a po-liceman,[96] and that a couple of the photographs in *How the Other Half Lives* are from a "Rogues' Gallery"?

But to this kind of suggestion, it might first of all be countered that not all gazes are alike. Crane does not stop any criminals, and Riis, who is much more often without than with a police escort, does not arrest any wrongdoers—except the ten-ement itself. Crane's "assassin" in "An Experiment in Misery" presumably goes off to beg his way to another dinner and another night in a lodging house. And two toughs of the Montgomery Guards (see front cover) go straight from a camera session with Riis to robbing a Jewish peddler and trying to saw off his head, "just for fun."[97] There are almost no limits to Crane's and Riis's viewing of the New York slums, but this does not mean that they establish a panoptic technology. A panoptic or disciplinary technology involves two elements besides surveillance: a strict regime of rules of movement and punishments for their smallest violation.

Crane and Riis do not stop deviants; on the contrary, their reporting and story-telling is quite likely to encourage them. As Riis himself admits, "[T]he newspa-pers tickle [the vanity of the tough] by recording the exploits of his gang with em-bellishments that fall in exactly with his tastes."[98] And if Riis is able to photograph toughs and to get them to confess their tricks, it is not because he threatens them with police force but because he offers them the possibility of a notoriety—and a confirmation—they seek. The Montgomery Guards "were not old and wary enough to be shy of the photographer, whose acquaintance they usually first make in the handcuffs and the grip of the policeman; or their vanity overcame their cau-tion. It is entirely in keeping with the tough's character that he should love of all things to pose before a photographer."[99] Here Riis is not exactly the tough's war-den but, rather, his ally. This gaze does not supervise; it flatters.[100]

Seltzer's mistake, it seems to me, is to try to deduce realism and naturalism from a phenomena that is not adequately global at the turn of the twentieth century: "disciplinary society" is being challenged and transformed by certain aspects of consumer capitalism, new forms of power that are not disciplinary but might be called "spectacular."[101]

Similarly, I would take issue with Maren Stange's interesting account of Riis in *Symbols of Ideal Life* (1989) because it classes his traditional moral reform and his tourism under the same category of "middle-class privilege": "Simultaneously titillating his audience with photographic versions of conventional urban subjects and exhorting them to take up tenement reform as a basis for class solidarity, Riis affirmed middle-class privilege, associating the images he showed with both entertainment and ideology." Stange construes Riis's moralizing and his entertaining as two harmonious expressions of the same middle-class privilege; what she misses is the tension, what I call the ethical conflict, between these two: the way Riis's touristic interest often undercuts and undermines his conventional "moral strictures" and asserts a new ethical relation to the poor.[102]

David Leviatin, in his "Framing the Poor" (1996), likewise stresses the continuities between Riis's approach to the slums and that of his moralistic predecessors: "Looking at the misfortune of others—even the picturesque and romantic images of the 1870s and 1880s that preceded and competed with Riis's more realistic view—helped the members of the new urban middle class to distinguish and define themselves." Though Leviatin too is aware of *How the Other Half Lives*'s other appeals (as tourism, entertainment, and vicarious adventure), he submerges all of these beneath the function of establishing "class distinction"[103] and so, like Stange, fails to see the tension between these different uses of the text.

For Stange and Leviatin, the salient, unchanging fact is middle-class, or new urban middle-class, superiority; but first of all, there are different forms of superiority, and second, this slum literature precisely marks the moment when that superiority is no longer monolithic. Riis does not simply affirm middle-class privilege; he helps change its terms. With his ethnographic and psychological understandings of the poor, he is part of what Jackson Lears has called "the revitalization and transformation of [his] class's cultural hegemony": "the shift from a Protestant to a therapeutic world view, which antimodern sentiments reinforced, . . . a key transformation in the cultural hegemony of the dominant classes in America."[104]

More strikingly, Riis even undermines middle-class superiority in certain ways. The new middle-class interest in slumming, Riis's presence in the slums, and especially his flirtation with the tough signal middle-class doubts about its own values and virility. Stange and Leviatin assume a middle-class completely confident of its vision of the good life of progress and prosperity—"of suburban bliss, spacious homes, bright churches, and tightly knit families."[105] But as Alan Trachtenberg has noted, by the 1890s, "in its very success, middle-class culture had come to seem stifling, enervating, effeminate, devoid of opportunities for manly heroism. The same nagging and nervous discontent which drove Roosevelt, Wister, and Remington to the West, Henry Adams to medieval France and the South Seas, . . . the offspring of Northern elite families into cults of arts and crafts, militarism, and Orientalism, . . . [William] James away from Chatauqua, 'wishing for heroism and the spectacle of human nature on the rack,'"[106] also took Riis and Crane, and some of their readers, to the slums.

Specifically, I cannot agree with Stange that Riis's spectacle of the slums is geared for a "tenderly refined" reader.[107] Not only do I find that his energetic and muscular aesthetic violates traditional moral strictures against vulgarity; I also claim that his spectacular entertainment shares much with a cheap aesthetic that is regularly attributed to the lower classes. In short, in my reading of Riis, the middle class is not simply expanding its usual privilege; it is also acting out of an anxious desire for excitement and going through its own ethical revitalization and conversion through its association with the slums. The slum is both a danger zone that provides opportunities for adventure and heroism, like the West and the battlefield, and a separate culture, like the Orient or medieval France, whose unrefined or more "primitive" virtues offer a tonic for a tired middle-class society.

Moreover, Riis is also nervous about this very conversion that he finds so invigorating, for it is a conversion to a spectacular aesthetic and ethic associated with the slum dwellers he is supposed to reform. Just as Amy Kaplan finds an "anxiety" in William Dean Howells's *A Hazard of New Fortunes* about "the line" between rich and poor neighborhoods in the city and the "collapse of class boundaries,"[108] it could be argued that Riis expresses an anxiety about the line between his documentary realism and the vulgar entertainments of tenement life—the difference being that he himself is participating in the collapse. Riis loudly denounces the cheap spectacle of the streets and insists on a moral difference between this aesthetic and that of his own work, but one might suggest he protests too much: this difference is often hard to find. Crane's work, meanwhile, is rejected by some publishers as being as morally suspect as popular dime novels; Crane, however, has no problem accepting his moral conversion, accepting, as he puts it, that he is a "bad man"[109] (in middle-class terms).

If, with realism—in reaction to a sentimentalism perceived as effeminate— "'reality' come[s] to be associated with depictions of brutality, sordidness, and lower-class life," as Kaplan points out, then it is a genre that always threatens to cross the line between middle-class "good" taste and lower-class vulgarity. Kaplan suggests that "Riis crosses over the line [into the tenements] not to abolish it but to make 'the other half' known . . . ; by doing so he conceptually reinforces the hierarchy between classes."[110] Leviatin would go further and consider the act definitive of the new urban middle class: "to define itself as a class, the new urban middle class needed to look at the new urban poor."[111] But it might also be argued that Riis crosses an aesthetic—and moral—line between the classes, thus blurring the distinction between them and undermining the traditional basis for the hierarchy. Previously, the urban poor were absolutely inferior, both morally and aesthetically, and held at a distance, but now the middle class is carrying on a more intimate contact with them, even borrowing from them, and so implicitly acknowledging that they are superior at least when it comes to the issues of excitement and toughness. The privilege of the middle class, the basis of its domination, and its power relationship to the poor are going through a transformation, and the realist author tends to be either caught in the middle and schizophrenic (Riis) or in the ethical vanguard and defiant (Crane). In any case, the realist text cannot simply participate in both disciplinary society and the society of the spectacle; constructing the slums as spectacle turns out to interfere with the discipline of both the urban poor and its middle-class readership.[112]

The first part of the book, "The New Ethnography of the Slum," places Riis's and Crane's ethnographic styles in the context of the practices of contemporary and previous charity writing and slum fiction, respectively. In the first chapter, Riis is seen to have much in common with his moralistic predecessors but also to exceed their analyses, with a new interest in sightseeing as well as new ethnographic categories of perception. In the second chapter, Crane is observed to make an almost clean break with previous and concurrent slum fiction and to develop an ethnography that is more profound than Riis's; he identifies not only alternative customs but also alternative ethics behind the behavior of the urban poor. The tragedy of *Maggie* is explained in terms of a clash between traditional and Bowery ethics. Thus Riis implicitly challenges, and Crane explicitly challenges, the universality of Protestant morality.

In Part II, "Slum Spectacle," Riis and Crane are shown to present the poor not merely in the traditional manner (as victims or threats that inspire Christian pity or civic concern) but also as spectacle that provides entertainment. Chapter 4 gives special attention to Riis's photography and explores this alternative ethical relation to the poor—the role of spectator or tourist—that Riis and Crane encourage their readers to assume. Chapter 5 goes on to show how this new ethical relation, with its investment in visual pleasure and excitement, interferes with the traditional moral and social aims of slum reform (to which Riis's work is ostensibly devoted).

Part III, "Slum Psychology," explores Riis's and Crane's new versions of subjectivity—or of ethical substance—that center around a notion of self-esteem in addition to (Riis) or instead of (Crane) the concept of moral character. Chapter 5 examines Riis's and Crane's psychological accounts of traditionally immoral behavior, with special attention to the figure of the tough, who is at once vicious and possessed of self-esteem. The demise of the title character in *Maggie* is elucidated in terms of her progressive loss of confidence in a world where there is a zero-sum competition for self-esteem, and Crane's slum tales are broken down into their typical episodes of this psychological positioning. In the sixth chapter, Riis's social programs and architectural prescriptions are shown to aim in part at nurturing self-esteem and providing entertainment—and thus to partake (unwittingly) of a new psychological ethics and politics. This chapter also asserts that Crane's conception of psychology is ultimately an ethical one, and it explores his moral romanticization of the tough and, more generally, his depiction of an ethical relationship to others and to oneself—involving a self-esteem that is not rooted in competition but, rather, is insulated by feelings of anger or rebellion and thus makes moral behavior possible.

The afterword follows up the sixth chapter with a brief, merely suggestive discussion of the bohemian and youth-culture descendants of Crane's rebel ethics and his flirtation with the slums. Finally, the afterword and the book conclude with a reassessment of Progressivism, a comparison between the different psychological moralities of the slum that Riis and Crane articulate, and a glance at what might be called our current mythology of the slums.

If I treat separately the new ethnographic, aesthetic, and psychological styles of describing the poor, this is for the sake of analysis: these, after all, are the terms we now use in thinking on the subject. But this is not to imply that these are somehow separate developments. They come together, and together they indicate a burgeoning alternative morality on the part of the middle class.

I

The New

Ethnography

of the Slum

1 ⮂ *Riis and Charity Writing*

*T*hough in many ways Jacob Riis's *How the Other Half Lives* follows in the tradition of nineteenth-century charity writing, portions of his book are unlike any previous American writings on poverty. His description of the infamous Mulberry Bend is one. It is touristic.

What a birds-eye view of "the Bend" would be like is a matter of bewildering conjecture. Its everyday appearance, as seen from the corner of Bayard Street on a sunny day, is one of the sights of New York.

Bayard Street is the high road to Jewtown across the Bowery, picketed from end to end with the outposts of Israel. Hebrew faces, Hebrew signs, and incessant chatter in the queer lingo that passes for Hebrew on the East Side attend the curious wanderer to the very corner of Mulberry Street. But the moment he turns the corner the scene changes abruptly. Before him lies spread out what might better be the market-place in some town in Southern Italy than a street in New York—all but the houses; they are still the same old tenements of the unromantic type. But for once they do not make the foreground in a slum picture from the American metropolis. The interest centres not in them, but in the crowd they shelter only when the street is not preferable, and that with the Italian is only when it rains or he is sick. When the sun shines the entire population seeks the street, carrying on its household work, its bargaining, its love-making on street or sidewalk, or idling there when it has nothing better to do, with the reverse of the impulse that makes the Polish Jew coop himself up in his den with the thermometer at stewing heat. Along the curb women sit in rows, young and old alike with the odd head-covering, pad or turban, that is their badge of servitude—her's to bear the burden as long as she lives—haggling over baskets of frowsy weeds, some sort of salad probably, stale tomatoes, and oranges not above suspicion. (43)[1]

"The Bend" from How the Other Half Lives, *by Jacob Riis (photo courtesy of the Museum of the City of New York)*

There is not much in the way of a traditional tableau of urban poverty here: no beggars, no drunks, no catalogue of vice, no exposure of crime, no ragpickers, no hungry and shivering children, no filthy rooms, no suggestion of the pathos of the situation. There is, rather, queer lingo, strange head-coverings, the proclivity to stay inside or head out for the streets, the bustle and activity of the sidewalks, a suggestion of romance. This is not the usual material of charitable writing.

For such material we might turn first of all to Charles Loring Brace's *The Dangerous Classes of New York and Twenty Years' Work among Them* (1872), the work that historians regularly cite as a predecessor to *How the Other Half Lives*. Here is Brace on the subject of the German immigrant poor:

> On the eastern side of the city is a vast population of German laborers, mechanics and shop keepers. Among them, also, are numbers of exceedingly poor people, who live by gathering rags and bones.
>   . . . I had many cheery conversations with these honest people, who had drifted into places so different from their mountain-homes. In fact, it used to convey to me a strange contrast, the dirty yards piled with bones and flaunting with rags, and the air smelling of carrion; while the accents reminded of the glaciers of the Bavarian Alps. . . .

From ignorance of the language and the necessity of working at their street trades, they did not attend our schools, and seldom entered a church. They were growing up without either religion or education. Yet they were a much more honest and hopeful class than the Irish. There seemed always remaining in them something of the good old German *Biederkeit*, or solidity. . . . The young girls, however, coming from a similar low class were weaker in virtue than the Irish. . . . [T]he poor German girls of the Eleventh Ward [were] not as ragged or wild as the Irish throng in the Fourth Ward, but equally poor and quite as much exposed to temptation.

Brace goes on, in the same chapter, to remark on the dwellings of "shanty families" ("the filth and wretchedness in which they sometimes live are beyond description"); the amount of intemperance ("liquor, of course, 'prevailed'"); the prevalence of disease, along with intemperance ("the few men there . . . were often disabled by disease and useless from drunkenness"); the "weakening of the marriage tie" ("many of the women had been abandoned by their husbands"); the loss of purity among the girls ("the life of a swillgatherer, or coal-picker, or *chiffonnier* in the streets soon wears off a girl's modesty and prepares her for worse occupations"). He tells anecdotes of charity successes (children he saved from the shanties) as well as of failures (poor people who could not be induced to stop begging or drinking or living in the tenement houses).[2]

One can identify in Brace's book the familiar themes of the genre of charitable writing. A small number of topics were taken up again and again in reports on the slums in the course of the nineteenth century: crime, the Protestant virtues and vices (especially intemperance, disorder, uncleanliness, idleness, beggary, vagabondage), disease, the miserable conditions of dwellings (especially filth, heat and cold, lack of air and sunlight, overcrowding), the loss of modesty (especially among girls), the dissolution of families, the forms of employment and their moral and physical ills and dangers, the institutions devoted to their uplift, and the reform that still needed to be done.[3] Riis, too, is fluent in this language of charitable writing.

In his description of the Italian immigrants, for example, he covers all of this ground. Here he is on the subject of order and cleanliness: "Certainly a picturesque, if not very tidy, element has been added to the population in the 'assisted' Italian immigrant. . . . [He] reproduces conditions of destitution and disorder which, set in the frame-work of Mediterranean exuberance, are the delight of the artist, but in a matter-of-fact American community become its danger and reproach." On the subject of vices, Riis notes: "Ordinarily he is easily enough governed by authority—always excepting Sunday, when he settles down to a game of cards and lets loose all his bad passions. Like the Chinese, the Italian is a born gambler." On the subject of crimes: "The only criminal business to which the father occasionally lends his hand, outside of murder, is a bunco game." On the subject of virtues: "With all his conspicuous faults, the swarthy Italian immigrant has his redeeming traits. He is as honest as he is hot-headed. . . . The women are faithful wives and devoted mothers. Their vivid and picturesque costumes lend a tinge of color to the otherwise dull monotony of the slums they inhabit. The Italian is gay, light-hearted." On the subject of housing conditions, Riis provides statistics on overcrowding and room temperatures, which he supplements with descriptions: "Look into any of these houses, everywhere the same pile of rags, of malodorous bones and musty paper. . . . Here is a 'flat' or 'parlor' and two pitch-dark coops called bedrooms. Truly, the bed is all there is room for. . . . The closeness and smell are appalling. How many people sleep here? The woman with the red bandanna shakes her head sullenly, but the bare-legged girl with the bright face counts on her fingers—five, six!" On the subject of disease, he cites mortality rates for various tenements and areas: "Here, in this tenement, No. 59 ½, next to Bandit's Roost, fourteen persons died that year, and eleven of them were children. . . . Out of the alley itself, No. 59, nine dead were carried in 1888, five in baby coffins." On the subject of their employment and its conditions, Riis writes: "Whenever the back of the sanitary police is turned, he will make his home in the filthy burrows where he works by day, sleeping and eating his meals under the dump, on the edge of the slimy depths and amid surroundings full of unutterable horror." Finally, Riis refers to agencies that work to aid the slums (the Society for the Prevention of Cruelty to Children, the Tenement House Commission, and the Health Department), and he closes his chapters on the Italians with an anecdote that indicates that the reformers' work is far from finished. A police raid failed to turn up any lodgers in one tenement apartment, but Riis knows that the investigation of illegal overcrowding "had been anticipated. The policeman's back was probably no sooner turned than the room was reopened for business" (37–52).

Riis's and Brace's styles of description have much in common. Not only do they favor the same subjects; they also rely on the same tropes. Both commentators make ethnic and racial generalities; they compare immigrant groups to one another (the German to the Irish, the Italian to the Chinese); they invoke images of the immigrant homelands, by way of contrast to the slums of New York (the glaciers of the Bavarian Alps, Mediterranean exuberance); they support and dress their claims with both anecdote and statistic; they acknowledge the limits of descriptive power in the face of extreme conditions (filth and wretchedness beyond description, surroundings full of unutterable horror).

Finally, a shared logic (at once Christian and civic-minded) organizes the genre's small set of subjects. Foul home conditions and miserable employments and diseases are bad in themselves, but they lead to things that are much worse: moral degradation and riot. In *Humanity in the City* (1854), the Reverend E. H. Chapin moves from physical to moral facts:

> The entrenched filth that all day long sends its steaming rot through lane and dwelling . . . Cold that encamps itself in the empty fire-place . . . Hunger that takes the strong man by the throat . . . [T]he fascinations of the bottle and the shamelessness of harlotry . . . And, with all this, may we not expect that fierce in-

stinct of selfishness which overwhelms every other impulse, and breaks out in crime? Ah![4]

Charles Loring Brace presents a full page of statistics on overcrowding and discusses hygiene but concludes with a report that emphasizes the moral sickness and contagion of the tenements:

> It need not be said that with overcrowding such as this, there is always disease, and as naturally, crime. The privacy of a home is undoubtedly one of the most favorable conditions to virtue. . . .
> Here, too, congregate some of the worst of the destitute population of our city—vagrants, beggars, nondescript thieves, broken-down drunken vagabonds. . . . Naturally, the boys growing up in such places become, as by a law of nature, petty thieves, pick-pockets, street-rovers, and burglars.[5]

Walter Channing's "Address on the Prevention of Pauperism" (1843), another example of the charitable writing genre, makes explicit the precedence of spiritual concerns. He describes at length the miserable conditions of the poor, only to conclude: "But I ask for no tear for the destitution, the physical suffering of poverty. . . . But I do ask for the helplessness of poverty . . . for its subjection to the lowest passions of human nature."[6] And Brace is very clear about the ultimate civic stakes of the social problem. He begins his account of the dangerous classes of New York with a warning: "Let the Law lift its hand from them for a season, or let the civilizing influences of American life fail to reach them, and, if the opportunity offered, we should see an explosion from this class which might leave this city in ashes and blood."[7]

True to this form, Riis introduces his book with the claim that the "worst crime" of the tenements is that "they touch the family life with a deadly moral contagion" (3), and on the last page, he threatens the reader with a scene of social apocalypse: "The sea of a mighty population, held in galling fetters, heaves uneasily in the tenements. Once already our city . . . has felt the swell of its resistless flood. If it rise once more, no human power may avail to check it. The gap between the classes, in which it surges, unseen, unsuspected by the thoughtless, is widening day by day" (226). In his study of the tenements, Riis is most of all concerned, like his predecessors, with moral disease and class violence.

But though *How the Other Half Lives* speaks the language of charitable writing, Riis is not constrained by its vocabulary or its grammar. He often exceeds its traditional subject matter and forms of judgment and sometimes even violates its logic.

While Brace's assessments and anecdotes all center on moral concerns and physical misery, some of Riis's wander into other territories. There is the passage with which we began, a passage that has very little to do with vice, crime, employment, physical misery, disease, or environmental design, all those themes that had exhausted the previous writings on urban poverty. Riis does recount instances of filth and overcrowding and vice, but he also describes the Italians hanging out in the street, doing their bargaining, their love-making, and their idling. Riis shows not just how the other half sins and suffers, keeps house and works, but also how it speaks and flirts and passes time: to use his word, more fully how the other half *lives*.

Riis's prose has a kind of descriptive exuberance that makes it frequently burst the limits of previous charitable writing. Even when Riis is ostensibly concentrating on the issue of tenement darkness and overcrowding, he turns the attention momentarily to a red bandanna and a pair of bare legs. Now, bare legs could perhaps be said to signify deprivation and thus emphasize his point (though this argument is undercut by the fact of the 115-degree temperature in the tenements), but a red bandanna is an object that in no way symbolizes poverty or degradation. What does it symbolize? Nothing traditionally moral or hygienic, to be sure. And its incoherence is precisely its significance: it is not part of a moral or sanitary economy. Riis's red bandanna is excessive: it exceeds his demonstration about overcrowding.

But Riis is interested in behaviors and objects that do not have a traditional moral or sanitary valence, such as ways of flirting and modes of dress. He goes to the Jewish market on "bargain days" because "then is the time to study the ways of this peculiar people to the best advantage" (85). With Riis, a whole new series of habits of the poor becomes remarkable.

Moreover, he introduces ethnographic terms into his account of the slums, terms that often overturn traditional moral explanations for behavior. At points, instead of abiding by the usual moral categories of vice and virtue, he employs such terms as "ways," "customs," and "fashions," and he uses traditionally ethical terms, such as "habit," in new, ethnographic ways. He challenges his readers to view the poor with a different set of categories that will yield a new perception. "Go into any of the 'respectable' tenement neighborhoods," he suggests; "be with and among its people until you understand their ways" (121). Instead of charging the people of "Cat Alley" with viciousness for their hostility to outsiders, he notes that the alley "had it standards and its customs, which were to be observed."[8]

Similarly, Riis finds that certain problematic slum habits are the result not of individual evil or moral weakness but of tenement ways or fashions. This is the case with the slum dwellers' penchant for lavish funerals. "Fashion, no less inexorable in the tenements than on the avenue, exacts of him that he must die in a style that is finally ruinous. The habit of expensive funerals—I know of no better classification for it than along with the opium habit and the similar grievous plagues of mankind" (132–133).

Something remarkable is happening here to the word "habit," a central term in the conventional language of moral responsibility. "Habit," which once referred to the traditional Protestant set of "universal" and individual virtues and vices (the habits of temperance, drinking and drugs, industry, idleness, etc.) is here being applied, self-consciously, to a local, group behavior outside this set. Riis extends the classification of habit to include a complex ritual of an urban community. Unlike the moral habits of previous charity writing—unlike, say, idleness or opium (which were often seen to have group causes, of a racial nature)—the expensive funeral is exclusively a group habit. One can be individually idle or smoke opium alone, so even if these activities are pursued in numbers, even if they are shared by all members of a race, each individual can be seen as separately having the habit. But the expensive funeral requires a crowd to be performed; individuals comprise the habit, but only the group can be seen to have it. A custom may still be called vicious, but the traditional sense of vice is lost: the collective quality of a custom vitiates the notion of individual moral responsibility. Such a use of the word "habit" is in itself a Progressive notion: it implies a direct relationship between the social environment and individual behavior.

Riis is not alone in his nontraditional, Progressivist use of the word "habit," and his isolated observations here unwittingly fit into the larger philosophical framework being constructed by the Pragmatists. By the end of the 1870s, C. S. Peirce was presenting an evolutionary account of the development of phylogenetic habits, and though he tended to focus on species-wide habits, rather than ethnic or group customs, he was thinking in terms of the communal aspects of methodic behavior and of social habits that govern an individual's conduct and interfere with sound reasoning.[9] The Pragmatists, in fact, were making explicit the moral implications of such a reconception of habit that Riis, who was by no means a philosopher, left only partially explored. A few decades later, John Dewey, Pragmatist *and* Progressive, would see habits as functions of individual impulses and the environment, both natural and social. He would state bluntly that "conduct is always shared. . . . It *is* social, whether bad or good." And "for practical purposes," he would explain, "morals mean customs, folkways, established collective habits."[10]

Again, Riis does judge the slum dwellers in conventional moral terms: he cites what he considers the Italians' bad passions (gambling) and their virtues (honesty and maternal devotion). He does judge them on sanitary criteria: he stereotypically refers to their lack of tidiness and notes that they are "content to live in a pigsty" (37). But he also assesses them on fresh ground, noting their appearances as well as their customs. This aesthetic contemplation of slum habits is something new. Among the Italians' "redeeming traits," along with their honesty, is for Riis the fact that "their vivid and picturesque costumes lend a tinge of color to the otherwise dull monotony of the slums they inhabit" (41). Their colorfulness is laid side by side with their probity. Riis is asserting a new type of virtue.

Riis does not couch the passage we began with, his description of the Italians working and selling and flirting and just plain hanging around, in a familiar moral lesson. Unlike a typical Protestant moralist, he does not criticize the population for being idle but understands that at times "it has nothing better to do." He is not scandalized by the community's open love-making; he does not scold the Italians for what he considers their lack of modesty and privacy. Nor does he scold them for what he considers their cutthroat bargaining practices. Rather, he goes on to detail, with obvious enthusiasm and enjoyment, a few of the tricks of these trades:

> Near a particularly boisterous group, a really pretty girl . . . has been bargaining
> long and earnestly with an old granny, who presides over a wheel-barrow load of
> second-hand stockings and faded cotton yarns. . . . One of the rude swains . . .
> to whom the girl's eyes have strayed more than once, steps up and gallantly offers to
> pick her out the handsomest pair, whereat she laughs and pushes him away with a
> gesture which he interprets as an invitation to stay; and he does, evidently to the sat-
> isfaction of the beldame, who forthwith raises her prices fifty per cent. without being
> detected by the girl. (45)

Finally, Riis does not turn the popularity of the street into another proof that
the buildings are uninhabitable; he does not turn the street scene back onto his ostensible theme, the tenement. When the subject of the tenements arises, he flatly
remarks: "[F]or once they do not make the foreground in a slum picture from the
American metropolis. The interest centres not in them, but in the crowd" (43).

"The interest": not the tenement, here, but the crowd. And not the crowd's
state of health, nor its viciousness, nor its menace. Riis states the criterion of interest very plainly, at the start of this passage. The Bend's "everyday appearance, as
seen from the corner of Bayard Street on a sunny day, is one of the sights of New
York" (43). The interest is in the sight. The interest is in behaviors, in objects that
have not been attended to before: strange ways, fashions, and collective habits, the
tendency to congregate in the street, the flirtatious play, the red bandanna. Between its morally concerned introduction and its apocalyptic ending, even within
its traditional sorts of passages on Protestant vices and social evils, *How the Other
Half Lives* takes its reader sightseeing. This sort of reporting was beyond Brace's
scope; this sort of assessment was irrelevant to him. Riis's book is not simply charitable writing: it is also an urban travel literature.

Spectacle for Its Own Sake

A red bandanna can interrupt, can exceed Riis's demonstration of overcrowding;
the sights of the Bend can steal the interest from the usual moral and social theme:
this is something new in slum writing. Previous charitable writers did sometimes
stray from a strict catalogue of vices and diseases and physical miseries and include curiosities of local color; they too presented a spectacle.[11] But their curiosities and their spectacles were subordinated to the social message, recuperated as
part of the moral theme.

Consider Charles Loring Brace's description of the Italians:

> Here, in large tenement-houses, were packed hundreds of poor Italians, mostly en-
> gaged in carrying through the city and country "the everlasting hand-organ," or
> selling statuettes. In the same room I would find monkeys, children, men and
> women, with organs and plaster-casts, all huddled together; but the women contriv-
> ing still, in the crowded rooms, to roll their dirty macaroni, and all talking excitedly;
> a bedlam of sounds, and a combination of odors from garlic, monkeys and the most

dirty human persons. They were, without exception, the dirtiest population I had met with.[12]

Here we find a parade of curiosities, to be sure. The Italians are living with monkeys; they are involved with hand organs and statuettes; the Italian women are exceptionally committed to dirty macaroni; a mix of strange smells lingers in the air. But these local colors are colored over with Protestant moral tones: modesty is violated, as adults and children, men and women, humans and animals share the same crowded room; order is disturbed and replaced by bedlam, as sounds and odors mix wantonly and senselessly; cleanliness is assaulted by "dirty macaroni" and "most dirty human persons," in fact "the dirtiest population."[13]

Brace's collation of a strange set of social objects does not lead to a touristic or ethnographic investigation of them. He makes no attempt to solve any of the mysteries he presents; he does not explain, for instance, that the monkeys play a role in organ grinding. In fact, the confusion of the assortment of objects (monkeys, men, macaroni, plaster-casts, garlic, all mixed together!) is more important than the objects themselves. The disparate (and interesting) objects are recuperated in an overarching sign that drains the individual things of their local color, their potential as sights or curios: the sign is disorder, and disorder, unlike monkeys or macaroni, has a traditional moral significance. Because these objects are distributed helter-skelter (the monkey is divided from its partner, the organ, and placed instead with the humans and then with the garlic), all potential ethnographic logic is obstructed or buried, and a conventional moral logic is engaged.

At work here, from our point of view, is a moral tunnel vision, a Protestant fetishism. Without a sign of vice, there was no interest in reform, or even description of the poor. To describe the social object was, in fact, to endow it with moral significance.

A. E. Cerqua, an Italian gentleman who collaborated with Brace in the description and reform of these impoverished Italians, explicitly confirms this tunnel vision. In 1855, this Italian immigrant community of Five Points in New York City, though horribly impoverished and overcrowded, was receiving no aid from charity organizations. Signor Cerqua explains why the Italians were able to fall through the cracks of the city's charity apparatus:

> Had they displayed the vices or criminal inclinations which prevail to a deplorable extent among the low classes of other nationalities, they would soon have been brought to public notice and taken care of by our benevolent and religious societies; but they cannot be reproached with intoxication, prostitution, quarreling, stealing, etc; and thus, escaping the enviable notoriety of the criminal, they fell into a privacy that deprived them of the advantages of American benevolence.[14]

Cerqua's account of the Italian community of Five Points presents a highly unusual case, in the annals of American reporting on urban poverty up until that time: a poor area unafflicted with vice. It can serve as a kind of litmus test of the era's social perception and obsessions. And what Cerqua suggests to us, in his quiet, logical way, is that signs of vice and crime alone catch the attention of the charity agencies, and that even glaring and unmistakable marks of poverty—let alone peculiar ethnic and urban sights—are of little interest in themselves.

What Cerqua does not say is how the Italians, so long overlooked, come to be attended to at last. In effect, the Italian community is brought into the fold of American benevolence and charitable writing precisely by working up a moral case against it, resorting to technicalities, as necessary. Though the Italians do not openly display the obvious vices and crimes—intoxication, prostitution, etc.—Charles Loring Brace is able, through a close and "generous" moral reading, to identify less blatant, less serious Protestant vices: uncleanliness, immodesty, disorder.

Previous charitable writing presented spectacle, even self-conscious spectacle, but it is of a different nature than that of Riis. The Reverend Edward Chapin, author of *Humanity in the City*, could certainly be said to strain for an aesthetic appreciation of the urban space. Some of the descriptions in his first chapter, "The Lessons of the Street," are downright grandiloquent: "[T]here is something finer than the grandest poetry, even in the mere spectacle of these multitudinous billows of life, rolling down the long, broad, avenue. It is an inspiring lyric, this inexhaustible procession." And Chapin does not restrict himself to a "lyric" of the streets; he takes up an "epic" of the population, attempting to describe the visible "diversities of human conditions":

> Here you may find not only the finest Saxon culture, but the grossest barbaric degradation. There you pass a form of Caucasian development, the fine-cut features, the imperial forehead, the intelligent eye, the confident tread, the true port and stature of a man. But who is this that follows in his track; under the same national sky, surrounded by the same institutions, and yet with those pinched features, that stunted form, that villainous look; is it Papuan, Bushman or Carib? Fitly representing either of these, though born in a Christian city, and bearing about not only the stamp of violated physical law, but of moral neglect and baseness. And no one needs to be told that there are savages in New York, as well as in the islands of the sea. Savages, not in gloomy forests, but under the strength of gas-light, and the eyes of policemen; with war-whoops and clubs very much the same, and garments as fantastic, and souls as brutal, as any of their kindred at the antipodes.

When Chapin turns his attention to the urban population, it becomes clear how his spectacle differs from Riis's. It is not merely that Chapin's description veers immediately to moralistic assessment (villainous look, moral neglect and baseness, souls as brutal) as soon as it tries to encompass the human: it also becomes abstract. He refers to nothing as specific, as visual, as the Italian woman's red bandanna or the Chinese man's braided pigtail (on which Riis also remarks); instead, we are told about fantastic garments and pinched features. These are signs of the primitive and the undeveloped, not particularities of dress or physical feature. The visual and auditory peculiarities are not only buried by traditional moral judgment; they are also smothered by metaphor. Chapin's metaphor—that of "degrees of civilization"—is a common one at midcentury. The imagery here is borrowed, stolen, abstracted, from the antipodes (war whoops are not native to New York): the color, that is, is not local. Riis's is. He does not rely on this metaphor to describe his subjects. Riis may be constantly returning to moral formula, but he is able, momentarily, to leave it and let another logic take over.

Chapin's spectacles are, initially, of urban scenes and types: the Civilized Man and the Savage, "Purity" and "womanhood discrowned," "the beggar" and the man "bloated with luxury."[15] The nature of his spectacle is quite different from that of Riis, even though Riis too has his categories and has plenty of "types." Riis uses categories that are more refined and more homegrown (the Italian, the Chinaman, the Street Arab, the cheap lodging houses, the stale-beer dives); simple Manichean distinctions between rich and poor, civilized and primitive man, pure and fallen woman, may be employed, but they are no longer adequate.

The overriding difference between these spectacles is that Chapin insists that all of his have ethical meaning. Some of Riis's—his red bandanna, his sights of the Bend—are not interpreted as morally significant. Chapin's binary urban types are retrieved as allegorical figures, because Chapin "would ascertain the practical purport of this lesson of human diversity which is so conspicuous in the street—the meaning of these sharp contrasts of refinement and grossness, intelligence and ignorance, respectability and guilt." He demands that the entirety of spectacles he describes has moral import. And he finds it: out of these spectacular diversities "come some of the noblest instances of character and of achievement. Ignorance and crime and poverty and vice . . . constitute the dark background against which the virtues of human life stand out in radiant relief." Similarly, "how could *Charity* have ever appeared in the world, were there no dark ways to be trodden by its bright feet, and no suffering and sadness to require its aid?" Chapin can speak of "the purpose of these diversities," but *How the Other Half Lives* presents diversities of which Riis would never speak in such terms: he is interested in the Bohemian's long beard and the Chinese man's braided pigtail, the Italian's red bandanna and the Jew's suspenders, but he would never dream of searching for a moral purpose in this variety.

There is a final difference: Chapin finishes up by denying the spectacle he has conjured. After laying out his collection of spectacular diversities, he finds that "differences between men are formal rather than real." He calls them "mere appearances." Even the difference between rich and poor "is merely *phenomenal*, merely appears." "But, say you, 'here is one who is returning to a home of destitution, of misery.' . . . And yet, in many splendid mansions you will find a more fearful destitution . . . a brood of evil passions that mock the splendor." What is left, when spectacle and appearance is peeled away, is an "essential *unity* of humanity," a humanity "balanced in the depths of the inner life," "the kindred spirit that is in every one of us," the "motives, sympathies, faculties, that run through the common humanity": a spiritual, and invisible, reality.

It is a strange but recognizably Christian trope: commentators describe the spectacles of the city and the physical conditions of the poor at length and in sensational language, and then, at some point in the argument, deny their importance and, in effect, deprive them of reality. The lurid corporal facts that engaged the reader moments before become incidental, accidental, contingent. Rags and mansions, imperial foreheads and pinched features, take on an epiphenomenal status.[16]

This makes for a dramatic rhetorical maneuver—the more shocking, the more extreme the diversities, the larger the gesture by which they could be reduced to nothing, the grander the spiritual fundament that could be laid bare. Spectacle in Chapin is nothing but the first term of a dialectic, something from which the reader must be weaned as he learns "another lesson of the street; a lesson which requires us to look a little deeper."[17] Meanwhile, for Riis, spectacle is often enough an end in itself.

Riis's publicity agent could advertise *How the Other Half Lives* as a good read and good "look." "No page is uninstructive," announces a blurb for the book, "but it would be misleading to suppose the book even tinctured with didacticism. It is from beginning to end as picturesque in treatment as it is in material."[18]

No such claim could be made for *Humanity in the City* or *The Dangerous Classes of New York*, which are steeped in didacticism, always pointing to the same problems, the same lessons, the same morals—at the expense of the potential "picturesqueness" of their materials. Brace himself implies at one point that his book gets repetitive and boring. Speaking of the poor children and the middle-class people who come to their aid, he writes:

> Beyond a certain point, the history of these various schools becomes *monotonous*. It is simply a history of kindness, of patience, of struggles with ignorance, poverty, and intemperance; of lives poured out for the good of those who can never make a return, of steady improvement and the final elevation of great numbers of children and youth who are under these permanent and profound influences.[19]

The tradition of poverty writing before Riis, then, is devoted to a small number of themes, abstract in its descriptions, tightly constrained by traditional moral formulas: it is impoverished.[20]

2 ❦ Crane and Slum Fiction

*I*n the early 1890s, Stephen Crane set out to reinvent the tenement novel. His inability to find a publisher for *Maggie* is an indication of his success—especially when one considers that at the time slum fiction was in vogue, and certain books about the poor were becoming veritable bestsellers.[1] The scandal of Crane's work was not its setting but, rather, his refusal to judge slum life according to middle-class standards. In order to appreciate Crane's innovations, we will need to turn first to the slum fiction conventions that he was defying.

Crane was by no means the first novelist, or one of a few, to look upon the slums with an ethnographic or aesthetic gaze; authors of the period were taking their readers on literary slumming parties.[2] Edgar Fawcett, in *The Evil That Men Do* (1889), describes a slum dance hall, a tenement shop, a billiard room, a wake, and the crowded and noisy Bowery streets, full of "ragged boys . . . yelling 'extra'" and "orange-and-banana vendors" crying out "in a kind of vocal sword-thrust."[3] *Timothy's Quest* (1890), by Kate Douglas Wiggin, portrays a tenement house full of "frowzy, sleepy-looking women hanging out of their windows."[4] Basil March, the protagonist of William Dean Howells's *Hazard of New Fortunes* (1890), rides an elevated train "into the gay ugliness—the shapeless, graceful, reckless picturesqueness of the Bowery," and he is fascinated by the "picturesque admixture" of immigrant faces as well as the "strident forms and colors" of "certain signs, certain facades, certain audacities of the prevailing hideousness."[5] A "slumming part[y]" in H. H. Boyeson's *Social Strugglers* (1893) reveals Italian "alleys . . . thronged with a dusky population, wearing ear-rings and gesticulating with the vehemence that was wholly un-American."[6] James W. Sullivan's *Tenement Tales of New York*

(1895) shows its readers an Irish wake and funeral, several sweatshops, an Italian fruit stand, an elevated-train ride, the scams of the young toughs and newspaper boys of lower New York, and, of course, "tenement-house life."[7] Irish brogue, a slum raffle and party, a dance hall, Ellis Island Immigrant Station, and the tricks, habits, and "way of life" of lodging-house bums fill the pages of *Meg McIntyre's Raffle and Other Stories* (1896), by Alvan Francis Sanborn.[8] *Poor People* (1900), by I. K. Friedman, represents a tenement house, a saloon, and a fortune-teller.[9] Theodore Dreiser's *Sister Carrie* (1900) takes its reader into a workshop and among "the motley company" of homeless men who beg during the day and spend their nights in lodging houses.[10] A few years later, Upton Sinclair's *The Jungle* (1907) would open with an extended description of a Lithuanian wedding feast, called a *veselija*.[11] Even the very refined Henry James visited the "swarming" streets of the Jewish "Ghetto" in his nonfiction travel piece *The American Scene* (1907).[12]

Some fiction writers even remarked upon their new anthropological mission—and its tension with the usual objectives of slum writing.[13] In *A Daughter of the Tenements* (1895), Edward Townsend expresses a wistful attachment to Mulberry Bend, which, thanks to Riis and others (he includes himself), is soon to be converted into a park:

> For the sunlight and air so introduced into that neighborhood we shall feel appropriately proud of our share in the achievement, yet I cannot but regret that even with all the deliberation our rulers may exercise in this matter, the transformation of the Bend into the park will have taken place before any American painter shall have found time from working up his "Naples sketches" and elaborating his "scenes from Cairo streets" into ambitious canvases, to step over into the Bend and *preserve its distinctive color and action* for those of us who care.[14]

(On a similar note, Henry James notes that as immigrants become Americanized, they are deprived of their "pleasant" native "colour"; the social uplift and Americanization of the alien "makes him for us," James writes, "a tolerably neutral and colourless image.")[15] The preservation of "distinctive color and action": this is a concise formulation of a joint aesthetic and ethnographic project for the slums, and Townsend's description of the Bend, though not a painting, is of course, such an act of preservation.

For most turn-of-the-century slum novelists, however, the representation of this distinctive action is a sideline, much as it was several decades earlier for Horatio Alger and Rebecca Harding Davis, two of the first practitioners of the genre. As with Riis, it takes a back seat to the objectives of social muckraking and moral edification, the traditional themes of the discourse on the poor.[16] It is not until Crane in the early 1890s—and then Sanborn and others a few years later—that the aesthetic and ethnographic stake goes beyond the intermittent pursuit of picturesque and exotic sights and becomes a holistic project.

The traditional novel of the poor was centered around a moral struggle and transformation. This drama usually involved a battle to resist the bad influences of the slums and the pressures of physical misery. One of the first, Rebecca Harding Davis's *Life in the Iron Mills* (1861), documents the struggle for health and survival in appalling living conditions, and the climax is a moral struggle with the temptation to a criminal act: the main character, a mill worker, must decide whether he will keep stolen money, and the inner battle drags on for half a dozen grueling pages:

> His brain was clear to-night, keen, intent, mastering. It would not start back, cowardly, from any hellish temptation, but meet it face to face. Therefore the great temptation of his life came veiled by no sophistry, but bold, defiant, owning its own vile name, trusting to one bold blow for victory.
>
> He did not deceive himself. Theft! That was it. At first the word sickened him; then he grappled with it. . . .
>
> The money,—there it lay on his knee. . . . A thief! Well, what was it to be a thief? He met the question at last, face to face, wiping the clammy drops of sweat from his forehead. . . .
>
> He folded the scrap of paper in his hand. As his nervous fingers took it in, limp and blotted, so his soul took in the mean temptation, lapped it in fancied rights, in dreamed of improved existences. . . .
>
> The trial-day of this man's life was over, and he had lost the victory.[17]

After his moral defeat, it is only a few short pages before he is sentenced to prison and dies.

Dime novels about slum girls would climax with a similar trial, but, of course, the heroine would triumph. The Bowery girl of *The Detective's Ward; or The Fortunes of a Bowery Girl* (1871) defies her tempter:

> I am but a poor shop-girl; my present life is a struggle for a scanty existence; my future a life of toil; but over my present life of suffering there extends a rainbow of hope. . . . Life is short, eternity endless—the grave is but the entrance to eternity. And you, villain, ask me to change my present peace for a life of horror with you. No, monster, rather may I die at once.[18]

Most slum novels of the 1880s and 1890s likewise focused on moral conflict and metamorphosis. *Poor People* centers around a poor artistic immigrant's son who "is addicted to the habit" of drink and struggles to give it up. His battle is not only against the influence of a perpetually drunk father and the lure of a saloon across the street; he also fights against the "inexorable . . . law of heredity." As he writes to his dead mother,

> [T]wice during the past year . . . have I let liquor make me gross as the beast of the fields; but you alone can know how I struggled and fought and battled before I submitted. The taint has been in my blood since birth; yet my will is strong, and before its persistent assaults, slowly, unwillingly, and step by step, does the enemy recede.[19]

The slum in these renditions is not so much a territory of strange habits and appearances as a den of vice and moral decay. *The Evil That Men Do*, for example, is filled with bad people whom the heroine Cora, the good and honest woman from the country, has no choice but to "mix" with. As she puts it, "I can't get rid of 'em; I sometimes wish I could."[20] The story chronicles its heroine's moral struggle and corruption: her temptations to vice (numerous men try to seduce her; various loose women hammer away at the pointlessness of virtue), her attempts to resist these temptations, her eventual yielding and fall into sin, her remorse and shame, her complete moral demise (she becomes a defiant prostitute), and finally her miserable death.

The slum novel is often elaborate in its description of moral transformation. The exploration of the experiences of sin and remorse is exhaustive; the lesson is not to be missed. Such is the case with Cora's experience, which goes through several stages. Immediately after her "boldly sinful bargain [sex with a man] . . . the pleasure of her purchase clothes [her] for weeks in a kind of brazen armor against remorse." But soon enough "regret had begun to grow at her heart with a fang that each new day sharpened and strengthened." Though she plans to leave her lover and "avoid further sin," she cannot pull herself away. When pregnancy and a miscarriage reveal her secret to the world at large, she is "pierced . . . with a recognition of her own repulsive sin. . . . She had tried very hard to be good; and she had failed hopelessly. This became the incessant haunting formula of her reflections." But then she revolts against her guilt, and "some particular levity had come into nature, giving her demeanor a . . . mild laxity and recklessness, that had never formerly marked it. Perhaps a new cynic impulse lay at the root of all this. . . . Her spiritual fatigue had begun subtly to show itself in a light, defiant waywardness." A "bacchanal revolt" soon follows, and "for a time she dwelt in luxury." But guilt eventually reasserts itself with a vengeance:

> She might have held her own through many seasons with a malignant magnificence, but for one cause—conscience. . . .
>   In her ears there were always whispers that waited to be dulled; in her memory there were always pictures that challenged effacement. . . . This part of the transgressor was one that she played ill; she had too much native nobility and chastity for it; she had gone to the devil ungracefully. . . .
>   The tragedy of her life was now dreadful.[21]

The moral transformation at the center of a slum tale might also be for the good. Horatio Alger's boy hero in *Ragged Dick; or, Street Life in New York* (1867), of course, swears off his bad habits, gives up his "vagabond life," seeks out an education, and makes himself into "a respectable man."[22] In "Slob Murphy," one of Sullivan's *Tenement Tales of New York*, the young title character experiences a "miracle of the spirit" as he approaches an untimely death. A fatal accident with a horse first leads to his metamorphosis from a "dirty, sneaking, suspicious, deceitful rogue" to "a cherub boy—confiding, honest, open-eyed, innocent."[23]

Ethnographic detail is basically a digression in these stories, which are devoted to Protestant moral exposition as well as social investigation. Touristic observations usually give way to reports of despicable living conditions. Townsend's *Daughter of the Tenements* is typical. His heroine and her middle-class missionary sidekick merely pass through the picturesque Bend on their way to "Tenement Hades"; the brightness and gaiety of the market become a foil for the darkness and oppression of a street of sweatshops, which Townsend goes on to decry: "As they turned down Bayard Street, and then into Baxter, Eleanor shivered as one who steps from sunlight into the silent, solemn shade of a vault. Every condition of life which could affect mind or body was reversed. The people, from the youngest to the oldest, were speechless and grave and hopeless-looking." When the friendly visitor sets foot in the tenement she cannot help but expostulate: "God in heaven! Can nothing be done for such as these?" The next ten pages are spent detailing the horrors of tenement overcrowding, hunger, filth, child labor, despair, and disease.[24]

The plot of moral struggle is accompanied by a general moral as well as social commentary on the slums. When Townsend wants to describe the Bowery as a whole, he falls back on the sort of abstract moral spectacle that the Reverend Chapin indulged in: "The Bowery! . . . [T]he Bowery presents . . . a microcosm. There is man in worldly condition from wealth to bitterest poverty; in morals, from him who is devoting his life to following Christ's example among the poor, to him to whom every crime and vice are familiar by practice."[25]

Usually the moral response is not so balanced or sanguine. When Basil March takes his Elevated ride through the Bowery in Howells's novel, "the whole at moments seemed to him lawless, godless," and an ethical lesson of New York's "frantic panorama" pushes itself toward consciousness. March begins to "perceive the chaos to which the individual selfishness must always lead."[26]

The language of moral disdain can get a good deal richer than this. The slumming expedition in *Social Strugglers* veers from the picturesque Italian sector to a dangerous and vicious neighborhood where "that most noxious growth of a great city, the New York tough, flourishes; here youthful gangs of criminals have their 'clubs' in the rear of saloons and dives, and plot burglaries and assaults; here vice and degradation of all kinds stalk abroad in hideous nakedness."[27]

Sometimes moral repulsion and social horror play off each other and become feverishly confused. In one passage, Fawcett starts out in an ethnographic manner, describing a tenement woman's peculiar adaptations to the conditions of the tenement (she sews at night by electric light for want of sunlight), but he abruptly veers into a tirade of moral condemnation and social expose. It is as if the subject of the tenement cannot be raised without certain axes being ground. The particulars of tenement habits first give way to garish metaphors of social misery:

> [S]he did her work at night, and took what rest she could get between morning and the hours that followed. Soon others in the house imitated her. . . . The late feasts of luxury and dissipation in other parts of town were copied here with tints of frightful parody and irony. These were revellers with cups of gall for their wine, and spectres of want to serve as footmen.

Then Fawcett seems to forget that he is spinning a metaphor about the social oppression of these women. An ideological dam seems to burst with the introduction
of his moralistic metaphors. The next sentence does not follow from the logic of
his present topic; it splashes on the page from another discourse:

> Sin rioted in the reeking house, whose very stairs had rotten creaks when you trod
> them, as though fatigued by the steps of sots and trulls. To enter some of the rooms
> was to smell infection and to face beastliness. Fever lived in the sinks and closets
> along the halls, where festered refuse more rancid and stenchful than stale swill, and
> so vile that to name it would be to deal with words which are the dung of lexicons.
> Those halls had nooks of gloom whence miasma might have fled in fright before the
> human grossness that spawned there. Little children dipped their chastity in poison
> between the scurfy-grained wainscots of every corridor, and twisted their soft lips
> into the shaping of oaths that would scare brothels.[28]

Rotten stairs seemingly worn down by drunks and prostitutes; infection together
with beastliness; miasma versus human grossness; scaly paneling and poisoned
chastity: the social and moral decay of the building is of a piece, or else there is a
contest between them, a contest in which spiritual degradation is the more powerful. The description of strange tenement habits is overwhelmed by a melange of
invective that is traditional in the literature of the poor.[29]

From its earliest sustained appearances in fiction, the slum was described with
just such a mixture of moral and physical disgust. In *Life in the Iron Mills*, Rebecca
Harding Davis begins with physical description:

> A cloudy day: do you know what that is in a town of iron-works? The sky sank
> down before dawn, muddy, flat, immovable. The air is thick, clammy with breath of
> crowded human beings. It stifles me. . . .
>   The idiosyncrasy of this town is smoke. It rolls sullenly in slow folds from the
> great chimneys of the iron-foundries, and settles down in black, slimy pools on the
> muddy streets. . . . The long train of mules, dragging masses of pig-iron through
> the narrow street have a foul vapor hanging to their reeking sides.

Her account then becomes blatantly symbolic: "[H]ere, inside, is a little broken figure of an angel pointing upward from the mantel-shelf; but even its wings are covered with smoke, clotted and black." And soon enough her chronicle moves into
literal moral estimation:

> [F]rom the street window I look on the slow stream of human life creeping past,
> night and morning, to the great mills. Masses of men, with dull, besotted faces bent
> to the ground, sharpened here and there by pain or cunning; skin and muscle and
> flesh begrimed with smoke and ashes; stooping all night over boiling cauldrons of
> metal, laired by day in dens of drunkenness and infamy; breathing from infancy to
> death an air saturated with fog and grease and soot, vileness for soul and body.[30]

Her description begins with men's bodies (faces, skin and muscle and flesh), the
pollutants that stain them (smoke and ashes), and finally the source of these pollutants (boiling cauldrons of metal). But then the paragraph takes a spiritual turn to

dens of iniquity: it leaves off of the bodily and brings up another sort of corruption, a kind that is not visible from her street window. Finally, she returns to the corporal register, now claiming that the physical pollutants have both material and moral effects. The circuit is completed. Spiritual corruption is made tangible, and visible, in the form of fog and grease and soot.

In most of this fiction, not much distinctive slum action is represented simply because it was too scandalous to report or view. (Henry James exemplifies the tender Victorian sensibilities of many of his literary contemporaries and their readers when he explains that his omission of the "grosser elements of the sordid and the squalid" from his description of the slums is due to the fact that he and his "fellow-pilgrims" in the ghetto themselves avoid places "of the 'seamy' order, an inquiry into seaminess having been unanimously pronounced futile.")[31] On the level of plot, this taboo against slum realism translated into a sort of deus ex machina that was familiar in the genre: the slum characters are often mercifully saved from participating in their surroundings.

Townsend can wax poetic, in a touristic mood, about "the gay companionship of the market-place," but when his title character, Carminella, in *A Daughter of the Tenements* reaches the age of fourteen and is expected by her Italian immigrant father to help at the fruit stand, the market is suddenly considered "a fixed evil" by her virtuous and dutiful mother. Townsend's reader finds out very little about the gay companionship of the market (which, it is indicated, involves a loose sexuality) because Carminella's mother Teresa sees that she works only during daylight hours and is properly chaperoned to and from work. Likewise, though Carminella becomes a Bowery dancer, the reader sees hardly anything of the life behind the scenes in the theater, again because Teresa had somehow managed always to keep her daughter from "the seamy side of stage folks' lives." In fact, her mother "had schemed and planned, ceaselessly and tirelessly, to keep Carminella from the people and the life in the Bend. . . . [S]he considered the whole life there an immitigable evil from which she strove to protect her child by care." Oddly enough, then, Townsend's "daughter of the tenements" is not *of* the tenements at all, and this is precisely what makes her a morally proper heroine for his story: she is "more intelligent, more companionable because of [a] mind and body untainted by the slums."[32]

Much the same can be said for Townsend's other hero in this romantic comedy of the tenements. Tom, Carminella's amorous counterpart, is said to have some "places on the surface of his character where the manners and morals of the Bend had cut in too deep to be polished out by a few years of casual rubbing against less rugged planes." And indeed, Townsend gives the reader a demonstration of these rough edges: at one point Tom beats up a sidewalk solicitor from a cheap-clothing house without much apparent provocation. Tom recognizes in the "puller-in" a menace that the reader does not, shows a seasoned skill in street-fighting, alludes to a gang of friends who would "have cleaned out the shop" if he had been jumped, and recounts "all this in an indifferent and somewhat feelingless manner." But this scene is practically the single indication that Tom possesses any manners or morals of the Bend; it is just about the only sequence in which he is a carrier of ethnographic detail. Usually the narrative heaps Tom with wholesome epithets: the reader is told that "he was industrious, sober and strong"; that he was "a stalwart, handsome boy"; that his father "was proud of his behavior, his good morals, his honesty about his wages"; that he was "unnaturally industrious"; that at four years old he was "early displaying a strength and independence of character which in latter years made him . . . our hero." Like Carminella's mother, Tom's father strives "to keep Tom off the street at night," to protect him from the immoral influences of the Bend.[33] In Townsend's novel, the almost magical moral rectitude of his protagonists functions as a sort of curtain that is continually brought down on the ethnographic action he stages.

An even more extreme operation is at work in Kate Douglas Wiggin's *Timothy's Quest*. The boy-hero, Timothy Jessup, though bred in an institution and the slums and though "somewhat ragged, all forlorn, and none too clean," was at the age of "ten or eleven" "a poet, philosopher, and lover of the beautiful." His tenement neighbors "had never discovered the fact; for, although he had lived in that world, he had never been of it." The tenement had been "helpless to defile him, such was the purity of his nature." And his first action in the novel is to gather up his baby sister (who also, despite "the sacred laws of heredity," has a "sunshiny nature . . . like Wordsworth's immortal babe") and to head for the train station: within three chapters, he has managed to leave the slums behind entirely.[34]

This dynamic of a moral proof against ethnographic detail is again evident in the literature of the slums from its first incarnations. In Alger's *Ragged Dick*, the reader learns that Dick was "fond of going to the Old Bowery Theater" and to "a noted gambling-house on Baxter Street." But these places are immediately relegated, by the narrator, to the category of "mean faults." And before the reader can accompany Dick to either of these slum haunts and thus see them in any detail, Dick's "noble" nature (with the help of some moral instruction from an upperclass boy) overcomes his bad habits, and he gives up these pastimes. The novel, though subtitled *Street Life in New York*, contains precious little of that life.

In the case of Townsend's *Chimmie Fadden* (1895), it is not exactly the hero's moral hardiness that stifles the distinctive action of the slums; rather, a lucky break removes a deserving boy from the Bowery once and for all. Because "Chimmie is a good boy if 'e only had a chance," a rich woman who does slum missionary work decides to get him hired as her father's footman. After a single scene in the streets of the slums (a scuffle in defense of the lady's honor), Chimmie is whisked away to "polite society," and in the course of the rest of the book, he ventures back into the slums only a couple of times.[35]

It is significant, though, that Alger's Ragged Dick smokes and gambles and goes to Bowery shows even briefly, that Townsend's Tom is allowed an episode of rowdy Bowery conduct while his Carminella is never anything but well-behaved, and that his mischievous vernacular hero (Chimmie Fadden) is a boy. Because they were young and because they were boys, their dubious slum exploits were not sexual in nature and so not taboo.

Late-nineteenth-century Protestant morality was sentimental and profoundly sexist. Bad habits were thought to leave a deeper stamp on women, and feminine vice was of greater repugnance; in the middle-class hierarchy of virtues, a woman's chastity, even a poor woman's, was highly fetishized. Charles Loring Brace, for instance, could sympathize with street boys, romanticize their pluck and resourcefulness, and admit that they often have "a rather good time of it," but he states plainly that "with . . . girl-vagrant[s] it is different." According to Brace, slum boys' characters could be redeemed with a change of environment and re-fined influences, but girls, in losing their purity, experienced a "deeper" fall, one from which they could never recover.[36]

Thus Sullivan's short fictions include picturesque comedies about the naughty exploits of slum boys, but his girls are a different story. The boy-protagonist of one tale, "Leather," commits a purse-snatching and then manages, entertainingly, to elude an improbable police dragnet, and "A Young Desperado, a Story for Boys" delights in the pranks and petty scams of a little tough named "Skinny," who, rather than being punished for his dubious deeds, is rewarded, at the end, with money and accolades. Meanwhile, Sullivan has no rough-and-tumble female heroines. In fact, he has two tales about slum women who get innocently caught up in the snares of immorality, and in both, the women contemplate suicide—and properly so, according to the author. Minnie Kelsey is spared, and her story ends happily when her would-be seducer suddenly proposes to marry her. Ernestine Beaulefoy's tale is a "Tragedy"; she throws herself down a hatchway in a sweat-shop after being physically molested by her "lascivious, brutal, and gloating" boss, and the narrator basically applauds her action. Upon her death, the narrator first experiences relief, and "as the shock passed away, this relief came to be almost gratification. . . . [I]nsult and temptation had followed her wherever she looked for employment; . . . she had chosen between death and degradation. So I re-joiced with her in her choice."[37] Whether by marriage or death, the distinctive sexual action of the slums is usually terminated quickly.

Occasionally a tale of premarital sex does drag on, and this is rare because it is scandalous. Fawcett tells such a story, but he is obviously nervous about potential outrage among his readership. At the end of his novel, it is as if he feels required to cite absolutely every virtue known to the middle class in order to counterbalance the sinfulness he has been busy representing, or, perhaps, in order to make it completely clear that he is not to be tarnished by the scurrilous events he has narrated:

> There was something measurelessly pitiable in the meeting of these two destitute and accursed human souls. Each had made its own earthly hell, and amid the horrors of such a doom they sat and gazed at one another. Not far from them the immense

hopeful push of human life was progressing. The innocence of childhood, boyhood, girlhood, kept its purity unsullied. Ambition, thrift, delight in life, blossomed like hardy flowerage on sturdy stalks. Household peace and ease, domestic love and joy, honor of self, parental tenderness, confidence in the future, wisdom of temperance, hatred of soiling habitude, calmness of virtuous old age, wifely and husbandly devotion, filial fondness and obedience—all, in short, that sums up what we name the nobility and worthiness of society flourished but a few streets away from these two outcasts, and yet all as so abysmally distant![38]

Fawcett also includes in *The Evil That Men Do* an explicit justification of his representation of rank immorality. Before the final, dreadful demise of his heroine, he interrupts the narrative to show two walk-on characters reading and commenting on his book in what is basically a high-class brothel:

> "How can you read this sort of stuff?"
> "That!" sped the astonished answer. "Why, it isn't stuff a bit! Jack, you can't have read 'The Evil that Men Do,' or you wouldn't talk so of it!"
> "I haven't read it," replied Jack, "but I've heard it's pretty bad."
> "Bad! *How*, bad?"
> "Oh, well . . . immoral."
> The brunette bridled. . . . "It's the plain truth—every line and every word of it!" she declared. "*We* oughtn't to call it immoral," she went on excitedly, with the manner of one who has a treasured cause to defend. "The very people that know how true such a book is are always the first ones to stamp on it and shout it down. It ought to do a great deal more good than harm, and I believe it will!"[39]

Even when a slum tale does delve into the taboo, as Fawcett's does with its sexual violation, it is only the conduct of the characters—not their desires, feelings, or ethics—that is distinctive of the slums. The slum women will share the same values as their middle-class counterparts; they will recognize the same code; they will agonize over it; and they will fall to a man who is attractive by middle-class standards. Such is the case in *The Evil That Men Do.*

Unlike Townsend's heroes, Cora Stang has no parent to keep her from the life of the slums; unlike Wiggin's heroes, she does not manage to escape from it; unlike Alger's, she is not able to earn her way out of it: she must constantly encounter it. She works for sweaters; she lives in a tenement and a lodging house; she attends a wake; she goes to a dance hall; she does domestic service; she gets employment as a shop girl.

But though the reader is told that the women at the shop occupy themselves with cheap novels and spend their money on fashion, when they converse, they hover around the subject of morals: "'Character!' laughed Lily. 'I had one once, but I'm afraid it's all gone to grass now.'" Lily, a young woman of skimpy "moral weight," who is "no taintless representative of her chaste-sounding name," is nonetheless obsessed with familiar questions of moral philosophy. She goes on for a full page in a blasphemous manner: "I think girls like us make fools of themselves . . . to fritter away their days tryin' just how good they can be. What's the use of it all? . . . Now, after all, who cares two pins whether I lark a little or don't? What's heaven ever done for *me*? . . . *Is* there any?"

Likewise, the slum woman's desire is circumscribed by a familiar moral and social context: she falls for a man who is not of the slums. Fawcett's novel fits the category which Friedrich Engels called the "old, old story of the proletarian girl seduced by a man of the middle class."[40] The heroine's virtuous resistance to her seducer is slowly broken down through promises of marriage and finally the imposition of alcohol, and importantly, her seducer is a cad from a higher class whose moral qualities and social trappings appear dazzling to a woman accustomed to mean and vicious surroundings. Though her sexual act is taboo, her sexual desire is perfectly acceptable and familiar: at one point Cora thinks excitedly to herself, "[H]ow handsome and strong he is, and what a *will* he has."[41] And finally, as we have seen, Cora's inner experience of temptation, sin, and remorse is textbook middle-class moral philosophy.[42]

Maggie: *Crane's Correction of the Slum Tale*

Stephen Crane is one among many fiction writers with an ethnographic interest in the slums, but his commitment to its "distinctive color and action" is something extraordinary.[43] As is well-known, Crane's representations of the slums never come in the form of moral sermons and social pleas; though he describes sweatshop drudgery and tenement disorder, he does not sound the traditional charity themes of vice and crime, filth and disease, unhealthy and unsafe labor practices. It is well-known that Crane claimed that "an artist has no business to preach"; we also know that he boasted to his friends that "you can't find any preaching in *Maggie*." As we have seen, he regarded the sentimental novels of his contemporaries as "pink valentines," and in a letter about *Maggie* he specifically derided Townsend's *Daughter of the Tenements*.[44] But the absence of moralistic and social preaching and the acid rejection of Victorian sentimentalism are only the beginning of what makes Crane's book unusual.

In addition, *Maggie* is not populated with individuals who are magically spared their slum environment; indeed, in an inscription on several copies of the original version, Crane claims that "it tries to show that environment is a tremendous thing in the world and frequently shapes lives regardless."[45] Even more striking, the book does not contain traditional moral drama of the sort Fawcett's Cora experiences. Crane chose for his plot an "old story" in the literature of the slums, as Frank Norris noted in review;[46] in fact, *Maggie* recounts the same basic tale as *The Evil That Men Do* and also shares a compelling resemblance with Reverend Thomas de Witt Talmage's *Night Sides of City Life* (1878) and Brace's *Dangerous Classes of New York*—depending on how one reads Maggie's death scene. Like Maggie, Fawcett's heroine is a slum girl subjected to the hardships of violent parents and menial labor; she is made love to and abandoned by a man, and she ends up as a prostitute and then a corpse (Cora is murdered). According to Talmage, a fallen woman must choose between the cold garret of a sewing girl and the East River;[47] Brace includes a drawing of a woman who is about to throw herself in the same river, which Maggie approaches in her last moments (perhaps to kill herself). But Crane's retelling is distinctive—and not simply because a girl's chastity, one of the most precious themes of sentimental literature and sentimentalized Protestant morality, draws from him no preaching.[48] Not only is the conduct of his characters scandalous, but their moral code and values are likewise particular to his slums—and anathema to the middle class.

Crane's ethnography is more profound than that of his contemporaries, not simply because it is more prevalent or because it is uninterrupted by conventional moral and social asides but because he imagines the distinctive codes and values— together, the distinctive ethics—that lie behind the distinctive slum action. An action is largely incomprehensible on its face, and this is why the action in the slum novels of the day can often appear exotic: it is unexplained; its cause is obscure; it has the ontological status of either a genetic disease or a freak of nature. To understand an action, one must also know the ethics: the ethical code (so one knows whether it is an observance or a violation) and the ethical values (so one knows why and how the actor engages in the action).

When Tom beats up the dangerous "puller-in" in *A Daughter of the Tenements*, the reader does learn something about the code: Tom's unfeeling reflection on the event indicates that fighting is not prohibited. But the sequence remains exotic because the reader is never given insight into the values that encourage everybody—and here, specifically, the puller-in—to engage in spontaneous violence.

Much the same distinction could be made about Riis's ethnography. As we have seen, he often acknowledges that the poor districts have their own "standards and customs." What is difficult for Riis, though, is a discussion of alternative values indigenous to the slums: in one strange passage, Riis dismisses as "a heathenish pessimist" the man who seems to explain to him that the extravagant wake is "a sort of consolation cup for the survivors for whom there is . . . 'no such luck,'" even though he accepts the explanation (132–133). For Crane, it is not just the living conditions and the ways of the urban poor that are other; so is their morality.

Crane proceeds in a programmatic fashion. His *Maggie* is a tour de force and a self-conscious one. It is a kind of counterdemonstration. He takes an old tale and retells it: to get it right. It is as if Crane is saying to his colleagues, yes, you got the basic plot elements, the basic action correct, but you completely misunderstand how it comes about; you do not understand just how distinctive this action is; you do not want to understand; let me show you. Yes, says Crane in *Maggie*, the slum girl has premarital sex. Yes, she becomes a prostitute. Yes, she kills herself or is murdered—Crane may be so deliberate in his attempt to set the record straight that he purposefully leaves Maggie's death ambiguous in order to cover both variants of this stereotypical story.[49] In any case, for Crane, the rough outline of the action is correct, but everything else is mistaken. The details of the sexual behavior are wrong: Maggie is not seduced, and not by a playboy of a higher class; she falls in love with a tough. The significance of the sexual action is misinterpreted because the local ethical code is not understood: a portion of Crane's Bowery has no prohibition against premarital sex. Finally, the girl's inner experience is misrepresented because her values do not correspond to those of the middle class—because, in particular, chastity is not an ethic for her: Maggie experiences no temptation and resistance to sin and no remorse for the act; rather, she is attracted to a tough because he is, in her ethics, a moral exemplar.

At each point in the narrative when the reader could expect resistance or regret from Maggie, Crane supplies none. First of all, when Maggie's beau Pete comes to fetch her for a date, her drunken, violent mother accuses her of having "gone t' d' devil" and being a "disgrace t' yer people," and she finally tells her daughter to "go teh hell an' good riddance." All we get of Maggie is: "Maggie gazed long at her mother," "the girl began to tremble" and, in the end, "she went" (30–31).[50] After Maggie goes off with Pete, the narrator raises the question of morality. In a bar, "a hall of irregular shape," we are told of Maggie's feelings: "As to the present she perceived only vague reasons to be miserable. Her life was Pete's and she considered him worthy of the charge. She would be disturbed by no particular apprehension so long as Pete adored her as he now said he did. *She did not feel like a bad woman.* To her knowledge she had never seen any better" (38–39, my italics). Crane make it absolutely clear that Maggie's "vague reasons to be miserable" are not moral compunctions; rather, they probably have to do with her mother's rejection. "To her knowledge she had never seen any better" may at first sound redundant, but it is not. What that curious-sounding sentence means is that Maggie may in fact have seen better women, but she lacks the moral conceptions to make such a judgment.

When Maggie returns to her home, some weeks after having left it and after Pete has gone off with another woman, a successful prostitute, her mother attacks her with righteous sarcasm, while a tenement crowd looks on:

> Maggie's mother paced to and fro, addressing the doorful of eyes, expounding like a glib showman. Her voice rang through the building.
>   "Dere she stands," she cried, wheeling suddenly and pointing with a dramatic finger. "Dere she stands! Lookut her! Ain' she a dindy? An' she was so good as to come home teh her mudder, she was! Ain' she a beaut'? Ain't she a dindy?" (48)

To this baiting and to the crowd's "jeering cries" and "shrill laughter," Maggie does not react with remorse. "The girl seemed to awaken," is all Crane tells us. She appeals to her brother: "Jimmie——." When he rebuffs her, "his lips curling in scorn . . . and his repelling hands express[ing] horror of contamination," all we hear is that "Maggie turned and went" (48). If Maggie's "awakening" here were a traditional moral one—if, that is, a sense of her own sin had dawned on her—she might then have asked for forgiveness or she might have gone off to excoriate herself, but she does neither of these. Instead, she seeks out a second opinion; she obviously hopes her brother will see it differently than her mother does. Maggie has awakened, rather, to the fact that her mother is dead set against her, that an appeal to her is pointless; she had not counted on such vehemence, or, presumably, she would never have returned home.

Maggie's next transition, into prostitution, has no spiritual correlative at all. The narrative elides her emotions entirely: chapter 16 ends with Maggie searching for help (now that her lover Pete has rejected her again, in addition to her mother and brother); at the beginning of chapter 17, the reader is presented with a girl who is already "of the painted cohorts of the city" (52). Her final transition, into death, does dip into subjectivity, briefly and vaguely, but Crane's prose reveals no trace of any guilt on her part. After she has been rejected by a number of potential clients (continuing her rejections of the last few chapters), she comes to the river, and her feeling is obliquely expressed in the last sentence of the death scene: "The varied sounds of life, made joyous by distance and seeming unapproachableness, came faintly and died away to silence" (53). The implication is that the girl would like to participate in the "joyous" "sounds of life" but feels she is an outcast from them. Meanwhile, the narration suggests that she is the victim of an auditory illusion: they only sound joyous because they are remote and inaccessible. And, true enough, most of the sounds the reader has heard in the novel have been violent, mindless, and argumentative. She dies with what the narrator has shown is an illusion, an illusion of human joy and togetherness. She also dies in the emptiness of silence. This sentence implies lonely despondency, but hardly compunction. The experience of Maggie, the protagonist of the novel, includes no moments of traditional moral drama or transformation.

Maggie's moral illiteracy stems from the fact that the ethics of character and purity, which are given frantic voice by her mother, have not been passed on to the younger generation in the Bowery. In Crane's novel, premarital sex does not have its usual status as an unforgivable sin, an irreparable degradation. In fact, it has no monolothic status. Rather, it is a sometime moral taboo, and this is part of Crane's ethnographic perspective: a moralist sees absolute good and evil, an ethnographer various codes and violations. In Crane's Bowery, the taboo against premarital sex has half-crumbled. While Mrs. Johnson may truly believe that her daughter has "gone t' d' devil," Maggie herself clearly has no such conviction, and her brother initially considers the affair a matter of "the rules of politeness" (31). When he finds himself harassed by the gossip of neighbors, he is not worried about the fact that Maggie's soul is in peril but, rather, as he says to his mother, that "dis t'ing queers us" (40). Likewise, Pete is concerned about protecting the "eminent respectability" of the saloon where he works (51). Like Maggie's mother, Jimmie and Pete turn Maggie away, but unlike Mrs. Johnson, they are not morally outraged. Rather, they are trying to follow rules of decorum they seem barely to understand.

Crane uses the word "respectability" four times in the course of three pages, and it is a term with ethnographic significance. Respectability is not a substantive virtue, nor does it belong exclusively to Protestant morality; it is merely the social acceptance that accompanies compliance with a code of ethics, whatever that code happens to be. For Jimmie and Pete, the Protestant prohibition against premarital sex is something vague and hazy; since they have not been brought up in this code (and routinely break it in their own lives), it is abstract and arbitrary for them. When the time comes for them to obey it, they act like visitors to a foreign country.

Crane never judges his characters in terms of traditional middle-class morality; rather, they are in part defined by their relations to its code (as well as to a local, homegrown code, as we shall see). As Crane says of a millionaire's family and his mansion in "An Experiment in Luxury" (1894), "there lived tradition and superstition. They were perhaps ignorant of that which they worshiped, and, not comprehending it at all, it naturally followed that the fervor of their devotion could set the sky ablaze."[51] Elsewhere, he frames the issue theoretically: "[S]ocial form as practised by the stupid is not a law," he writes. "It is a vital sensation. It is not temporary, emotional; it is fixed and, very likely, the power that makes the rain, the sunshine, the wind, now recognizes social form as an important element in the curious fashioning of the world."[52] Crane is interested in the curious fashioning of the world, and thus, in the cases of *Maggie*, *George's Mother* (1896), and his city sketches, he is interested in the social forms—or ethical rules—that operate in the slums: here the taboo against premarital sex. Crane's characters are not philosophers; they are stupid. They are victims and enforcers of this social form: uninformed violators (Maggie), superstitious believers (Mrs. Johnson), and hypocritical advocates (Jimmie) of this ethical rule.

In *Maggie*, it is not that women are susceptible, as in traditional moral thought, to a deeper fall than men. It is, rather, that they are subjected to more stringent ethical rules and treated as carriers of moral infection. Pete's own premarital sex with Maggie does not harm his reputation with his boss as long as he can henceforth keep her away from him; likewise, Jimmie can preserve his Protestant respectability with the tenement crowd as long as he avoids his child-bearing girl-friends and his notorious sister.

The significance of this sexual taboo in Crane's story comes as much from the ease with which it is broken as from the savage punishment for its violation. In presenting Maggie and Pete's love affair, Crane's ethnography pushes beyond the familiar moral rules and plunges into the alternative code of the Bowery that was exotic and threatening to its middle-class reader. Another code exists in Crane's Bowery, among the younger generation, that accepts premarital sex. And this code is just one aspect of an entirely alternative morality.

Pete, with his "enticing nonchalance," his "hair curled down over his forehead in an oiled bang," his "bristling mustache," his "red puff tie, and his patent leather shoes" (17), suggests, as one editor of *Maggie* notes, "the Bowery B'hoy (Boy), a tough of the Lower East Side who dressed as a 'dandy.'"[53] And in addition to a bizarre dress code, Pete embodies an ethical philosophy that is foreign to the middle class. Maggie, a true daughter of the tenements, recognizes an ethics in Pete and respects him for it. She observes that

> there were valor and contempt for circumstances in the glance of his eye. He waved his hands like a man of the world who dismisses religion and philosophy and says "Fudge!" He had certainly seen everything, and with each curl of his lip he declared that it amounted to nothing. Maggie thought he must be a very elegant and graceful bartender. (17–18)

> When he said, "Ah, what d'hell!" his voice was burdened with disdain for the inevitable and contempt for anything that fate might compel him to endure.
> Maggie perceived that here was the beau ideal of a man. (19)

> Here was a formidable man who disdained the strength of a world full of fists. Here was one who had contempt for brass-clothed power; one whose knuckles could ring defiantly against the granite of the law. He was a knight.. . . .
> To her the earth was composed of hardships and insults. She felt instant admiration for a man who openly defied it. She thought that if the grim angel of death should clutch his heart, Pete would shrug his shoulders and say, "Oh, ev'ryt'ing goes." (20)

> She thought he must live in a blare of pleasure. (21)

Maggie's attraction to Pete, a character whom the middle-class reader would have recognized as uncouth, is another of Crane's representations of distinctive action in the slums. Maggie's relationship to Pete can hardly be called a seduction. In her reaction to Pete, she is not hampered by moral qualms. On the contrary, for her he is an ethical paragon, "a knight." Her attraction to Pete is instant and spontaneous; unlike the cad in Fawcett's novel, he does not need to promise marriage or administer alcohol to win affection. Much more shocking, he has no real "elegance," that is to say, no middle-class moral or social appeal to recommend him. Pete is a Bowery tough, and Maggie falls for him on this basis.[54] What Maggie's idealization of Pete suggests is that the two of them subscribe to values that are different from those of the middle class.

Maggie's brother Jimmie, an angry young truck driver, might seem quite particular and quirky until one notices that he has nearly all of the traits that Maggie finds so admirable in Pete. He exhibits the same physical bravado: he is getting in fights from the very beginning of the book, in which Crane represents a rock skirmish among rival gangs of kids. He is fearless: "He was afraid of neither the devil nor the leader of society." He is likewise worldly and cynical: "He studied human nature in the gutter, and found it no worse than he thought he had reason to believe it." He has contempt for his social betters and all those things he is supposed to respect: "He maintained a belligerent attitude toward all well-dressed men. . . . Above all things he despised obvious Christians and ciphers with the chrysanthemums of aristocracy in their buttonholes." In fact, he has contempt for everything: "After a time his sneer grew so that it turned its glare upon all things. He became so sharp he believed in nothing" (13–14).

Physical prowess, fearlessness, worldliness, contempt, defiance, pleasure, and Bowery bravado and style: these are the qualities that are valued in Crane's slums, among the younger generation at least, and they show up again in his other novel of the slums, *George's Mother*. In much the same way that Maggie is awed by Pete, George looks up to a gang of "young men who stood in the cinders between a brick wall and the pavement, near the side door of a corner saloon," and he eventually joins their group. What makes them attractive is their worldliness (they "knew more about life than other people"; "they were like veterans with their wars"), their toughness and their disdain for their social superiors ("they sometimes inaugurated little fights with . . . well-dressed men"), and their defiance of the laws that usually governed slum existence ("they were all too clever to work"). "One lad in particular" is respected because "he whipped his employer, the proprietor of a large grain and feed establishment," a man of "wealth and social position." As with Jimmie and Pete, "their feeling for contemporaneous life was one of contempt. Their philosophy taught that in a large part the whole thing was idle and a great bore. With fine scorn they sneered at the futility of it." Just as Pete would do no more than shrug his shoulders if the angel of death should grip his heart, they had "the courage to stand still and let the skies clap together if they will."[55]

This is a philosophy that is not only quite foreign to the middle class but also, in fact, an inversion of traditional Protestant ethics. What the middle class officially values (to borrow some expressions from Fawcett's *The Evil That Men Do*) is "the innocence of childhood, . . . peace and ease, . . . tenderness, confidence in the future, wisdom of temperance, . . . [and] obedience," whereas what Crane's younger generation in the Bowery idealizes is worldliness at an early age, physical power and violence, toughness, contempt for the future, the wisdom of pleasure, and disobedience. The proper relation to the self is no longer denial; it has been replaced by indulgence. Jimmie does feel "obliged to work," but not because of the Protestant work ethic. Rather, "when he had a dollar in his pocket his satisfaction with existence was the greatest thing in the world. So, eventually, he felt obliged to work" (14).[56] The ethical strategy and aim for the self is no longer to be industrious and to avoid and resist temptation so as to keep one's character pure, but to be "in life and of life"—to "menace . . . mankind" on the streets (14), even to work—in order to feel good.

There is a profound ethnographic quality to Crane's representation of Maggie's romance of Pete, Jimmie's street activities, and George's emulation of a neighborhood gang. Most slum literature was organized on the conventional nineteenth-century moral distinction between the worthy and the unworthy poor. Characters in slum stories would be dressed up in exotic local clothing, vernaculars, and customs, but these distinctive colors and actions were superficial trappings that had little to do with the essential ethical identity that lay beneath. Slum writers again and again taught their readers to disregard the ethnographic surface and pierce through to the moral substance. Underneath Ragged Dick's tattered clothing and vulgar street dialect is an honest nature; Tom's unruly Bowery manners in *A Daughter of the Tenements* are nothing but dressing on his fundamentally noble character; beneath Jurgis's strange Lithuanian rituals, in *The Jungle*, is a fierce Protestant work ethic; and the socially ostracized Jews in Sullivan's *Tenement Tales of New York* turn out to be paragons of moral virtue. The narrator in Sullivan's tale converses with the Jewish mother and discovers that despite her miserable English, she speaks the same moral language as he does, full of expressions such as "honestness", "gharagder," and "hard-vorrukin'": "Through her uncouth words shone a conscience and a true heart in the right place. Her thought and her manner were the last remove from vulgarity. I lost sight of her broken English and followed her reflections, sound as they were; and her moral feelings, unperverted as they were."[57] In depicting slums types, from bootblacks to meat packers, from Jewish tailors to Italian fruit peddlers, typical fiction writers eventually placed them somewhere along a moral continuum that stretched from virtuous to vicious (there was the honest, hard-working slum girl, the industrious young man, the boy tough, the beggar, the drunkard, the male libertine, the woman loose in morals). Crane, meanwhile, never pierces beneath his ethnographic representations, and he never puts his characters on the traditional moral map. Rather, he suggests that the younger generation in the Bowery lives in a separate ethical universe, a world that does not recognize the traditional Protestant values of sobriety, discipline, chastity, and so on but operates according to an alternative morality— with its own ethical geography.

Maggie's tragedy, as critics have often noted, is not that she experiences a traditional moral fall into sin but that she is ostracized for her immorality. Apparently for selfish reasons of her own, Maggie's drunken, abusive, and hypocritical mother morally denounces her in front of the tenement crowd, and the girl henceforth becomes untouchable in the community. What is overlooked in this version of Crane's tale is that Maggie has already received a second and completely different moral denunciation—this one in front of her only remaining ally, Pete, and by a representative of the alternative ethics of the Bowery.

Nell, "the woman of brilliance and audacity" (44), who sets herself up as an ethical judge in much the same way that Mrs. Johnson does, curses Maggie with the younger generation's ethical equivalent of the older woman's "gone t' d' devil." For Mrs. Johnson, Maggie has thrown aside her goodness and lost her soul; for Nell, Maggie has "no spirit" and has an air about her of "pumpkin pie and virtue" (49). In the Bowery beer-hall world, Nell's words, like Maggie's mother's in her own milieu, are the kiss of death: Pete will no longer have anything to do with her.

Nell's ethical diagnosis seems to be borne out by Maggie's subsequent failure as a prostitute. Crane's critics have often been baffled by a seeming contradiction in Maggie's last scene: she is wearing expensive clothes that bespeak success at her profession, but she is rejected by a long series of potential clients.[58] The answer may in part be very simple. Maggie did well enough at the beginning, when she was a new item on the streets, but now her novelty has worn off, and she does not have what it takes. Or so the novel suggests, in no uncertain terms: her first and best potential client "stared glassily for a moment, but gave a slight convulsive start when he discerned that she was neither new, Parisian, nor theatrical" (52). To say that she is neither Parisian nor theatrical is to say that she lacks style and flair, or perhaps what Nell would call spirit. Men who smoke cigarettes with "a sublime air" and wear "a look of ennui" (52) do not want to have sex with prostitutes who suggest "pumpkin pie and virtue"—once they are no longer "new."

If the client's terms are not obviously ethical, it is undeniable that Nell's terms are moral ones; they could hardly be more resoundingly moral, and it is also pretty clear that they are inversions of the familiar Protestant ones. We have a glimpse of just how severe the ethical divide is between the older and younger generations in Crane's Bowery. These groups have different values, if by values we understand not only the kind of self one is supposed to develop (modest or "theatrical," humble or "audacious," honest or "brilliant," and so on) but also the very aspect of the self that is valued. Soul and spirit here are not the same "ethical substance": the Bowery spirit is akin to passion or pride, the enemy of the Protestant soul or conscience; conversely, that soul or virtue throws a wet rag on slum spirit.

Crane's Bowery is split between two opposing moralities. It is a society in ethical war. The division between opposing camps seems so extreme that it borders on the artificial: the older and younger generations appear hardly to communicate. Each code is mysterious to those outside of it, and only Nell, perhaps, seems to be aware of the conflict; at least her language is informed. But Crane needs this extreme separation so that Maggie can fall through the cracks, so that she can be a casualty of the war. She does not know how to be conventionally virtuous because she was never told; she is drawn to the values of her generation, but she does not seem to possess the spirit to embody them herself.

If at the end she is bordering on the suicidal (whether she actually commits suicide or simply has lost the ability to exert any precaution),[59] this is because she appears ethically repulsive to both camps and is repeatedly rejected by both of them. The ignorance that makes possible her Protestant sinfulness is clear enough, if somewhat fantastical. What remains to be seen is why she is ethically ill-equipped to succeed in the beer-hall and streetwalker world of the Bowery. For this, we will have to turn to Maggie's inner experience. She has one, all right; it just does not happen to be the traditional moral one.[60]

II

Slum

Spectacle

3 ❧ The Touristic Ethic
and Photography

When *How the Other Half Lives* was advertised, it was not marketed strictly as a reform piece, exclusively as "an indictment of the tenement system." One advertisement for the book declared:

> No page is uninstructive, but it would be misleading to suppose the book even tinctured with didacticism. It is from beginning to end as picturesque in treatment as it is in material. The author's acquaintance with the latter is extremely intimate. The reader feels that he is being guided through the dirt and crime, the tatters and rags, the byways and alleys of nether New York by an experienced cicerone. Mr. Riis, in a word, though a philanthropist and philosopher, is an artist as well. He has also the advantage of being an amateur photographer, and his book is abundantly illustrated from negatives of the odd, the out-of-the-way, and characteristic sights and scenes he has himself caught with his camera. No work yet published—certainly not the official reports of the charity societies—shows so vividly the complexion and countenance of the "Down-town Back Alleys," "The Bend," "Chinatown," "Jewtown," "The Cheap Lodging-houses," the haunts of the negro, the Italian, the Bohemian poor, or gives such a veracious picture of the toughs, the tramps, the waifs, drunkards, paupers, gamins, and the generally gruesome population of this centre of civilization.[1]

The blurb for Riis's book promised picturesque art and ethnic and social sight-seeing. It instructed the reader to approach a sociological study with touristic stakes in mind. These were novelties that set his work apart from the official reports of the charity societies.

In 1896, Crane ended a letter to a concerned and perhaps baffled woman who wrote him about the objectives of his slum novel with a painfully simple explanation: "I had no other purpose in writing 'Maggie' than to show people to people as they seem to me. If that be evil, make the most of it."[2] Crane's final, defiant quip here is not as gratuitous as it might sound to our modern ears. How could it possibly be evil merely "to show people to people as they seem" to one? Precisely because it leaves so much out. To have "no other purpose" was to eschew the traditional, respectable, and righteous purposes of slum writing—those of Protestant moral accounting, social protest, and political muckraking. Moreover, to the middle class, the poor were not simply people like any other people; they were a special breed (racially, economically, morally, socially) that required a special brand of discourse. The slums were the domain of clergymen, police reporters, sanitation officials, and reformers; novelists were relative latecomers to the terrain, and when they arrived they naturally took up the issues and campaigns that went with the territory. Showing people to people was certainly part of the literary project of the slums, but this spectacular element was an accessory, an accomplice of traditional moral and social demonstration: part of the project of showing poor people to middle-class people.[3] Riis and Crane were providing middle-class readers with a new way of approaching the slums: as spectacle for its own sake.

To be sure, the representation of the poor is not altogether new in either Riis's or Crane's works. In *How the Other Half Lives*, the poor man is often the (sentimental) victim of greedy landlords, sweatshop bosses, and public neglect; at other times, he is hopeless (186) and has no one but himself to blame; at still other points, he is "The Man with the Knife" (199). Riis creates sympathy for the poor, but he also confirms contempt and fear of them. It is a common enough schizophrenia among social reformers of the turn of the century: to call for both social justice and social control. In Riis's book, the poor are sometimes worthy and pathetic, sometimes despicable, sometimes menacing. More comprehensively, Riis inhabits all the postures that were regularly taken up toward the poor at the end of the nineteenth century: righteous condemnation for viciousness, civic concern about crime and riot, and brotherly sympathy for physical deprivation and social exploitation.[4] And though Crane does not sermonize or call for reforms of any sort, *Maggie* arguably stirs up this set of emotions as well, as the reader encounters dishonest beggars, violent toughs, abused children, and exploited workers.[5]

But sometimes, to be sure, Crane's novel does not offer any of these familiar footholds. Likewise, Riis's *How the Other Half Lives* at times does not occupy any of these positions. Riis's description of Mulberry Bend, for example—where he consciously overlooks the "unromantic" tenements for the romantic street scene— is not accusatory, nor very menacing and offensive, nor even particularly sympathetic. Similarly, Crane's detailed account of Pete's and Maggie's various outings to museums and beer halls could hardly be said to elicit pity, contempt, or fear. In their writing, the poor are not just victim or menace but also curio. To the opposition between pity and empathy, on the one hand, and fear and contempt, on the other, a third alternative can be added: fascination or amusement.

Clearly, something pitiable or menacing might also be fascinating. The point is that the traditional material of slum writing might have inspired powerful emotions, but it always had a moral and social meaning: these emotions fed into proper moral and civic responses. Fascination with the ethnic and social other—for its own sake—was not appropriate in a presentation of the slums. This was the stuff of dime novels and newspaper crime stories that presented titillating accounts of lawlessness, including sexual crimes.[6] Their tales were menacing but had little or no redeeming social value; they induced horror in their audiences without inspiring moral or civic consciousness.

The same charge might be leveled against Riis and was in fact leveled against Crane,[7] but this sort of charge is hard to prove. However, what is clear in the cases of both of these authors is that they presented some simply amusing spectacles—ones that did not play on the traditional emotions of pity, contempt, and fear and thus could hardly have led to social concern.

Riis's urban curiosities are sometimes merely clownish (though no less racist). Riis excavates the light side of alien habits for the entertainment of his reader. One example is his "mystery of Jewtown":

> The suspender peddlar is the mystery of the Pig-market,[8] omnipresent and unfathomable. He is met at every step with his wares dangling over his shoulder, down his back, and in front. Millions of suspenders thus perambulate Jewtown all day on a sort of dress parade. Why suspenders, is the puzzle, and where do they all go to? The "pants" of Jewtown hang down with a common accord, as if they had never known the support of suspenders. It appears to be as characteristic a trait of the race as the long beard and the Sabbath silk hat of ancient pedigree. I have asked again and again. No one has ever been able to tell me what becomes of the suspenders of Jewtown. Perhaps they are hung up as bric-a-brac in its homes, or laid away and saved up as the equivalent of cash. I cannot tell. I only know that more suspenders are hawked about the Pig-market every day than would supply the whole of New York for a year, were they all bought and turned to use. (86–87)

Suspenders, suspenders everywhere, but none holding up pants. This is the mentality of the Polish joke. In ethnographic details, Riis discovers a new source of urban exoticism. Such details are easily curious because they can defy moral evaluation (what is the morality of a long beard?) and frustrate a utilitarian assessment. Immigrant customs can easily be opaque to the outsider: they may simply stem from a milieu that has been left behind; in this case, long beards and silk hats refer to a religious practice or ethics to which Riis has little or no access. Suspenders, long beards, silk hats: the Jews have no obvious utility for any of them. The racist humor is that they might just carry this excess baggage around out of some misguided aesthetic or, in the case of suspenders, out of their celebrated racial instinct for thrift: the implication, in the context of Riis's typical stereotyping of the Jews, is that their habit of saving might here again have gotten out of control.

The image here is certainly not a sympathetic portrait; Riis is having fun entirely at the expense of the Jews. But neither is the portrait menacing; on the contrary, it could be said to sublimate anxiety. This kind of racist humor serves as a re-assurance that the immigrant is more ridiculous than threatening.

A similar dynamic animates Crane's city sketch called "An Experiment in Misery." A youth dons ragged clothing and heads downtown to uncover the mystery of pauperism. The bum he meets is not a virtuous victim—by the end of the tale the reader learns that this bum is dedicated to "easy livin'"—but neither is he a menacing criminal. The narration at first seems ready to attribute to him threatening traits: "his eyes peered with a guilty slant"; his mouth has "cruel lines"; "he appeared like an assassin steeped in crimes." But this description is laced with humor. His guilty eyes peer from "a fuddle of bushy hair and whiskers"; his cruel mouth "looked as if its lips had just closed with satisfaction over some tender and piteous morsel," and finally, he actually "appeared like an assassin steeped in crimes *performed awkwardly*." For the remainder of the tale, the narration refers to this harmless bum as "the assassin," an ironic epithet that fits the tone of much of the piece. "The assassin, tottering about on his uncertain legs, and at intervals brushing imaginary obstacles from before his nose, entered into a long explanation of the psychology of the situation. It was so profound it was unintelligible."[9] It is as if Crane is consciously out to poke fun not only at the bum but also at the middle-class reader's fearful conception of paupers. His "Experiment in Misery" is also, in part, an experiment in mockery.

Riis's photographs were obviously the most spectacular, the most fascinating aspect of *How the Other Half Lives*, and perhaps of any slum literature published in the 1890s. They were the first snapshots of the slums to appear in an American book,[10] in a culture that was not at all familiar with photographs to begin with. As Alexander Alland has noted, Riis's was the first book on any subject to use a large number of halftone reproductions from photographs.[11] Newspapers did not have photographs until the 1880s, and they did not appear there with any frequency until after the publication of Riis's book.[12] Before the last two decades of the nineteenth century, they were scarce indeed: for instance, Abraham Lincoln had been unable to get a snapshot of himself to send to supporters during the election of 1860. In the press, there was also a dearth of pictures in general. The absence of photographs was due to technological limitations and, on top of that, a journalistic prejudice against pictures throughout most of the nineteenth century (they were thought to be clutter and a waste of space); many newspapers did not print images of any kind until the 1880s. Finally, when pictures and photographs of the city did occasionally appear, proprietary conventions were usually observed. As Thomas Leonard puts it:

> In America . . . , illustrated magazines at mid-century had only a topographer's vision of the growing cities. This was a journalism of proud panoramas. Streets were uncluttered, buildings and people were isolated; the bustling activities in an industry or a neighborhood were not allowed to get in the way of what the reader was

supposed to see. One looked down on people and up at imposing buildings. Only the important people met the reader at eye level. The poor and the "dangerous classes" were swept from the city. The earliest daguerreotypists broke some of these rules, but urban photographers quickly found an angle of vision to make streets fit the dream of the town booster.[13]

All of this would change beginning in the late 1880s with Riis. In his excellent history of American urban photography, Peter B. Hales finds that between 1885 and 1895 the tradition of "celebratory, monumental style . . . , the urban grand-style taxonomy," would be challenged by "an entirely new vision of the city." He asserts that these years, with their radical innovations in photographic technology, mark "the great division in American urban photography," and he claims that "from that revolutionary decade, one name stands out clearly— that of Jacob Riis."[14] Due in large part to his unprecedented photographs, Riis's book was an instant success, and reviewers paid a good deal of attention to them. A typical review claimed that "his descriptive powers paled" before his photographs.[15]

Hales recognizes the social contribution of Riis's photography: "[T]he photographs Riis made . . . firmly linked photography to the cause of social reform, making it . . . the preeminent mode of proof in the rhetoric of social and urban reformers for the next ninety years."[16] Riis's introduction of photography into the domain of the poor was of course a major tactical discovery in the ongoing battle for social justice, but it was at the same time a powerful event in the reconstitution of the slums as an aesthetic or spectacular space.

It is true enough that despite their newness, many of Riis's photographs were pictures of recognizable urban types and had clear moral and social messages (often hammered home by captions): one finds a photo of lodgers crowded into a single room, a woman with her child in a squalid tenement, "typical toughs," boys in a "gang," the "Black-and-Tan Dive" and the "Stale-Beer Dive," "street Arabs," a "tramp," a man smoking opium "in a Chinese joint," immigrants working in a "sweatshop." These are certainly images of helpless victims and menaces to society; they were no doubt meant to inspire pathos and fear. The *Chicago Times* could thus call Riis's book "a gallery of pictures, each one reeling with horror of its own kind."[17] But these denotations did not exhaust the content of his snapshots—not for a readership who had never seen such photographs before. What I have said about the opportunities for fascination in reading his text is above all true of his photography.

As we have seen, the *sights* of the Bend can momentarily crowd out, for Riis, the tenements and all the injustice they imply; a red bandanna can flash, irrelevantly, at a moment when he is describing the horrible overcrowding of an apartment. In a similar way, his photographs suffer from distractions. The excessiveness of Riis's prose style is similar to the logic of his photographs, even to the logic of photography in general, for documentary photographs cannot help but show

"Street Arabs in Sleeping Quarters" (*Street Arabs at night*), *by Jacob Riis* (*photo courtesy of the Museum of the City of New York*)

everything in the line of vision of the camera: they cannot help reproducing "irrelevant" details along with the subject at hand.

Take Riis's photograph "Bohemian Cigarmakers at Work in Their Tenement," a snapshot that would indeed have been menacing to his reader. One sees the father, the mother, the boy, all but the smaller children rolling cigars in their apartment. The reader may have heard about the existence of tenement sweatshops, so perhaps he will not be shocked by the fact that immigrants have to work long hours in their homes, but he cannot help, at least, seeing the blatant violation, the offense. The home, he knows, is supposed to be exempt and remote from labor; the domestic sphere is supposed to be a haven from the cold world of commerce.[18] Also, children should not be put to work so young (Riis takes up the outrage of child labor in his *The Children of the Poor* [1892]).[19] Father should be relaxing, perhaps smoking a cigar, but certainly not rolling one; mother should be reading to the children or cooking or cleaning house (not forms of labor in the popular myth of the home); the children should be studying their lessons or playing. Here, surely, is Alan Trachtenberg's version of Riis's slum: "the antithesis of the home . . . , an offense to all notions of the clean, the sanitary and the civilized."[20] The duty of motherhood, the entitlement of childhood, the sanctity, the very meaning of the home: they are all menaced by this scene.

But the scene is not yet exhausted. There is also, unmistakably, the father's long and bushy beard, the son's suspenders. These are strange things to behold for the middle-class audience: they are curious. They too are violations—of the norms of appearance—but these offenses are not particularly menacing.

Beyond the "obvious" moral and social meaning of the photograph, then, there is another content, another point of interest. Besides the reactions of condemnation and fear (these people are a threat to the American home) or sympathy (these people are being deprived, by this system of employment, of the joys of the home), there is another reaction: fascination (these people look so strange, dress so strangely). Like the red bandanna in the description of overcrowding, this secondary ethnographic content supplements the overt social message and distracts from it.

It could be argued that this dynamic is simply an interesting accident of the photograph, or the accidental nature of photography. After all, it could be asserted that the interest in the father's beard is greatly subordinated to the threat of work in the home. But as with the passages on the sights of the Bend and the mystery of the Jewish "Pig-market," Riis also includes photographs where the touristic content seems primary. One such photograph is "'The Official Organ of Chinatown.'"

"Bohemian Cigarmakers at Work in Their Tenements" from How the Other Half Lives, *by Jacob Riis (photo courtesy of the Museum of the City of New York)*

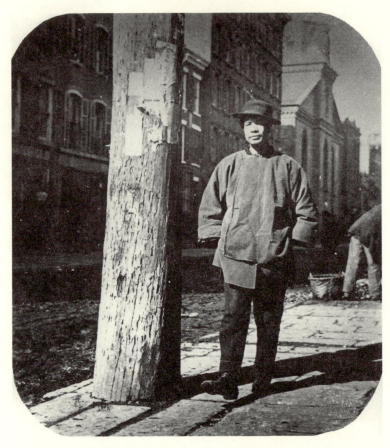

"'The Official Organ of Chinatown'" from How the Other Half Lives,
by Jacob Riis (photo courtesy of the Museum of the City of New York)

The "official organ" is a telegraph pole with notices tacked up (the notices look blank because of the light); next to the pole is a Chinese man. Now, we might reasonably suspect that this photograph, like the "Bohemian Cigarmakers" photograph, was somewhat menacing for Riis's reader. Unreadable messages in a foreign language are at the very least mysterious, but Riis has given these signs a sinister flavor: the reader has been led to think of notices about illegal gambling and strange political plots on the telegraph pole. Riis's text has revealed that "every day notices are posted upon it by unseen hands, announcing that in such and such a cellar a fan tan game will be running that night, or warning the faithful that a raid is intended on this or that game through the machination of a rival interest. A constant stream of plotting and counter-plotting makes up the round of Chinese social and political existence" (74). Perhaps on this pole, the reader might even imagine, is pasted up a subversive plot against the government of the United States!

Then, the snapshot also shows the Chinese man himself, a figure of no little suspicion: after all, further Chinese immigration been restricted by an act of Congress.[21] Riis himself has asserted, pessimistically, that "all attempts to make an effective Christian of John Chinaman will remain abortive in this generation; of the next I have, if anything, less hope" (67). Moreover, the Chinese immigrants are responsible for the helpless victim of the previous photograph—a man crashed out on a mat and some pillows with a pipe in front of him, a slave of the dreaded opium. Riis has plainly stated that "Chinatown stands" for this ultimate "dissipation," this "moral, mental and physical death" (76). The Chinese man in this photograph, and the mysterious telegraph pole along with him, cannot help but take on all these other associations, the associations of Riis's descriptions and other photographs, as well as of national policy. Riis has colored the reader's vision so that the reader will see a menace even in this seemingly innocent photograph.

But this is not all that the reader will see, for though Riis considers the Chinese a serious threat, he also has his moments, as usual, of sympathy. He suggests at one point that the secretiveness of the Chinese in New York may be due to "the attitude of American civilization toward the stranger" (69). And on the political status of the Chinese, he concludes in their favor: "Rather than banish the Chinaman, I would have the door opened wider—for his wife; make it a condition of his coming or staying that he bring his wife with him. Then, at least, he might not be what he now is and remains, a homeless stranger among us" (76). In this light, the reader may glimpse in this photograph a somewhat lonely figure, out alone in the streets (not, significantly, at home), shunned by Anglo-Saxon culture, and now cut off from his family by harsh laws of immigration.

However, the reader will be invited to see even more than these two images, of the menace and the outcast. For Riis is also interested in Chinatown as a sight: "Chinatown as a spectacle is disappointing" (68), he comments. Disappointing or not, he goes on to report on what can be seen there:

> The bloused pedlars who, with arms buried half to the elbow in their trousers' pockets, lounge behind their stock of watermelon seed and sugar-cane, cut in lengths to suit the purse of the buyer, disdain to offer the barbarian their wares. Chinatown, that does most things by contraries, rules its holiday style to carry its hands in its pockets, and its denizens follow the fashion, whether in blue blouse, in gray, or in brown, with shining and braided pig-tail dangling below the knees, or with hair cropped short above a coat collar of "Melican" cut. All kinds of men are met, but no women—none at least with almond eyes. A few, very few, Chinese merchants have wives of their own color, but they are seldom or never seen in the street. (70)

Cut sugarcane, blouses, hands in pockets, long pigtails, Chinese pronunciation of the word "American," almond eyes, the absence of Chinese women; goods, dress, hairstyle, physical features, ways of holding one's body, ways of saying things, ways of treating wives: these are neither menacing nor pathetic. They are notes in a travelogue, features in a fast-and-loose ethnography—which also help the reader (who has probably never before seen a Chinese man or a picture of one) appreciate the oddities of the photographic object. Riis is the connoisseur of the immigrant slums, and his written description is in part insurance that the viewer will not miss a modest but important sight, a wonderful opportunity for fascination.

Likewise, if the telegraph pole is somewhat menacing at one point in Riis's description, it is elsewhere unmistakably curious or even silly: "Chinatown has enlisted the telegraph pole for the dissemination of public intelligence, but it has got hold of it by the wrong end. . . . [T]he wires serve us" (74). And it is this light, touristic tone that characterizes the caption to the photograph of the telegraph pole and the Chinese man: "'The Official Organ of Chinatown,'" reads the caption. Riis is having a joke at Chinatown's expense—the word "official" pokes fun—and the viewer is invited to join in. "That is *his* official way of communicating!" says the reader to himself. "He uses the telegraph pole too!" It is funny, and it is curious.

Sympathize or fear: Riis states the alternative plainly enough in *The Children of the Poor*: in regard to "the tough," he remarks, "we have the choice of hailing him man and brother or of being slugged and robbed by him."[22] But Riis presents a third option, even if he does not state it outright: the reader can also read about the tough and look at pictures of him.

And if Riis himself does not make this option explicit, the publicity agent for his book does, with a blurb that promises the "picturesque," "the odd, the out-of-the-way, and characteristic sights and scenes."[23] Riis's written and pictorial tourism might be considered a sort of comic relief from the tragedy of his documentary report; his art might be thought of as a social leisure that gives his reader a break from his philanthropy and philosophy, the social "work" of the book.

But Riis's sight-seeing also does its work. To read about the strange habits of the poor, to view the poor, the immigrant, the tough in photographs, is also to develop a particular relationship to them. One becomes not only or necessarily brother to the poor or moral reformer of the poor or potential victim of the poor; one also becomes a spectator of the poor.

What relationship does a spectator have to her spectacle? Alan Trachtenberg says of late-nineteenth-century journalism, "[I]n providing surrogate experience, the newspaper only deepened the separations it seemed to overcome—deepened them by giving them a precise form: the form of reading and looking. . . . The form in which it projected its reader's assumed wish to overcome distance concealed its own devices for confirming distance, deepening mystery, and presenting the world as a spectacle for consumption."[24] Walter Benjamin noticed that the presentation of the news in the columns of the newspaper serves "to isolate what happens from the realm in which it could affect the experience of the reader."[25] Guy Debord writes, "[T]he spectacle is the *affirmation* of appearance and the affirmation of all human, namely social life, as mere appearance."[26] William Dean Howells found the slums—their "stenches," their "fouler and dreadfuller poverty-smell," their savagery, their "squalor," their "ugliness"—too overwhelming in person, but he noted that "in a picture [they could] be most pleasingly effective, for then you could be in it, and yet have the distance on it which it needs."[27]

A spectacle, then, provides vicarious adventure while it remains at a safe distance: when one assumes the position of a spectator, which the newspaper and the photograph encourage, the poor are banished to the world of pictures and print, the realm of mere appearance, where they no longer threaten the viewer or demand her aid. Riis's book, then, is doubly schizophrenic in regard to slum dwellers. Not only does it vacillate between sympathy and suspicion; it oscillates between intimacy and estrangement.

How the Other Half Lives offers several conflicting messages. The poor are abused, overcrowded, and poorly housed, so feel for them; they are just like you and me, but they are deprived of a good home. Alternatively, the poor are abused, overcrowded, and poorly housed, so condemn and fear them; their home life is a threat to our American traditions, and their anger may be unleashed: they may rob you or rebel en masse. Then, as an alternative to this first pair of alternatives: the poor look different from us, they live differently, and they do things in strange ways, so enjoy their peculiarities and thrill to their bizarre conditions of life, but do not worry; they are remote from you and there to be looked at.

This last alternative, this third term in the series (sympathy, revulsion, fascination) cuts back against the other two, undermining the overt messages of the book. The first two messages call for some form of political activism: moral and social justice (better housing) or social defense (better policing or further immigrant restriction). The third and implicit message is not activist: it reassures, even encourages passive viewing.

Though they contradicted each other, the alternatives of sympathy and suspicion—justice and defense—were at least options that had the same aim of social and traditional moral order. That is why Riis can go about procuring social justice for the tough precisely by playing the contradictory alternatives of fear and sympathy against one another. He claims that the tough "is to be preferred to the born pauper any day" and asserts that he "has the making of something in him." He assures his reader that he is "weak rather than vicious," that "he even means well," that "after all, he is not so very different from the rest of us." Riis makes "a remorseful review of the chances he has had." Then he reminds his reader, though it is hardly necessary, that the tough will do "the very same evil deed over again the minute he is rid of restraint." Pathetic versus menacing: two contradictory accounts of the tough, but the threat can work to inspire concern and to demonstrate the need for sympathy. In the end, Riis gives the reader a choice, and occasionally he makes it explicit: "[W]e have the choice of hailing him man and brother or of being slugged and robbed by him,"[28] Riis concludes of the tough. No one chooses to be slugged and robbed. If the pathetic image does not win the reader's sympathy naturally, the fearful one will enlighten him of its practical benefits.

Something else happens when the third option of entertainment is introduced.

Now there are two different ways in which the poor man can be assimilated: as a sibling or as a spectacle. Roland Barthes has noted, in a different context:

> Sometimes—rarely—the Other is revealed as irreducible: not because of a sudden scruple, but because *common sense* rebels: a man does not have a white skin, but a black one, another drinks pear juice, not *Pernod*. How can one assimilate the Negro, the Russian? There is here a figure for emergencies: exoticism. The Other becomes a pure object, a spectacle, a clown. Relegated to the confines of humanity, he no longer threatens the security of the home.[29]

In regard to the Chinese immigrant, Riis starts off as he does with the tough. "All attempts to make an effective Christian of John Chinaman will remain abortive," Riis begins, but if we open up the immigration door wider and make him bring his wife, then "he might not be what he now is and remains, a homeless stranger among us." After Riis's assertion of hopeless difference and division comes a vision of sympathy, similarity, brotherhood: give the Chinese man a family and a home like us, and we will be able to hail him, like the tough, as man and brother.

But that tack of Americanization is far off. Right now the law prevents it; moreover, at the moment the Chinese man is secretive and criminal (remember the fantan game and the opium den). So in the meantime, "there is a figure for emergencies," as Barthes says. Riis presents the Chinese peculiarities of appearance and dress and habit and manages a snapshot of a Chinese man: consciously or not, he helps assimilate the Chinese man as a curiosity, a pure object, a spectacle, a clown (remember how he uses "the wrong end" of the telegraph pole), because he cannot yet be assimilated as an American. Visions of brotherhood and spectacles of curiosities both serve to reassure the reader that the Chinese man is perhaps not ultimately a threat to home and country. Aesthetic assimilation has its practical benefits.

But these options correspond to two very different ethical orders—that is to say, two completely different types of relation to others. They cannot be said to reinforce one another. Exoticism not only makes traditional moral and social assimilation that much more difficult to achieve. It also turns the poor into an object of entertainment, the middle-class reader into a spectator. Americanization or immigrant restriction versus aesthetic exoticism, intimate sympathy or condemnation versus remote fascination. This is an absolute choice between ethics.

It can be argued that Riis still largely operates in terms of a traditional ethical relation to the poor, but the same cannot be said about Crane. Crane's reader, of course, is not exhorted to help reform the slums. Moreover, she is invited to enjoy not only the spectacle of the poor but also the spectacle of the middle class trying to relate in its traditional ways to the poor. The righteous preacher in the mission church in *Maggie* is laughably oblivious to the disinterest and disdain of his congregation, and the minister who sidesteps Maggie in order to "save . . . his respectability" (51) is another occasion for irony.

Mockery is a general antidote to conventional moral feelings of pity, righteousness, and fear, and it is much more extensive in Crane's work than in Riis's. While irony can be allied to traditional moral postures of condemnation (consider Crane's exposure of a beggar-woman's fraud),[30] in his texts it is usually leveled against Protestant moralizing (recall Mrs. Johnson's hypocritical denunciation of Maggie, which approaches burlesque); conventional civic worries (remember Crane's mockery of middle-class fears in his "Experiment in Misery"); and a sentimental pity for the poor (Crane makes it difficult to construe Maggie as a pure victim because she herself exhibits the harsh prejudice against prostitutes that will later come to haunt her).[31]

Irony or mockery—so important in Crane's work—is a sort of guarantee against the conventional relationships to the poor. Irony about the poor helps keep them, their suffering, and their menace at a distance; irony about middle-class morals rules out righteous condemnation. Crane not only encourages touristic fascination as an alternative ethical relation to the poor. He also teaches his reader an ironic attitude about the slums, which is an "ethical" defense against civic concern and sentimental moral feeling and an "ethical" proof against the temptation of moralizing. Though Crane's novel does at points encourage these conventional responses to the poor, it might be argued that it does so partly in order to neutralize them, to make these postures untenable for the reader, and to replace them with a sort of universal skepticism and irony, which, it should be added, is perfectly compatible with spectatorship.[32]

4 ⤨ *"In Search of Excitement"*

The Ethics of Entertainment

*O*ne editor who turned *Maggie* down did so because "it closely approaches the morbid and the morbid is always dangerous." "It produced its effect upon me," he told Crane, "the effect, I presume, that you wished to produce, a kind of horror." Horror—or some similar sensation—for its own sake was exactly what the dime novels were after, and "in itself it is unpleasant and in its tendency unhealthful."[1] Crane could hardly have been surprised. He had inscribed several copies of the original edition of *Maggie* with this warning: "It is probable that the reader of this small thing may consider the Author to be a bad man, but, obviously, this is a matter of small consequence to *The Author*."[2]

Part of Crane's refusal to sermonize in his novel was his refusal to recognize the traditional distinction between moral and immoral art, between the decent art of high culture and the vulgar art of the dime novel and the slums. (Riis pays lip service to this difference in his *Children of the Poor*; there he criticizes "the ways of the street that are showy always," associating a street aesthetic with despicably "trashy novels and cheap shows." He adopts the usual moral distinction between "cheap trash" and "real works of art." "The ideal of the street is caricature, burlesque, if nothing worse," and Riis contrasts this aesthetic of the cheap spectacle with that of "the beautiful.")[3] Crane was intent on absorbing the street aesthetic into his own writing. He goes on for pages in *Maggie* detailing the numbers in a Bowery theater—bawdy songs, melodramas, ventriloquist acts, comedy routines, "negro" melodies, and ribald dances—he describes the dress and mannerisms of his slum characters, and he reproduces their slang, including profanity such as "hell," "damn," and "fudge."[4] Meanwhile, he dismisses the "beautiful" novels of

74

his contemporaries as "pink valentines,"[5] much the way Nell dismisses Maggie as "pumpkin pie." Crane openly embraces "cheap trash" and ridicules Victorian high art as sentimental and saccharine.

And though at some points Riis dutifully acknowledges traditional aesthetic standards, he also indulges in a spectacular imagination that would certainly be trashy according to his own distinction. His interest in spectacle not only provides an alternative to his concern about reform. His aesthetics is, by conventional measure, immoral.

As we have seen, Riis's documentary is torn between the claims of traditional moral and social reform and those of aesthetics.[6] But even more strikingly, Riis's pursuit of spectacle—"cheap" as it is—can explicitly contradict his supposed moral and social message. The fact is that his "habits of . . . style"[7] do not simply coexist side by side with his high-minded causes. His alternative morality of spectacle implies a set of values that overturns the traditional Protestant one.

Consider Riis's critique of Chinatown:

> Chinatown as a spectacle is disappointing. Next-door neighbor to the Bend [the Italian area], it has little of its outdoor stir of life, none of its gayly-colored rags or picturesque filth and poverty. Mott Street is clean to distraction: the laundry stamp is on it, though the houses are chiefly of the conventional tenement-house type, with nothing to rescue them from the everyday dismal dreariness of their kind save here and there a splash of dull red or yellow, a sign, hung endways and with streamers of red flannel tacked on. (68)

What Riis finds disappointing about Chinatown is the cleanliness of the place. This is a strange sort of disappointment for a man who approvingly quotes the first legislative committee that looked into the tenements and recommended "'for every man a *clean* and comfortable home.'" Cleanliness is a standard Protestant virtue, and moreover, the tradition of charitable and sanitary writing with which Riis associates himself has long identified filth as one of those "'conditions and associations of human life and habitation [that] are the prolific parents of corresponding habits and morals.'"[8] Riis is ostensibly concerned with rescuing the tenements from the conditions that breed pauperism and "touch the family life with deadly moral contagion" (3), but here he is interested in "rescu[ing] them from the everyday dismal dreariness." Filth is a social danger and a traditional sin, but in search of "spectacle," Riis finds cleanliness an aesthetic vice. "The laundry stamp" here is a kind of visual stain. "Clean to distraction": Riss asserts that a place can be too clean. In this phrase is an inchoate sense of a negotiation between traditional social and moral imperatives and alternative standards, as if there is a level of filth that, while picturesque, is still pretty harmless by conventional moral measure, and a degree of cleanliness that, while essentially socially prophylactic, is still aesthetically pleasing.

Previous charitable writers had routinely conjured up the filth of shanties and tenements; it was a regular theme of the genre. It could be argued that their very preoccupation with the subject marked a fascination, an obsession, a fetishism—that dirt was a metaphor for vice and also its usual accompaniment, that it became a visible substitute for vices that were often hidden. But these writers did not explicitly praise filth, nor did they ever condemn cleanliness. Riis is one of the first connoisseurs of urban filth. Spectacle is not eschewed even when it is obviously "cheap" and threatens Protestant virtues; his aesthetic appreciation is allowed to play havoc with his traditional moral crusade.

All of this indicates a new premium on entertainment—in fact, an alternative set of values—for this havoc is by no means limited to the issue of filth. The "outdoor stir of life" for which Riis lauds the Bend and which he misses in Chinatown is just the sort of phenomenon that many charity workers and, later, social workers found so threatening to the "'ordinary wholesome influences of home and family'" (2, Secretary of the Prison Association of New York, 1865). The streets versus the home: the traditional moral opposition here was becoming as pronounced as the social opposition between the workplace and the home. If the home meant wholesome influences, the street certainly meant vicious ones—the tendency to idleness, the dangerous anonymity of crowds, the clandestine circulation of criminals, the wanton mixture of the sexes.[9] Riis regularly shares these views. Elsewhere, he construes "the street and its idleness as factors in making criminals of . . . boys." Even the factory, outlawed for children because it introduces them to health hazards, maintains them in ignorance, and brings them in contact with unsavory influences, "is to be preferred to the street." Riis describes new social reforms that make "war upon the streets" and identifies himself with that crusade.[10]

But in the chapter on "The Bend" in *How the Other Half Lives*, Riis notes approvingly, of the Italians, that "when the sun shines the entire population seeks the street" (43), an observation that would make the average charity worker—and Riis himself, perhaps, in a different mood—edgy. Here he is not nervous or disapproving in the least; in fact, he goes on to describe, with some relish, a flirtation between "a really pretty girl" and "one of the rude swains": just the sort of sexual interchange that the guardians of Protestant decency feared.

Of course, it is the crowding and the resulting lack of privacy—so characteristic of the streets—which Riis attacks in the tenements and because of which he would have them torn down: he says simply, "[T]he absence of [privacy] is the chief curse of the tenement." He himself draws the analogy between the streets and the tenement: "The hall that is a highway for all the world by night and by day is the tenement's proper badge. The Other Half ever receives with open doors" (119). For Riis, the tenement means precisely "'homes [that] had ceased to be sufficiently *separate*, decent and wholesome to afford what are regarded as ordinary wholesome influences of home and family'" (2, Secretary of Prisons, my italics). Family life is impossible because there are no proper boundaries between families, and decency is impossible because there are no proper boundaries between adults and children, males and females. For Riis, the tenement is not a collection of separate, autonomous families but a crowd housed in a building. Family influences are overwhelmed by the tendencies of the tenement crowd, such as pauperism: "[P]auperism grows in the tenements as naturally as weeds in a garden lot. . . . All the surroundings of tenement-house life favor its growth." Without domestic boundaries, without further separations within the family space, no family life is possible, and without family life, moral character is impossible as well. That's why Riis calls "the tenement, the destroyer of . . . character everywhere" (186).

Tenement homes are insufficiently separate from each other—and thus from the street and its rules. The home was supposed to be a haven: from work, from the streets. With tenement sweatshops, the world of work has transgressed the domestic boundary line, and with the crowds and lack of privacy, it is as if the streets have overflowed into the home. Even if they are not the source of the home's disintegration, the streets at least share and exaggerate the conditions that Riis so fiercely condemns. Yet he does not decry these same conditions—the overcrowding, the lack of boundaries—when he finds them out of doors. On the contrary, he celebrates them. Why? What do the streets have over the tenements? The air is better, to be sure; there is more light; no doubt more room is available; but there is also something that has nothing to do with health or traditional morality: more visibility.

Riis continues his aesthetic critique of Chinatown:

> Red and yellow are the holiday colors of Chinatown as of the Bend, but they do not lend brightness in Mott Street as around the corner in Mulberry. Rather, they seem to descend to the level of the general dullness, and glower at you from doors and windows, from the telegraph pole that is the official organ of Chinatown and from the store signs, with blank, unmeaning stare, suggesting nothing, asking no questions, and answering none. Fifth Avenue is not duller on a rainy day than Mott street to one in search of excitement. Whatever is on foot goes on behind closed doors. Stealth and secretiveness are as much part of the Chinaman in New York as the cat-like tread of his felt shoes. His business, as his domestic life, shuns the light, less because there is anything to conceal than because that is the way of the man. Perhaps the attitude of American civilization toward the stranger, whom it invited in, has taught him that way. At any rate, the very doorways of his offices and shops are fenced off by queer, forbidding partitions suggestive of a continual state of siege. The stranger who enters through the crooked approach is received with sudden silence, a sullen stare, and an angry "Vat you vant?" that breathes annoyance and distrust. (69)

The problem with Chinatown here, the source of its dullness, is simply that it is private. It does not yield itself up as a spectacle for the public. But should not domestic life shun the public eye and keep to itself? Riis knows that the moral ills of the poor become contagious because there are no closed doors in the tenement, but here "closed doors" are viewed with hostility. Elsewhere in his book Riis is alarmed at the dearth of boundaries—between families, between the sexes, between the worthy poor and the pauper—but here he finds partitions "queer" and "forbidding." Privacy, the very linchpin of a decent home, of character itself, according to Riis, here becomes vicious: it becomes "stealth and secretiveness." The inference is that there is too much privacy in Chinatown, just as there is too much cleanliness.

Too much privacy in a book whose principle message is that the tenement has deprived the poor of the necessary amount? Yes, partly because, as Riis indicates elsewhere, the privacy signals seclusion from proper American influences. Chinatown's privacy does not insulate family life; for Riis, there are no homes here because there are no Chinese wives. "A continual state of siege" suggests an occupying army, and, indeed, there are obvious candidates for the analogue of a military force: police, health officials, social reformers. What is it that the Chinese are hiding, protecting with their privacy? The reader finds out later in the chapter that they are carrying on fan-tan games and, much worse, running opium dens. "[I]n their exclusiveness and reserve," Riis declares, "they are a constant and terrible menace to society" (75). In this subsequent version of Chinatown, Riis unearths a secret threat to Protestant morals and a consequent need to exercise powers of surveillance and arrest.

But oddly enough, this is not the way that Riis construes Chinese privacy in the first instance. He simply asserts, rather, that the Chinese shun the light "less because there is anything to conceal than because this is the way of the man." The reason Riis settles here on the racial stereotype is that here he is looking not for signs of opium traffic but for signs of "brightness." He is not reading the signs on the telegraph pole to see if they remark on the whereabouts of an illicit fan-tan game; he is not reading them at all, but remarking on their color, considering them for their visual appeal. At this point, he is not a charity agent in search of vice or illegality: he is, openly, "one in search of excitement." His frustration with the Chinese here is not that they are hiding terrible opium dens; his frustration is that they are hiding at all—hiding themselves. He is down on the Chinese here not because they seduce white women with opium but because they do not make themselves visible.

From a touristic perspective, privacy and cleanliness turn out to be allied. Both prevent the Chinese from being enjoyed as spectacle. Privacy thwarts tourism for the obvious reason. Cleanliness, meanwhile, might make the Chinese interesting to the visitor: Chinatown is an oasis of cleanliness in the desert of filth that is the tenements, hence it seems to be outside the social laws of dirt. Chinatown's cleanliness might even be held up as a spectacular sight, in the context of the slums. But Riis, the aggressive tourist, is suspicious of Chinese cleanliness, just as he is suspicious of their privacy. He seems to construe both as barriers to his viewing: it is as if he considers cleanliness as another kind of cover, as if he imagines that he could penetrate through both privacy and surface cleanliness, not here to criminality but to a secret filth and picturesqueness.

For excitement, one needs people—ideally, crowds—and there must be mess; Riis finds only impersonal, orderly colors, and he imagines, as only a frustrated viewer could, that the colors themselves stare back at him: they "glower at you from doors and windows . . . and from store signs, with blank unmeaning stare." Another stare, this time a sullen one, and more silence, this time a sudden one, greet him when he enters a Chinese residence. People staring back at Riis: this is believable, but colors glowering at him? He sounds here as if he has lost his bearings. But in fact, this is a reasonable feeling to entertain once one adopts the rationality of the tourist, once one enters the ethics of entertainment. In the logic of spectacle, everything is either viewer or object. Thus Chinatown, refusing to yield itself up as an aesthetic object, turns the tables on Riis, becomes a generalized spectator, and turns Riis into the spectacle, accusing him of voyeurism.

An issue of power and resistance is at stake here, but it is not the familiar game of policing or of reforming; it is the game of viewing. Riis is not a police reporter or a social reformer at this moment; he is a tourist. And tourism, it turns out, is only passive viewing when the sights are out in the open to see. Here Riis is, more precisely, an activist on behalf of tourism. To be sure, Riis generally wants to assert American influence over the the Chinese, but part of that influence centers around turning them into objects to be viewed.

Privacy and cleanliness, so central to Riis's moral reform, are here experienced as a stumbling blocks to his touristic project. Likewise, Riis is willing to overlook the dangerous filth and crowding of the Italian streets for the sake of entertainment. What is good for traditional morals and Americanization—cleanliness and privacy—is bad for sight-seeing. And what is bad for Protestant virtue—filth and crowds—is good for viewing pleasure. Amalgamation in the moral community and the social body—Americanization—is at odds with assimilation in what might be called the "spectacular body." Riis's loyalties are sorely split between two competing ethics.

Preoccupation with Color

Riis's bizarre preoccupation with color here is provocative, especially when one remembers that Crane is a well-known and obsessive colorist; one need only think of the titles of some of his most famous works: *The Red Badge of Courage*, *The Black Riders*, "The Bride Comes to Yellow Sky," "The Blue Hotel." I would argue that Riis's and Crane's desire for color gives us some insight into the source or perhaps the nature of their quests for excitement: they reveal here a visceral sort of revulsion to dullness. Perhaps, indeed, they are recoiling from what John Higham calls "the sheer dullness of an urban-industrial culture" and "the restraint and decorum of the 'Gilded Age,'" which he claims spurs the more general search for intense experience in the 1890s.[11] We have seen Riis, in regard to color in Chinatown, refer with evident irritation to the neighborhood's "clean[liness] to distraction," its "everyday dismal dreariness," and "the level of general dulness" that seem to swallow up what little color the area offers. He feels confronted by this dullness; it is experienced as a kind of threat or assault.

At points in Crane's work one feels an analogous sort of battle between bright and dreary colors, not unlike the antinomy in Riis's description between the reds and yellows in Chinatown and the general dullness there, which saps these colors of their brightness. Interestingly, in both the opening scene of *Maggie* and the title character's last scene, Crane's prose makes use of a similar palette and also a similar progression from the same vibrant color to sickly and dismal hues. At the center of the rock fight that opens the book, the little boy Jimmie is delivering "great, *crimson* oaths." As the camera-eye of the narrator pulls back to nearby spectators and finally to the distant periphery of the scene, we encounter "a worm of *yellow* convicts," who "came from the shadow of a *grey* ominous building and crawled slowly along the river's bank" (3–4, my italics). It is as if Jimmie's youthful, crimson "fury" is diluted or discolored in the course of the passage, as the reader is shown the larger, older, more established environment: the "grey ominous" unnamed prison building (ominous perhaps because it may be the slum child's future home) and the sickly yellow wormlike row of convicts that this building has created and out of whose "shadow" they emerge. Strictly in the light of Crane's use of color here, Jimmie's crimson passion can be read as the doomed effort of the child to remain vibrant and alive in a gray world that looms nearby and threatens to change one from combatant to prisoner, from enraged to jaundiced.

The end of Maggie's final scene contains a similar color progression. We begin with "the girl of *crimson* legions." She is being followed by "a huge fat man," but it is not this man or, more precisely, his colors that finish the sequence. Again Crane moves the point of focus away from the character to the larger environment, and again that environment is ghastly and sickly. What follows is the "deathly *black* hue" of the river, and then "some hidden factory sent up a *yellow* glare, that lit for a moment the waters lapping oilily against timbers" (53, my italics). Here black replaces the gray of the initial scene, and what was then only "ominous" is now "deathly." And as in the previous passage, the black and yellow are allied. (The black and yellow are also allied in another way. The factory's color, here yellow, was in the preceding paragraphs black, a disturbing and claustrophobic black: "[T]all black factories shut in the street" in the "gloomy districts," and in "the blackness of the final block," "the shutters of the tall buildings were closed like grim lips" [53].) The world of the living individual—apparently driven again to a drastic crimson in its own self-defense or struggle for survival, though now the crimson not of ritual violence but of commercial sex—is superseded by the lifeless, poisoned, and strangling world of industrial production and pollution.

In Crane's life and writing, the insistence on excitement seems more pronounced than in the case of Riis, even frenetic or desperate, and I would argue that it informs his unusual and frequent use of color words. Mark Van Doren has remarked upon Crane's "need to live, at least as an artist, in the midst of all but unbearable excitement"[12]—an extreme but not isolated example is his purposefully exposing himself to rifle fire during his coverage of the Spanish-American War[13]—and it seems to me that his colorism is linked to this need. Michael Fried shrewdly finds surfacing in Crane's prose a "repressed" fear of "the deathliness of the blank upward-staring page,"[14] and this reading is sensible if one considers Crane's writing as both an antidote to lifelessness and also—because of the colorlessness and emptiness of the actual blank sheet of paper—a potential reminder of it. Like his animism, which according to John Berryman "is like nothing else in civilized literature,"[15] Crane's colorism is a (no doubt unconscious) strike against the dullness, the flatness, and, as with Riis, the cleanliness—"the nicely-laundered lives"[16]—he finds in the middle-class industrial culture around him. He is feverishly attempting to animate and color what is for him a wan, deadening world.

What the Middle Class and Poor Have in Common: Entertainment

According to an editor of *How the Other Half Lives*, Riis's "straining for the picturesque . . . seems but a partial discount against [his] wide sympathy for the men, women, and children of New York's slums."[17] But was his interest in the picturesque really at odds with his empathy? I want to argue, on the contrary, that Riis's appreciation of the picturesque, his desire for spectacular entertainment, was rather a source of his sympathy for the poor. It was something—perhaps even the main thing—that he and the poor had in common.

Riis writes, in perhaps the moment of greatest sympathy in the whole of the book:

> Perhaps of all the disheartening experiences of those who have devoted lives of unselfish thought and effort . . . to the lifting of the great load, the indifference of those they would help is the most puzzling. They will not be helped. Dragged by main force out of their misery, they slip back again on the first opportunity, seemingly content in the old rut. The explanation was supplied by two women of my acquaintance in an Elizabeth Street tenement, whom the city missionaries had taken from their wretched hovel and provided with work and a decent home somewhere in New Jersey. In three weeks they were back, saying that they preferred their dark room to the stumps out in the country. But to me the oldest, the mother, who had struggled along with her daughter making cloaks at half a dollar apiece, twelve long years since the daughter's husband was killed in a street accident and the city took the children, made the bitter confession: "We do get so kind o' downhearted living this way, that we have to be where something is going on, or we just can't stand it." And there was sadder pathos to me in her words than in the whole long story of their struggle with poverty; for unconsciously she voiced the sufferings of thousands, misjudged by a happier world, deemed vicious because they are human and unfortunate. (131)

A story much like this one—of the poor who refuse to be "helped"—appears twenty years before in *The Dangerous Classes of New York*, and for Charles Loring

Brace it is not only disheartening but apparently stupefying. He ventures no guess as to why a poor girl "would not take a situation away from the city."[18] But Riis has come to understand the conundrum and anticipates that his reader will understand it too: being "where something is going on" is a consolation for poverty. It is the same dynamic that has led to the popularity of extravagant Irish wakes among the entire population of the slums: "[I]t has taken root among all classes of tenement dwellers . . . who have taken amazingly to the funeral coach, perhaps because it furnishes the one opportunity of their lives for a really grand turn-out with a free ride thrown in" (132). What Riis sympathizes with most of all here (what he finds the "sadder pathos" in) and what prompts him to call the poor "human" (rather than "vicious") is their desire for entertainment, and especially, in the case of the two women, for the sights that the city provides. William Dean Howells succinctly explains this love of the city: "[T]he place . . . affords [the poor] for nothing the spectacle of the human drama, with themselves for actors."[19]

Not only will poor women prefer to live in a dark room rather than a decent home for the sake of urban action; we also learn from Riis that newsboys and other poor city children will spend their hard-earned money—improvidently—to watch plays about city figures, with titles very much like Riis's own chapter headings, such as "The Bowery Tramp" and "The Thief." Slide shows with the "magic lantern"—with which Riis engrossed middle-class audiences in his presentations on "the other half," before and after the publication of his book—are also the slum "boy's dear delight."[20]

This is a delight that Riis, and his publicity agent, have all along been counting on his middle-class readers to harbor; some of his descriptions, as we have seen, are specifically geared for "one in search of excitement" (69). Now it becomes clear not only that the other half have this desire in excess, that they have a large enough appetite for city spectacle to suffer for it, but also that they value excitement above traditional virtue.

Crane's slum characters are, like Riis's urban poor, conspicuously preoccupied with spectacle. Nearly every event in *Maggie* becomes an occasion for spectatorship.[21] The rock fight that opens the book is watched by "a curious woman" in an apartment-house window, "some laborers, unloading a scow at a dock," and "the engineer of a passive tugboat," as well as Jimmie's comrades from "Rum Alley" and Pete (3–4); the Johnson family, with its various fights and drinking binges, provides an ongoing spectacle for the tenement population as well as for "a group of urchins" who wait for Mrs. Johnson outside a saloon (28); Jimmie and Pete's fight attracts a crowd that bends and surges in "absorbing anxiety to see" (37). And Maggie's final confrontation with her mother devolves into a theatrical event: "Children ventured into the room and ogled her as if they formed the front row at a theater" (48).

Crane, again like Riis, seems to understand that the love of entertainment is a natural outgrowth of slum conditions. Spectacle provides the poor with a consolation for their hardships and an escape from them. At one of the theaters where Pete takes her out, "Maggie lost herself in sympathy with the wanderers swooning in snow storms beneath happy-hued church windows, while a choir within sang 'Joy to the World'" (27). Later in *Maggie* the theater is referred to simply as "a place of forgetfulness," and this sort of place has salutary effects: "An atmosphere of pleasure and prosperity seemed to hang over the throng, born, perhaps, of good clothes and of two hours in a place of forgetfulness" (51). In a newspaper sketch, "The Men in the Storm" (1894), men waiting in line for the doors of a shelter to open get some relief from the cold and their own competitive pushing for warmth when a spectacle momentarily appears: "[O]nce the window of the huge dry-goods shop across the street furnished material for a few moments of forgetfulness."[22]

As with Riis's poor men and women who give up decency and providence for the sake of entertainment, Crane's characters often pursue excitement at the expense of traditional moral values. The title of Crane's city sketch "When a Man Falls a Crowd Gathers" (1894) turns out to be a virtual proverb about the process of spectacle—not charity. The crowd in this sketch is so interested in its ability to watch that it mostly forgets that the fallen man is in physical danger. People push and shove to see better; they deprive the man of air, scare his child companion, and oblige the latter "to put his hand upon the breast of the body to maintain his balance." It is not until "after the first spasm of curiosity had passed away" that some in "the crowd . . . began to bethink themselves of some way to help." And at the end of the sketch, when the ambulance has taken the fallen man away and disappeared, some "still continued to stare . . . as if they had been cheated, as if the curtain had been rung down on a tragedy that was but half completed; and this impenetrable blanket intervening between sufferer and their curiosity seemed to make them feel an injustice."[23] Crane's slum inhabitants seem to feel that they actually have a right to spectacle, a right that supersedes the duty to charity—as if they were citizens of an entertainment community with a notion of spectacular justice. In any case, Crane makes clear that his characters experience their curiosity or excitement as something other than a passion that ought to be restrained, as in traditional morality. It is experienced as an ethic in its own right.

There is never any sense of unseemly voyeurism or violated decorum among the aggressive spectators in Crane's Bowery, because excitement and pleasure are values there. The gang members in *George's Mother* have a "philosophy" that condemns modern life as "a great bore." "They longed dimly for a time when they could run through the decorous streets with crash and roar of war" in "revenge for pleasures long possessed by others, a sweeping compensation for their years without crystal and gilt, women and wine."[24] The ideal Bowery relationship is based on having "a good time together" or "a heluva time" (44), as Nell puts it to Pete: thus Jimmie and Pete go out to "a boxing match" (17), and Maggie and Pete's courtship is little more than a series of cheap and progressively seedier entertainments, centered around spectacle and alcohol—theaters, beer halls and their shows, "the Central Park Menagerie and the Museum of Arts," and finally "dime museums" with "freaks," which Maggie finds "outa sight" (26). The new moral value of pleasure or entertainment is registered in the Bowery slang, which Crane faithfully reports and which, having entered general use, is now taken for granted: a pleasureful experience is "a *good* time" or, its inversion, "a *heluva* time," which can mean the same thing. As we have seen, Crane's Bowery values are essentially a reversal of Protestant ethics, and this is often represented in the jargon; just as Maggie's "virtue" is denigrated by Nell as a lack of "spirit," "a hell of a time" now means something good. The centrality of vision or spectacle to this new ethic of pleasure is likewise implicit in the vernacular: something incredible is beyond the visible, "out of *sight*."

Crane is of course sardonic about the rabid pleasure-seeking of his Bowery characters, and *Maggie* might be described as one of the first novelistic renditions of individuals essentially stupefied by mass-culture entertainments.[25] But while Crane is derisive about his characters' thirst for spectacle, his relationship to Bowery entertainments is not simply critical, but complicit. He was also a consumer. We know that he partook of the very nightlife and street life that he describes— and not merely as an objective researcher. Before he proved his allegiance to the Bowery life by actually moving there, he extolled its cheap virtues to scandalized family members and middle-class acquaintances, at one point bragging about a black eye he had received by a bottle tossed in a barroom brawl, at another asking dinner guests if they had ever had the pleasure of seeing "a Chinaman wandering in Mott Street."[26] Often, in his bitter irony about his characters, Crane is also attacking himself, and that may very well be true here: where Riis is indulgent of himself and the slum residents who are dependent on slum spectacle, Crane is unforgiving of his Bowery characters and himself alike. Also, Crane is certainly a more sophisticated consumer of Bowery action than his characters: they watch the staged shows and the spontaneous fights, while he watches the shows, the fights, and the watchers. Nonetheless, Crane too was an avid consumer of the spectacles of the slums.

The Reverend E. H. Chapin and other charity writers had asserted that the "essential unity of humanity" had a spiritual basis. Victorian reform practices for the poor, such as Sunday schools and friendly visiting, and later Progressive settlement houses in slum neighborhoods,[27] were supposed to reunite the scattered urban classes on the grounds of shared spiritual interests. But again and again throughout the nineteenth century, reformers were "disheartened," to use Riis's word, about the indifference of the poor to their own moral and social state and to the efforts of the middle class to "befriend" them. Charles Loring Brace found, for instance, that the street girls' "worst quality is their superficiality. There is no depth either to their virtues or vices. They sin, and immediately repent with alacrity; they live virtuously for years, and a straw seems suddenly to turn them."[28]

What is deep among the poor, according to Riis and Crane, is their regard for excitement. As Riis remarks of the funeral party, it has "taken root." Riis and Crane suggest that one profound thing the middle class and the poor have in common—part of their humanity—is not a concern for self-restraint and ultimate salvation but an interest in pleasure and immediate entertainment. If Riis and Crane are right, and the slums in fact go a step further and nurture an *ethic* of excitement or "good times," then it might be said that it is the urban poor that eventually convert the middle class to their morality—not the other way around, as preachers such as Chapin had hoped. The fact that the Bowery slang of Crane's day, with its separate ethical bent, has come into middle-class usage is one sign of this conversion.

This ethical transformation of the middle class is of course made possible—if not irresistible—by the new entertainment technology. For, indeed, a common ground for all classes was finally being discovered precisely there, in the new or expanded media: the large daily newspaper, the photograph, the advertisement, live entertainment,[29] and the motion picture, which D. W. Griffith called "a universal language." Unlike the case of previous media and amusements, the audiences for these media would come from all classes and all ethnic groups: these were mass media. Immigrants did not have to speak English to understand snapshots, song-and-dance numbers, and moving pictures, and middle-class kids seemed to enjoy movies so much that their parents publicly expressed worry about what their children were seeing.[30] With the appeal of photographs and bold headlines, the large dailies were able to make inroads into neighborhoods served by the foreign-language press.[31] And soon silent movies, marketed first of all for urban immigrants in the form of shorts that were often ribald and rebellious, were made attractive to lower-middle-class clerical workers, and even respectable bourgeois men and women, through the introduction of longer photoplays, national censorship, and campaigns against foreign films.[32]

Progressive reformers had high hopes for the spiritual possibilities of the motion picture medium, hopes which today seem quaint: films could teach immigrants Anglo-Saxon values and draw them away from saloons and other vicious entertainments. One reformer suggested that the movies could function as a "grand social worker," and D. W. Griffith called them "a power that can make men brothers and end wars forever."[33] But if the motion picture—and the still photograph—had a unifying power, it was not in any traditional moral message. The new media did not unite and uplift the social body; they did not do social work, although they did unify the urban classes in another body. If they had the power to make men brothers, they made them not brothers of charity but brothers of the spectacle. They did not have the power to end wars, but they had the power to let people watch them in complete safety, eventually in their own homes.

Daniel J. Boorstin has written about the new and democratic "consumption communities" that started to replace the older fellowships of craft in the second half of the nineteenth century, about how men came to be "affiliated less by what they believed than by what they consumed." "Nearly all objects," he wrote, "from the hats and suits and shoes men wore to the food they ate became symbols and instruments of novel communities."[34] To this list of objects I would add the newspapers, photographs, and films they saw. Along with belonging in collectivities of ownership, what rich and poor, Anglo-Saxon and immigrant came to share was membership in a community of viewers—belonging to a body of spectators. And this membership implied subscription to a new ethic of entertainment.

In Crane's representation of Bowery slang and profanity, in Riis's "odd and out-of-the-way" photographs, in his readiness to praise filth and crowds while condemning privacy and cleanliness, in his sympathy for the slum dwellers who want and value spectacle above a decent home, and in both of these writers' appeal to that desire on the part of their middle-class readership: in all of this there is a new aesthetic and a new ethic. The traditional moral instruction of slum writing is put aside; the conventional distinction between moral art and cheap trash is largely ignored. The old demand for virtuous restraint is sacrificed to the new objective of excitement.

Cheap entertainment was not, of course, new to literature; dime novels had long stirred up the passions of the lower classes. But Riis's and Crane's books were aimed at a middle-class audience whose morality had previously forbidden anything but high-minded and moralistic accounts of the poor; here were books that gave middle-class readers the cheap street spectacle of the lower classes and affirmed the middle-class desire for what in some circles was still called "morbid" entertainment. Even when looking at the poor, these new books said, it was fine to trample traditional moral concerns and search for excitement.

And the old Protestant morality cannot accommodate a new aesthetic of excitement. After all, aesthetics was always a traditional moral issue. Not only is excitement an unhealthful passion; it naturally undermines other traditional ethical imperatives, most obviously self-restraint, decency, and modesty but also privacy, cleanliness, providence, and charity. The search for excitement is an ethic incompatible with conventional morality.

The editors who rejected Crane's book on moral grounds were by no means hysterical. They recognized the threat that such literature posed, and they made a pious decision. Riis's book was published and sold to the middle class because it was more insidious. It explicitly upheld traditional moral values even as it implicitly encouraged an alternative ethic that undermined them.

Social Policy and Entertainment

But, it might be objected, Riis's commitment to traditional moral and social reform won out, in the last analysis, over his search for excitement: Mulberry Bend, which

Riis alternatively enjoys and condemns for its crowds and filth, was in the end, thanks largely to Riis, razed and made into a park. I would put it differently: Riis succeeded as a social reformer because of his commitment to excitement, and beginning, at least, with Riis, social programs have been conditioned by an ethics and a politics of spectacle and entertainment. A compromise between moralities has taken place.

Looking back from the vantage point of the 1980s, Daniel Levine has assessed Riis's limitations as a reformer: Riis's solutions were narrow, did not stress broader socioeconomic causes, and so did not cure poverty. "Clearly Riis, as a visitor to rather than a resident amidst poverty, found his cure in the most visible aspects of slum life. Obviously better sewage and clean running water could eliminate some disease and filth; but neither then nor now has cleanliness or better housing cured poverty. Riis asked explicitly for justice rather than charity, but he seemed to think that justice could be a product of the architect's drawing board."[35]

I would go further and suggest that this problem of limitations seems to be endemic not simply to Riis's visitor status but to a general practice of slum representation whose most conspicuous stylistic feature is sensationalism. Riis may indeed have concentrated on the visual aspects of slum life because he was a visitor to poverty, but the fact is that the visual aspects were also the most appealing and accessible for a reading or viewing audience. If Riis's call for reform got tangible results where others' had failed,[36] it was because his book included dramatic photographs and depicted slum life in a sensational manner. That is, the general public was, like Riis, disposed to find the "cure in the most visible aspects of slum life" because only a presentation that exploited the slum's spectacular aspects could seize its attention. Riis's visual concentration and his focus on dramatic slum habits—his tunnel vision, according to Levine—was a condition of his book's success, its popular reception. Much the same could be said for the entire antislum movement of the 1890s.

And I would argue that we have never really surpassed the terms and styles of the slum representation of this era. It is true that we no longer describe the tenements as "picturesque" and that slumming parties have long gone out of fashion; today we find these practices repulsively insensitive and inhuman. But we continue to be thrilled by the exotic spectacle of the slums, and the media and the various arts continue to play on our fascination: with television, we can now enjoy slumming parties without ever leaving our homes. The media and the arts no longer fetishize "the picturesque" or "the racial and ethnic stereotype" in the slums, but they do still fetishize otherness (whether social, psychological, moral, or cultural).[37] Riis's tunnel vision is, in large part, also ours.

This is precisely why our present reporting on the slums is under attack by today's progressive scholars. And the critique of popular magazine articles and televised programs (including the *Time* piece with which we began) for their "lurid" descriptions of ghetto residents is not academic. For progressive scholars, such reporting is not just gratuitously sensational; it puts emphasis on the "individual attributes" of ghetto residents and "the so-called culture of poverty" and thus steals attention from more fundamental—and, I would add, less titillating—economic inequalities.[38]

Would-be crusaders for slum reform, it seems, are faced with a conundrum: the very means and terms of description that can draw the necessary attention to the problem of the slums also structure reform options, and the policies they suggest may not be the best methods of amelioration. The most accessible and attention-getting devices—exotic visuals, narratives of strange lives—seem necessary to drum up interest in the plight of the slums in a country where social rights are not assumed, not inalienable, but depend on the marshalling of public opinion; these devices are certainly endemic to a media that is always fighting for market share. (Discussions and statistics about social and economic structure, for instance, can hardly compete for publicity; they are abstract and tedious by comparison, and the social structuring of slum poverty is hard to visualize.) Meanwhile, these attention-getting devices are not simply matters of taste; they tend to condition possibilities for reform. Methods of publicity contain within themselves a certain logic of diagnosis and thus of cure. Levine might argue that we call attention to the symptoms of our social ills—because they are visible and dramatic—and thereby end up treating symptoms, not causes. Social policy in the United States today is conditioned by a politics of entertainment; or, to put it another way, in this country the cure of the social body is now tied to a healthy spectacular body.[39]

And entertainment does not only enter into publicity and thus determine the problems that need to be solved. Social solutions are themselves sought, in part, in entertainment. Consider, for instance, the park that replaces Mulberry Bend: it is meant to have an aesthetic and entertainment value (as well as a health value) for its visitors. Riis's reforms, as we shall see, are part of a movement that inaugurates social programs within a new ethics.

III

Slum

Psychology

5 ⋙ Self-Esteem and the Tough

Riis has a strange investment in the tough—what we would today call the thug. "I have certain theories concerning toughs which my friend the sergeant says are rot," Riis declares in *Out of Mulberry Street*.[1] For one thing, he claims that he prefers the tough to the pauper, despite the fact that the tough regularly robs, injures, and even kills, while, as Riis admits, the pauper is rarely violent. Riis has no illusions about his favored subject: within half an hour after a camera session with an accommodating gang of toughs, Riis found at the police station "two of my friends . . . under arrest for robbing a Jewish pedlar who had passed that way after I left them, and trying to saw his head off, as they put it, 'just for fun'" (168–169). It was one thing to romanticize or sympathize with harmless "street Arabs" and mischievous newspaper boys, as Charles Loring Brace and Horatio Alger did. It was another to spend time with and entertain an empathy for the accomplished tough, thief, or gang member, as Riis does.

Riis says of the boys in the juvenile asylum: they "were rather the victims than the doers of a grievous wrong, being in that place, no matter if they *had* stolen." In a chapter of *The Children of the Poor* called "What It Is That Makes Boys Bad," Riis explains that for these boys in the asylum, "it was a case of mis-direction, or no direction at all, of their youthful energies." "Even the tough, with all his desperation," says Riis, "is weak rather than vicious." His existence is first of all a "protest" against his miserable "conditions of life" (176). The gang represents "all the high ambition of youth caricatured by the slum and become base passions." A boy named "Mike was a tough, but with a better chance he might have been a hero."[2] For slum kids, "opportunities of mischief are greater than those of harm-

91

less amusement; made so," says Riis, "it has sometimes seemed to me, with deliberate purpose to hatch the 'tough.'"[3] In a chapter called "The Genesis of the Gang," Riis explains that "the average boy is just like a little steam-engine with the steam always up. The play is his safety-valve. With the landlord in the yard and the policeman in the street sitting on his safety-valve and holding it down, he is bound to explode."[4]

Clearly, Riis's genealogies of the tough are psychological, as opposed to conventionally moral. And these sympathetic notions concerning the tough, though they are perhaps some of the most dramatic of his ideas and certainly the most difficult for his police acquaintances to swallow, are not aberrations from his general analyses of slum behavior. He regularly challenges Protestant moral stereotypes and finds immoral behaviors to have natural, psychological motivations.

Like young boys who become toughs, young girls who become prostitutes may be implicated in vice, but they are not culpable.

> There was before them starvation, or the poor-house. . . . [O]f the thousands, who are travelling [this] road . . . , with the hot blood of youth in their veins, with the love of life and of the beautiful world to which not even sixty cents a day can shut their eyes—who is to blame if their feet find the paths of shame that are "always open to them?" (182)

Similarly, the poor who buy things on the installment plan and then cannot pay for them are not imprudent; the "specimen wages of the tenements . . . [are] seemingly inconsistent with the charge of improvidence" (130). Or, if they can nonetheless be called improvident—for Riis waffles on this point—then tenement living, and not they themselves, are to blame: "There is nothing in the prospect of a sharp, unceasing battle for the bare necessities of life, to encourage looking ahead, everything to discourage the effort. Improvidence and wastefulness are natural results" (130).

In each of these cases, Riis weakens the moral judgment, even if he cannot entirely discard it. In his rendition, the notion of vice becomes tenuous, even paradoxical. Moral labels are still possible, but moral responsibility is thrown out: people who hide from the debt collector are improvident but blameless; prostitutes still walk "the paths of shame," but they are not guilty for it; boys who steal are bad, but they are the victims rather than the doers of wrong; toughs are weak, vain, and idle but not vicious. And the category of vice is significantly watered down, not only by the consideration of objective, social factors (such as miserable conditions and low wages) but also by the simultaneous inclusion of other subjective categories.

The notion of a moral character, challenged by the passions, beset by temptations, and assaulted by deprivations—a concept central to Protestant mental philosophy—is being altered. "The hot blood of youth in their veins" or "the love of life" is something other than the vicious passion of lust. This lyrical description does not smack of moral condemnation; it romanticizes lust, naturalizes it. Likewise, the phrase "youthful energies" naturalizes the impulse that has led boys to theft, and the expression "high ambitions" legitimizes it: the drive is no longer seen as a base passion. "There is nothing in the prospect of a sharp, unceasing battle for the bare necessities of life, to encourage looking ahead": what is being described is something other than the twin dynamic of deprivation and temptation that one finds in previous charity writing; it is more like the psychological impact of living hand-to-mouth.

"Go into any of the 'respectable' tenement neighborhoods," Riis suggests; "be with and among its people until you understand their ways, their aims, and the quality of their ambitions" (121). These are the sorts of subjective categories that Riis contributes to the discourse on the urban poor. He overturns a host of moralistic cliches, sometimes, as we have seen, with ethnographic explanations of "ways" or "fashions," and also with psychological accounts of "aims" and "ambitions."[5]

If Riis is associated with a single breakthrough in the conception of poverty, it is with the "environmentalism" that the Progressive Era supposedly discovered and developed. His famous solution to pauperism was to tear down the tenement: change the environment and you will produce different kinds of individuals. Riis stated quite plainly, at the beginning of *How the Other Half Lives*, that "the tenements . . . are hot-beds of . . . epidemics . . . [and] the nurseries of pauperism and crime," that "they touch the family life with deadly moral contagion" (2–3). But Riis did not discover the idea that the environment shapes lives both morally and hygienically, and neither did the Progressive Era: this brand of environmentalism had been common to charity writing since the middle of the century. Two decades earlier, for instance, Charles Loring Brace asserted that "the packing of human beings in [tenements] . . . sows pestilence and breeds every species of criminal habits."[6] What Riis discovered was another brand of environmentalism, another theory of environmental influence.

Charity writers imagined both a physical and a moral exchange between the environment and the individual. Physically, the poor were susceptible to contagion in tenement crowds; accidents in unsafe work places; and poor health from filth, overwork, and lack of sunlight, warmth, and food. Morally, the slums were a hothouse of vice. The moral mode of influence was conceived of as infection; the metaphors were biological or botanical: one caught vice like a disease or absorbed it like a plant does polluted air. And though Riis partook of these terms and metaphors of transmission, he also imagined different ones.

"In self-defense, you know," says Riis, "all life eventually accommodates itself to the environment, and human life is no exception" (122). Riis's genesis of the tough may begin on traditional moral ground—the physical deprivations of the slums, the childhood foibles that can turn into adult vices, the lack of a disciplinary environment. But soon it veers into unfamiliar analytical territory, a sort of social psychology in which identity is not a function simply of the individual soul in the face of temptations, or even of the individual body and its physical environment, but also of healthy ambitions and natural impulses blocked by the social environment. In regard to the individual's response to the environment, it is one thing to speak of falling prey to a "moral contagion," quite another to talk of "self-defense."

Riis's most famous and important charge against the tenement partakes of his more complex conception of individual identity and begins to elucidate it. "'It all comes down to character in the end,' was the verdict of a philanthropist whose life had been spent wrestling with the weary problem. And so it comes down to the tenement, the destroyer of individuality and character everywhere" (186). This passage can be read as a succinct formulation of the moral environmentalism which Riis and the whole Progressive Era popularized. It does not entirely disagree with the philanthropic or ultramoralistic position; it respects that position but stands it on its head. Yes, says Riis, pauperism does come down to character, but that is not the end of it; character, in turn, comes down to environment.

But there is something strange about Riis's sleight of hand here, something that exceeds the traditional environmentalist twist. Riis adds a term to the philanthropist's character equation: individuality. It is an interesting formulation, for character is apparently being supplemented by another category of identity, and it is not an accidental formulation, for Riis repeats this charge several times in his writings.[7] But is individuality just another term for character?—is this simply a rhetorical flourish? It would appear not.

In leading up to his powerful charge, Riis voices his surprising and scandalous preference for the thief over the pauper. "The thief," he writes, "is infinitely easier to deal with than the pauper, because the very fact of his being a thief presupposes some bottom to the man. Granted that it is bad, there is still something, a possible handle by which to catch him. To the pauper there is none" (186). Elsewhere Riis reiterates the comparison, this time between the pauper and the tough. "When it comes to a choice, the tough is to be preferred to the born pauper any day. The one has the making of something in him, unpromising as he looks; seen in a certain light he may even be considered a hopeful symptom. The other is just so much dead loss."[8] In what light—besides a sadistic one—does the tough appear promising? What is this "bottom to the man," this "making of something in him," this "possible handle"? What do the thief or the tough have that the pauper does not? Certainly not character. Neither has that: the tough is conspicuously bad, by most accounts worse in character than the pauper.

What, then, does the tough have that the pauper does not? The implication is that the tough has individuality, the other aspect of subjectivity that the tenement stamps out in the production of the pauper. And what is this individuality? Riis gives a hint when he follows up his famous charge about the tenements with a quote from the federal commissioner of education: some people, says the commissioner, "become criminal because of lack of individuality and the self-respect that comes with it."[9] Elsewhere in *The Children of the Poor*, Riis talks of the "unconquerable vanity" of the child, which, "if not turned to use for his good, makes a tough of the lad with more muscle than brains."[10] And he explains that "a young man . . . trains with a gang, because it furnishes the means of gratifying his inordinate vanity; that is the slum's counterfeit of self-esteem."[11] Riis gives another hint about the nature of individuality when he talks about the refusal of tenants transferred to a model tenement to use communal washtubs as "an encouraging sign," "a sign that the tenement that smothers individuality left them this useful handle." He concludes, in regard to this "useful handle," that "every peg of personal pride rescued from the tenements is worth a thousand theories for hanging the hopes of improvement on."[12] The "handle," the "bottom to the man," that both the tough and the thief share turns out to be vanity, or personal pride, a well-known moral flaw which Riis himself, at one point, calls "not admirable."[13] But this same "bottom to the man," when seen outside a traditional moral light, is also self-respect or self-esteem. As Riis suggests of the child, his vanity can be "turned to use for his good."

Although Riis gets his notions about self-respect from the current psychology and criminology, his conception of the criminal, in fact, seems to differ radically from that of the federal commissioner of education whom he quotes. Whereas the commissioner attributes criminality to "a lack of individuality and the self-respect that comes with it," Riis attributes it to the child's unconquerable vanity gone astray, which, though perverse, is still a form of self-respect, "the slum's counterfeit of self-esteem." Furthermore, Riis finds that it is precisely the possession of individuality and self-respect that distinguishes the thief from the pauper.[14] These qualities are what prevent the thief from begging on the streets like the pauper. Lacking self-esteem or personal pride, the pauper is willing to humiliate himself in any way at all; there are no limits to his behavior, no bottom to his self. In this light, the bottom to the self is equivalent to the level of self-respect or self-esteem. The pauper has no self-respect, so his self is an abyss, an emptiness: he lacks individuality.

In the traditional moral version of identity, the pauper has no self (no moral character) because he has no industry and no independence, because he is idle and helpless,[15] and the thief has no self because he is idle and violent and also because he is vain. But that same overblown pride is what gives the thief a self (an individuality) and keeps one from the pauper, in Riis's other version of identity. In a psychological light, pride, even vanity, is a plus.

Built into Riis's simple and powerful slogan about the tenements are two separate versions of subjectivity—or two versions of ethical substance—and two separate ethics. That these versions are not consonant is obvious upon analysis. Riis's terse slogan involves an unwitting paradox. In traditional morality, pride, especially vanity, is a weakness in character. In the morality in which the tough is preferable to the pauper, pride or vanity is the very basis of individuality.

Crane, like Riis, gives his reader a psychological genealogy of the tough. His portrait of the boy Jimmie in *Maggie* includes a history of the boy's belligerent sensibility. After witnessing three chapters of child abuse and street scuffles, the reader of the novel is told:

> The inexperienced fibres of the boy's eyes were hardened at an early age. He became a young man of leather. . . .
> He clad his soul in armor by means of happening hilariously in at a mission church where a man composed his sermon of "yous." . . .
> He maintained a belligerent attitude toward all well-dressed men. To him fine raiment was allied to weakness, and all good coats covered faint hearts. . . .
> Above all things he despised obvious Christians and ciphers with the chrysanthemums of aristocracy in their button-holes. He considered himself above both of these classes. . . .
> After a time his sneer grew so that it turned its glare upon all things. He became so sharp he believed in nothing. To him the police were always actuated by malignant impulses and the rest of the world was composed, for the most part, of despicable creatures who were all trying to take advantage of him and with whom, in defense, he was obliged to quarrel on all possible occasions. He himself occupied a down-trodden position that had a private but distinct element of grandeur in its isolation. (13–15)

Crane's genesis of the Bowery tough is not a traditional Protestant one. He does not portray the streets of lower New York as sites of moral infestation that his characters wisely avoid or resist or, conversely, that insidiously poison them or slowly wear down their spiritual immune systems. He does not adopt the traditional metaphors of a moral epidemiology, as do other novelists at the time. He does not, like Edgar Fawcett, claim that "human grossness . . . spawned" in the tenement[16] or, like James Sullivan, describe a boy "whose budding character had suffered from a poisonous moral atmosphere."[17] Rather, like Riis when he considers the hatching of the tough, Crane portrays the tenement neighborhood as hostile and threatening and shows his characters steeling themselves against it.

Jimmie's experience in the slums is not one of temptation. He does not fall and then, like Fawcett's Cora, develop an "armor against remorse"; rather, he is simply "hardened" against a hostile environment. He does not build up armor against a soul that is the seat of conscience and remorse; it is instead his soul[18] that is "clad . . . in armor" against the external world, in self-defense. Jimmie struggles to preserve a sense of worth and superiority as he is subject to the abuses of drunken parents, the insults of religious missionaries, the spectacle of wealthier and better-dressed men, and the insurmountable powers of the police. "In defense," he becomes a "man of leather"; he turns "his sneer . . . upon all things"; and he feels "obliged to quarrel." In the interest of his self-image, he considers himself "above" Christians and aristocrats; he feels that his "down-trodden position . . . had [an] element of grandeur."

Crane inscribed several copies of the original 1893 version of *Maggie* with the following remark: "This book . . . tries to show that environment is a tremendous thing in the world and frequently shapes lives regardless. If one proves that theory one makes room in Heaven for all sorts of souls (notably an occasional street girl) who are not confidently expected to be there by many excellent people."[19] Crane suggests that to take the power of environment seriously implies that some prostitutes, as well as other wrongdoers, are completely innocent of moral wrong. This may seem like an obvious, logical corollary to environmental determinism, but it is precisely the step that moral environmentalists refused to take. Crane is not merely copying Progressive ideas in this note; he is pushing them to their logical conclusion—something not even Riis ever managed. Riis went further in his Progressivism than previous charity writers but, as we saw, still waffled on the issue of culpability.[20]

While Riis weakens the prerogatives of Protestant moral judgment, Crane does away with them completely. While Riis offers a moral epidemiology in regard to tenement family life and provides a psychological genealogy of the tough and the prostitute, Crane's behavioral accounts are consistently psychological. While Riis supplements and thus deemphasizes the notion of moral character in his account of human identity, Crane jettisons the notion entirely.

As we have seen, the apparatus of character that was thought to structure life and indeed structured literary slum action—the experiences of temptation, a guiding conscience, resistance to passion, sin, remorse, and so on—is conspicuously absent from *Maggie*, whose plot was stock material in traditional moral slum fiction. In the course of her premarital sexual affair, her vilification, and her movement into prostitution, Maggie experiences no conventional moral feelings or transformations. Now we can add that ultimately, Crane's first slum novel is more than an excavation of alternative ethical codes and values in the Bowery and therefore an ethnographic assault on the universal status of Protestant ethics: it is a psychological challenge to the very notions of moral character and conscience.

The cornerstone of the moral philosophy of human identity was the supremacy of the moral sense among all the different parts of the mind. As Thomas Upham put it in his popular textbook *Elements of Mental Philosophy* (1845),

> [T]he moral sensibilities . . . hold, in our estimation of them, a higher rank than the appetites, propensities, and passions. . . .
> The moral sensibility appears to hold . . . the position of a consultative and judicial power; it stands above . . . and over . . . , in the exercise of a higher authority; it keenly scrutinizes the motives of action; it compares emotion with emotion, desire with desire; it sits a sort of arbitress, holding the scales of justice, and dispensing such decisions as are requisite for the due regulation of the empire of the passions.[21]

Now, Crane's characters are far from devoid of moral notions: Pete and Jimmie embody a native Bowery ethics of fearlessness and defiance, and Maggie's mother, as critics have regularly noticed, gives shrill voice to the middle-class moral taboo against premarital sex. In the world of *Maggie*, however, there is no such thing as a moral sensibility with sovereign status, as there is in middle- and upper-class moral philosophy. To borrow Upham's language, there is no hierarchical division of morals, propensities, and passions. Crane's slum characters engage in very little of the intellectual abstraction that makes possible such distinctions; the material world is always present, always making itself felt.

For example, Maggie's moral evaluation of her sweatshop boss is thoroughly grounded in physical impressions. The result is an undifferentiated appraisal:

> She felt she would love to see somebody entangle their fingers in the *oily beard* of the *fat foreigner* who owned the establishment. He was a detestable creature. *He wore white socks with low shoes.*
>
>   He sat all day delivering orations, in the depths of a cushioned chair. (25–26, my italics)

The enlightened middle-class reader might agree with Maggie that her slave-driving employer is "a detestable creature," but hardly because he wears white socks with low shoes. For Maggie, though, her boss's footwear, his girth, his foreignness, the oiliness of his beard, and his unsympathetic attitude are all equal manifestations of his hateful nature.

Crane's rejection of the supremacy of the intellect is consistently registered at the level of his style. The wanton mixing of moral and material terms, which conventionally have been kept separate, is a characteristic device that runs through all of his writing. For instance, in a letter about *Maggie*, Crane says that the bum "thinks himself superior to the rest of us because he has no job and no pride and no clean clothes":[22] "no pride" is sandwiched between "no job" and "no clean clothes." No logical progression orders the three terms; they do not move from most material to most spiritual, or vice versa. Rather, a leveling tendency is at work: the implication is that these terms have a psychological and ethical equivalence for the pauper. Like the bum, the men in the short story "The Open Boat" (1897) fail to distinguish between material and spiritual things. The very physical waves are attributed moral qualities usually reserved for human beings: they are "most wrongfully and barbarously abrupt and tall."[23]

Crane's style likewise eschews intellectual abstractions and, in doing so, sometimes arrives at bizarre metaphors. The characters in "The Open Boat," as they struggle against drowning, desire "to nibble the sacred cheese of life."[24] "Life" is not allowed to stand naked as an abstract notion; in order to ground it in intimate physical existence, Crane compares it to cheese; the adjective "sacred" then saves it from being mundane, which cheese normally is. And, again, "sacred cheese" is a concentrated mixture of spiritual and material terms. The collapse of typical categories is sometimes accompanied by a breakdown in Crane's syntax, as he strains always to tie his own intellectual terms to the ever-present material world. Thus, in the same letter about *Maggie*, he writes, "In a story of mine called 'An Experiment in Misery' I tried to make plain that the root of Bowery life is a sort of cowardice. Perhaps I mean a lack of ambition or to willingly be knocked flat and accept the licking."[25] After speaking abstractly of "a sort of cowardice" or "a lack of ambition," Crane strives for a gritty material metaphor and lets his syntax fall apart, adding, "or to willingly be knocked flat and accept the licking." It sometimes seems as if his grammatical mistakes are a kind of counterbalance for his high-sounding formulations, or at least a proof of the fact that his ideas are ultimately down-to-earth.

With Crane's characters, then, the moral sensibility has no privileged status, and no mental faculty stands above the emotions or the desires and scrutinizes them. Moral feelings certainly do not occupy the exalted position of a judicial authority; they are emotions like any others. For this reason, the characters in *Maggie* do not have a traditional relationship to their own ethical codes (whether Protestant or Bowery "beer-hall" codes): unequipped with a supreme faculty for moral scrutiny, they are not susceptible to the classic experiences of temptation (to break their moral code) and remorse (for having done so), the inner experiences that lay at the heart of moralistic slum literature. These characters violate their own apparent ethics, but they do so without remorse.

Maggie's mother's hypocrisy, for instance, is painfully evident to the reader, but it never bothers her in the least. She righteously blames her daughter for having "abused an' ill-treated her own mudder—her own mudder what loved her," without the tiniest qualms for the regular beatings she gave Maggie when she was young. Without the smallest degree of self-reflection or sense of responsibility, Mrs. Johnson loudly wonders how Maggie could have gone so wrong: "When a girl is bringed up deh way I bringed up Maggie, how kin she go teh deh devil?" (40).

Jimmie's hypocrisy is simply more subtle. Though Jimmie is supposed to be contemptuous of everything, he ultimately submits to public opinion against his sister. After Maggie has gone off with Pete, "Jimmie . . . began to wriggle about with a new and strange nervousness" (40). New indeed: Jimmie is not supposed to be nervous about anything; he is supposed to be "a young man of leather" (13). He finally says to his mother, "shamefacedly," "[D]is t'ing queers us! See?" His terror over the opinions of others is in direct contrast to the defiant way he has conducted himself in his truck driving. Suddenly, he is no longer able to be disdainful of "opprobrium" and feels "queered"; supposedly fearless, he is frantic about his reputation. He further sins against his prized defiance by "publicly damn[ing] his sister [so] that he might appear on a higher social plane" (40, 42) and later, when she appeals to him on her return, by drawing "hastily back from her" to avoid the "horror of contamination" (48).

Yet he never seems to be aware of his about-face. He experiences only a couple of brief and murky moments of self-consciousness about his own womanizing. First, "it occurred to him to wonder vaguely, for an instant, if some of the women of his acquaintance had brothers" (32), and later, "he was trying to formulate a theory that he had always unconsciously held, that all sisters excepting his own could, advisedly, be ruined" (33). These short and vague reflections are as close to conscience as anybody comes in the book. It never occurs to Jimmie to question his acquiescence to the judgment of the mob. Though his belligerent indifference to the world and its opinions is in the process of caving in completely, he seems to feel just as defiant as ever when he damns his sister in public; as usual, "his lips [were] curling in scorn" (48).

Pete undergoes a similarly seamless about-face. His general contempt first crumbles with the appearance of a successful prostitute named Nell. When she taunts him about Maggie, the previously fearless man "squirmed" (44). And when Maggie comes to the bar he tends, after her family has rejected her, he has not only Nell's opinion to fret about but also that of his boss. Pete "gave a great start, fearing for the . . . eminent respectability of the place" (50). Though he previously gave the impression of being indifferent to the very angel of death, Pete now claims to be worried that he will "lose me job" (50), and he fearfully turns Maggie away. Maggie is shocked by Pete's metamorphosis. When Pete first goes off with Nell, Maggie "could dimly perceive that something stupendous had happened. She wondered why Pete saw fit to remonstrate with the woman, pleading forgiveness with his eyes. She thought she noted an air of submission about her leonine Pete. She was astounded" (45). Maggie is "dazed" because Pete has completely failed to live up to the ideal that he claimed for himself and that Maggie perceived in him: he is not brave and defiant but pleading and submissive. Pete, meanwhile, remains oblivious to his betrayal of his convictions; like Jimmie, he lets his proud defiance melt away without a shudder of conscience.

The characters in *Maggie* do not struggle to uphold their ethics in the face of temptation, nor are they subject to shame when they violate them. Rather, they are regularly terrified by the prospect of a loss of esteem and are continually striving for respect from a variety of quarters, each of which has its own standards of conduct. Pete wants recognition not merely from the Jimmies and Maggies and Nells of the younger generation of the slums, who value defiance, prowess, and elegance, but also from his boss, who expects orderliness. Likewise, Jimmie wants to impress the traditional tenement community as well as other toughs. The driving force behind Bowery behavior—and behind Maggie's tragedy—is not a particular morality or ethics but a pursuit that transcends them: a constant pursuit of respectability, acceptance, or admiration. What looks like ethical assertion or behavior is really nothing but self-promotion, usually at another's expense.

While the characters around Maggie succeed to some degree in their quests for acceptance and a sense of superiority, often at her expense, the book chronicles Maggie's increasing feelings of inferiority and finally her social ostracism. Her initial admiration for Pete suggests the possibility of a new and elegant life for her, but it also throws her into doubt about her present life and herself. As she gazes "rather wistfully upon Pete's face," she becomes nervous about the "general disorder and dirt of her home." She begins "wondering if he was feeling contempt" (19). The more she raises Pete in her estimation, the more she feels inferior: "She vaguely tried to calculate the altitude of the pinnacle from which he must have looked upon her." She feels that her attempts to keep house, "to freshen the appearance of a dingy curtain," are "piteous" (20) and beneath Pete. When he promises to take her out, she imagines "the golden glitter of the place" and becomes "afraid she might appear small and mouse-colored" (21). In the "great green-hued hall" where he takes her and where he has obviously been "many times before," she feels "little and new" (21–22). Her consolation is what she considers Pete's "condescension" to her (23).

After her mother accuses her of having gone to the devil and tells her to get out, the girl's self-doubts become more severe. When we next see her, "Maggie was pale. From her eyes had been plucked all look of self-reliance. She leaned with a dependent air toward her companion. She was timid, as if fearing his anger or displeasure. She seemed to beseech tenderness of him" (38). His condescension to her is now not merely heart-warming; it is a "marvel" (38). Three weeks after having left home, Maggie's "air of spaniel-like dependence had been magnified" (43). When Nell appears at the hall and coaxes Pete away, when her mother and brother denounce her in front of the tenement neighbors, and when Pete tells her to leave his bar, Maggie never once puts up a fight. She is remarkably passive; she doesn't pursue Pete and Nell or even open her mouth; she says nothing more in the confrontation with her mother than her brother's name; at Pete's bar, she must "struggle with herself" just to "find speech" (50).

She clearly lacks the confidence to battle for her prospects, and this is not surprising in light of the psychological course of her relationship: from the very start of her involvement with Pete, from the very moment she begins to admire him, she begins to doubt herself severely. Her sense of inferiority is more important than the particular reasons for the feeling; her self-doubt can arise in relation to any number of standards: at one point she even fears that she will appear to have a poor coloring. Like Pete's drive for respectability, Maggie's doubts about herself are ethically indifferent. The relationship progressively diminishes her and leaves her vulnerable to complete misuse. That is why, when people throw her away, she seems passively to accept their valuation. She becomes suicidal not because of a traditional moral degradation but because of a lack of self-respect.[26]

What is unbearable for Crane's hero in *The Red Badge of Courage*, as for Maggie, is the thought that he is "one of the unfit."[27] Likewise, what brings on the emotional climax in "The Open Boat" is the disturbing recognition that nature does not share man's view of his self-importance: "When it occurs to a man that nature does not regard him as important . . . , he feels, perhaps, the desire to confront a personification and indulge in pleas, bowed to one knee, and with hands supplicant, saying, 'Yes, but I love myself.'"[28]

Maggie's last word in the novel is "Who?" (50): not "who is responsible?" but, more likely, "who can I now turn to for acceptance or affirmation?" After her spate of rejections, prostitution no doubt seems more promising than sweatshop labor: at least prostitution offers the allure of a community. But even as a member of "the painted cohorts of the city" (52), Maggie must still undergo regular, systematic rejection by the men she solicits. A suicide in one of Crane's poems, when asked by the people in the sky why he did it, explains, "Because no one admired me."[29]

What Crane has chronicled in Maggie is not (as in the case, say, of Cora in the conventional *The Evil That Men Do*) the deterioration of her morals and her fall into sin, but the demise of her confidence and her fall into abuse and finally suicidal behavior. Her "struggle with herself" throughout the novel is not a battle with temptation and sin (as is the case, for example, of the hero of the moralistic *Life in the Iron Mills*), but a battle with doubts and feelings of inferiority. Here, self-doubt replaces temptation; self-hatred replaces sin. A struggle to be virtuous has been replaced in *Maggie* with a battle for self-respect. Edgar Fawcett's Cora "tried very hard to be good" but gives in to "repulsive sin"; Rebecca Harding Davis's mill worker "grappled" with his "hellish temptation . . . face to face," but "his soul took in the mean temptation." Meanwhile, Maggie struggles to prove herself worthy of Pete and later simply to assert herself but falls into suicidal self-loathing. Maggie, as we saw earlier, lacks a traditional moral experience, but she does not lack an interiority. With Crane, inner conflict has not disappeared: it has become a psychological struggle for self-esteem.

Crane's Revision of Mental Philosophy

Crane, like Riis, was a pioneer of our principally psychological version of subjectivity. Riis drew on a notion of individuality, pride, or self-esteem to supplement character, the classic moral version of identity. For Crane, egotism or self-esteem or selfishness or conceit—all terms used in his oeuvre[30]—becomes the master principle of subjectivity. As he says bluntly and unapologetically in "The Blue Hotel" (1899), "[T]he conceit of man was . . . the very engine of life."[31] Though Crane did not invent the notion of self-esteem or even its more central place in the discourse on the mind, he goes further than other thinkers of his day— including Riis—in both the importance he places on it and the absolute challenge he sees it pose to the traditional Protestant concept of will or conscience. Riis, who was not a rigorous thinker, did not discuss the tension between "individuality" and "character," even though it is evident in his work. But others did, and they attempted to fit their discoveries about self-esteem into the traditional Protestant moral framework.

The trouble with self-esteem—or its equivalent—had some history. At one point in his *Elements of Mental Philosophy*, Thomas Upham noticed a small contradiction in the tradition of mental philosophy that threatened to upset the entire moral system. In the course of his argument, he had duly noted that the propensities are "all subordinate, in the determination of their respective claims, to the intimations and the decisions of that paramount faculty," conscience. Upham had gone about painstakingly showing that each of the propensities ("self-preservation," "curiosity," "imitativeness," "emulation," "desire of esteem," "possessory desire," "desire of power," "self-love," "selfishness," "pride, vanity, and arrogance," and "sociality") was "innocent and useful when restricted within the limits of its appropriate sphere of action" and evil when it passed those limits. But the propensity of emulation presented a peculiar problem. Along with the others, it too was generally considered an "implanted and original" propensity in the human mind, and this troubled Upham deeply:

> If Emulation be the desire of *superiority*, as it is generally understood to be, we do not readily perceive how it can by any possibility subject itself to that rule of subordination which is a first principle in the structure of the sensitive or active mind.— The desire of superiority, if it actually exists implanted in the human constitution, must, from its very nature, throw defiance at the doctrine of subordination. Whatever, in virtue of any rule of comparison that can possibly be applied, sustains a higher rank, at once brings this principle into conflict. . . . And as [man] is surrounded by beings that are in some respects superior, either physically or mentally . . . in some of the situations and circumstances of existence, he finds no rest to the sole of his foot; it is his misery that he cannot, even if he had a disposition to, close his eyes to his situation; the sight of every object above him . . . kindles a consuming fire in his bosom. . . . It is not easy to suppose that such a principle, leading to such fearful results, and placed so far beyond the regulation of any controlling influence, is implanted, as an original and essential element, in the mental constitution.[32]

Faced with a desire that would logically overturn the entire command structure of the human mind (with the conscience ruling), Upham simply denies "emulation" its usual status "as an original and essential element." He preserves the traditional Protestant version of subjectivity by ignoring a desire that does not fit.

William James's *Principles of Psychology* (1890), the work that supplanted Upham's as the classic text on the subject,[33] did away with his cumbersome subdivisions of the emotions of the self and took issue with such attempts to deny the elementary or instinctive nature of some or all of these emotions. Nonetheless, while James's radical psychological revisions of traditional mental philosophy move in the same direction as Crane's, they stop short of his.

James can stare the problem straight in the face: he can note that self-interest "may be a moral riddle" yet insist that "it is a fundamental psychological fact." He can recognize that "we have an innate propensity to get ourselves noticed, and noticed favorably, by our kind." He can identify "pride, conceit, vanity, self-esteem, arrogance, vainglory, on the one hand; and on the other modesty, humility, confusion, diffidence, shame, mortification, contrition, the sense of obloquy and personal despair" as "direct and elementary endowments of our nature" and assert that no emotions "are more worthy of being ranked primitive than the self-gratu-lation and humiliation attendant on our own successes and failures." He can over-turn philosophical "Associationists [who] would have it that they are . . . sec-ondary phenomena arising from a rapid computation of the sensible pleasures or pains to which our . . . personal predicament is likely to lead," and he can re-verse in particular the philosopher Alexander Bain, who "does scant justice to the primitive nature of a large part of our self-feeling, and seems to reduce it to reflec-tive self-estimation of [a] sober intellectual sort." James, like Crane, "knows how the barometer of our self-esteem and confidence rises and falls from one day to an-other through causes that seem to be visceral and organic rather than rational." And again like Crane, who creates some characters given to self-doubt (such as Maggie and Henry Fleming) and others absolutely incapable of contrition or shame (such as Maggie's mother), James recognizes that

> there is a certain average tone of self-feeling which each one of us carries about with
> him, and which is independent of the objective reasons we may have for satisfaction
> or discontent. That is, a very meanly-conditioned man may abound in unfaltering
> conceit, and one whose success in life is secure and who is esteemed by all may re-
> main diffident of his powers to the end.

But James, like Upham, is not ready to leave the scene of selfishness in a state of contentious chaos. He too insists on an orderly mental system. The famous psy-chologist finds that "a tolerably unanimous opinion ranges the different selves of which a man may be 'seized and possessed,' and the consequent different orders of his self-regard, in an *hierarchical scale, with the bodily Self at the bottom, the spiri-tual Self at top, and the extracorporeal material selves and the various social selves be-tween.*" He claims that through "ethical judgment," through "judgments originally called forth by the acts of others," and finally through the "tortuous" "moral edu-cation" of experience, which teaches us that we cannot aggrandize all of these selves, "we learn to subordinate our lower selves to our higher." James's language soon shifts from description to prescription: "We *must* care more for our honor, our friends, our human ties, than for a sound skin or wealth. And the spiritual self is so supremely precious that, rather than lose it, a man *ought* to be willing to give up friends and good fame, and property, and life itself."[34]

Though his commitment to empirical psychology is profound, James, like tra-ditional mental philosophers before him, colonizes his psychological insights with traditional moral judgments—judgments that he at least never claims are instinc-tive or elementary endowments of our nature.[35] Crane would call these judgments "social forms," which vary from social class to social class and from subculture to subculture. James's "we" refers, it appears on closer inspection, certainly to the middle and upper classes, but not to the entirety of the urban poor; he is consider-ing those into whom "the moral generalities . . . from childhood have been instilled."[36] In his slum writing, Crane excavates just those portions of society that James ignores, just those portions of society that prevent James's "tolerably unanimous opinion" about the hierarchy of selves from being simply unanimous. And in his other tales—of war, the West, and monstrous mutilation—Crane likewise examines social situations in which the niceties of Protestant moral education have little influence.

Crane does not, like Upham or James, subordinate his psychological impressions to the imperatives of the traditional moral system. He does not produce characters who distinguish between their material and spiritual selves and put higher value on the latter. He does not shy away from the contradiction, articulated by Upham, between the moral rule of subordination and the propensity for unending self-promotion; rather, he explodes it. The result, roughly speaking, is that Upham's hastily suppressed nightmare about the desire for superiority comes true half a century later in Crane's fiction.

A Typology of Crane's Events of Egotism

In Crane's fictional worlds, a contest of all against all basically replaces a stable moral order, as his fictional characters[37] compete for superiority. The struggle for self-esteem is, for Crane, generally a zero-sum game. Episodes of egotistical inflation are normally allied to those of deflation in Crane's writing: self-assertive action can usually take place only at the expense of other egotisms. This is, in general, Crane's brutal physics of self-esteem. Crane's fiction does include important exceptions to the competition for superiority, but these are rare.[38]

The primacy of self-esteem for Crane not only recasts ethical behavior and judgment;[39] it often reinterprets the other social bonds that are supposed to hold a community together. Friendship, in most cases in Crane's oeuvre, is not a fundamental of human existence; it can be further broken down into the dynamics of mutual admiration or alliance in battle against a threatening third party. For the most part, love seems to be a euphemism for fantasies of prowess and self-promotion, dreams of distinguishing oneself and rejecting those things that have put one down.

The primacy of self-esteem for Crane also makes the development of individualized fictional characters a secondary concern: fictional characters are reconceived, to a large extent, as sets of typical experiences of egotism. As many of his critics have noticed, Crane was not interested in character in the traditional literary sense. Michael Warner, for instance, has observed that "characters in Crane almost never function as realistic representations of people; they are abstractions and surfaces";[40] R. W. Stallman has said of the characters in *Maggie* that they are "less individuals than types."[41] Indeed, characters in his writing are often referred to by abstract epithets: Henry Fleming is "the youth"; *The Red Badge* also features the "loud soldier," the "tall soldier," and the "tattered soldier." Likewise, *Maggie*'s name drops out by the end of that slum novel; she becomes simply "a girl of the

painted cohorts," while Nell is the "woman of brilliance and audacity." The characters in "The Open Boat" are "the correspondent," "the oiler," "the cook," "the
captain," and so on. In fact, in an initial, unpublished manuscript of *Maggie*, Crane
had no proper names at all. He grudgingly acceded to the advice of one of his
brothers to include them.[42] Crane's fictional characters are flat; they lack particularities of taste and biography that make characters rounded. But this does not
simply indicate, as Stallman has suggested of *Maggie*, that Crane was interested in
"aesthetic anonymity rather than sociological immediacy," that "if Crane had but
one intention, it was the display of his effects."[43] The flatness of Crane's characters
also occurs because his stories are largely thought experiments in the physics of
self-esteem. Crane is not writing about particular individuals so much as about
egotism and its variations and permutations, and he is doing so in a manner that is
certainly artistic but nonetheless nearly mathematical.[44]

Crane is as fanatical about his psychological model of behavior as the traditional slum novelist was about his or her Protestant mental philosophy. Crane's
tales imagine a few recognizable sources of self-esteem, and as a result, certain
types of scenes repeat themselves again and again in his slum oeuvre. Just as one
can reduce a moralistic tale to a few structural components (scenes of temptation,
virtuous resistance, sin, remorse, and so on), one can begin to break Crane's slum
fictions down according to several events of egotism.[45]

1. Sequences of Boasting or Showing Off

Such scenes are legions in Crane's tales because they are the most effective means
of self-aggrandizement. For example, Pete brags about his prowess to Maggie and
Jimmie near the beginning of *Maggie*. Bleeker tells "three tales of the grand past,"
and Jones gives "speeches on various subjects" under the influence of alcohol in
George's Mother; George recites his own tale to the street-corner gang (about a
fight in which he appears "prominent and redoubtable"); George's mother talks up
her son to her neighbors.[46]

2. Sequences of Mockery or Scorn and Their Apotheosis, Ostracism

Boasts and bravado generally bring an opposite and then perhaps an equal reaction. The witnesses to self-promotion feel small in comparison, and if they need to
and can protect themselves, they rebel against the show-off or the powerful and
bring him down with mockery. Putting down others —especially those who assert
themselves—is a way of protecting oneself against personal diminishment and
generally a way of elevating oneself.

Thus, the Bowery works up contempt for its well-dressed "betters," and members of the street gang in *George's Mother* scorn those who work. Maggie's mother
and brother can feel better about themselves and gain the respect of the community in denouncing Maggie. As Jimmie pushes his sister away, "radiant virtue sat
on his brow," and Mrs. Johnson wears "a terrible look of indignation" (48). However passively or meekly, Maggie has asserted herself by going off with Pete; she is

scorned and ostracized.[47] In Crane's worlds, even seemingly modest instances of self-assertion often involve bravado and are usually attacked.[48]

Scorn is a simple and direct way of deflating an ascendent egotism (or at least inflating one's own to the same size) and restoring the equal distribution of self-esteem; it is an extremely frequent emotion among Crane's characters, a kind of egotistical reflex.

3. Episodes of Mutual Admiration

Crane carries this sort of episode furthest with the drinking gang in *George's Mother*:

> They exchanged compliments. Once old Bleeker stared at Jones for a few moments. Suddenly he broke out: "Jones, you're one of the finest fellows I ever knew!" A flush of pleasure went over the other's face, and then he made a modest gesture, the protest of a humble man. "Don't flimflam me, ol' boy," he said, with earnestness. But Bleeker roared that he was serious about it. The two men arose and shook hands emotionally. Jones bunted against the table and knocked off a glass.
>
> Afterward a general hand-shaking was inaugurated. Brotherly sentiments flew about the room. There was an uproar of fraternal feeling.

In the case of mutual admiration, the game of self-promotion does not stop; rather, it is no longer zero-sum. All parties win. Self-assertion takes the form of complimenting the listener, so scorn on the latter's part is not necessary to maintain self-esteem, even though he must temporarily submit. Thus, the drinking gang in *George's Mother* "had no bickerings during the evening. If one chose to momentarily assert himself, the others instantly submitted."[49]

4. Fight Sequences

A fight becomes a definite possibility when two inflated egotisms confront one another and scorn has failed to deflate one of them. "The critical battle" in *George's Mother* occurs when, one morning, George's mother's "valorous" scolding of her son's swearing fails to cow him.[50] Conversely, when a fight is desired, it is prepared for by almost ritual exchanges of insult and boasting. In *Maggie*, Jimmie decides to fight Pete because Pete has ruined his sister. He takes a friend with him to Pete's bar, and they go about instigating a confrontation.

> "Say, Jimmie," demanded [the friend], "what's dat behind d' bar?"
> "Looks like some chump," replied Jimmie. They laughed loudly. . . .
> Hot blood flushed into Pete's face, and he shot a lurid glance at Jimmie. "Well, den we'll see who's d' bes' man, you or me," he said. . . .
> Jimmie began to swell with valor.
> "Don't pick me up fer no tenderfoot.[51] When yeh tackles me yeh tackles one of d' bes' men in d' city." (35)

5. Sequences of Awe, Fear, and Panic

Upon perceiving a vastly superior and threatening force, Crane's characters are susceptible to unreasoning acts of self-protection. In *Maggie*, Jimmie "achieved a respect for a fire engine. As one charged his truck, he would drive fearfully upon a sidewalk, threatening untold people with annihilation" (15–16). George panics when his mother finally coaxes him into church:

> When Kelcey entered with his mother he felt a sudden quaking. His knees shook. It was an awesome place to him. There was a menace in the red padded carpet and the leather doors, studded with little brass tacks that penetrated his soul with their piti-less glances. . . . The multitudinous pairs of eyes that turned toward him were implacable in their cool valuations. . . . Kelcey was in agony. . . . He could have assassinated [his mother].[52]

6. Sequences of Admiration (of Others) and Corresponding Self-Doubt and Self-Accusation

Boasts and bravado can be impressive, and they can result in admiration as well as scorn. But in the zero-sum game of self-promotion, admiration means an unequal distribution of egotism, and if the imbalance is not redressed, if the admiration is not mutual, the admirer is in danger of self-devaluation. As we have seen, Maggie admiringly takes Pete at his brave word and immediately begins to feel small and worthless. Pete himself ends up in pathetic self-doubt at the end of the novel as a result of his intimidation by Nell; he drunkenly tries to convince Nell, her friends, and himself that he is a "goo' f'ler" (good fellow), and his voice betrays "deep anxiety" (55, 56).[53]

7. Sequences of Self-Pity or Commiseration

Since, as we have seen, true self-loathing is intolerable and thus leads to suicidal feelings, and since any sense of inferiority is at least painful, Crane's characters experience a strong compulsion to rationalize all errors, failings, inferiorities, or sins and to recoup them, however perversely, as marks of greatness.[54] Thus, in *Maggie*, Jimmie's lower-class clothes become signs of a hidden superiority: "To him fine raiment was allied to weakness, and all good coats covered faint hearts" (14). Jimmie's downtrodden position has "grandeur in its isolation" (15).[55]

8. Fantasies of Grandeur

Fantasies generally serve as consolations for miseries, defenses against self-deni-gration. George's mother's "dreams were her solace. . . . [T]hey shed a radi-ance of gold upon her long days, her sorry labor. Upon the dead altars of her life she had builded little fires of hope." Likewise, George's dream of "an indefinite woman" "saved discomfort for him and for several women who flitted by him."[56]

These dreams, whether they ostensibly concern love or honor, are actually fan-tasies of grandeur. George's romantic dreams, for example, are actually fantasies of personal prowess.

> An indefinite woman was in all of Kelcey's dreams. As a matter of fact it was not he whom he pictured as wedding her. It was a vision of himself greater, finer, more

terrible. It was himself as he expected to be. . . . [H]e was icy, self-possessed; but she, the dream-girl, was consumed by wild, torrential passion. He went to the length of having her display it before the people. He saw them wonder at his tranquillity. . . . In these long dreams there were accessories of castle-like houses, wide lands, servants, horses, clothes.

Likewise, George's mother's dreams are not simply visions of familial love. They are vicarious fantasies of superiority: she liked to believe that "she was the perfect mother, rearing a perfect son."

> She rejoiced at qualities in him that indicated that he was going to become a white and looming king among men. From these she made pictures in which he appeared as a benign personage, blessed by the filled hands of the poor, one whose brain could hold massive thoughts and awe certain men about whom she had read. She was feted as the mother of this enormous man.[57]

Maggie's romantic visions also have an element of social self-promotion, though they too are largely vicarious. When she lets herself dream about Pete, she focuses on the "wealth and prosperity . . . indicated by his clothes," his capacity to sweep her up into his aristocratic life and to remove her "from all that she previously had experienced" (39).[58]

9. Scenes of Assertion over Inanimate Objects

For the downtrodden, dominion over objects is a desperate resort of self-promotion. George's mother savagely cleans house, wielding a broom and a dustpan "like weapons."[59] And Maggie's mother "broke furniture as if she were at last getting her rights" (26).

10. Scenes of Abusive Self-Assertion

When power over another is consolidated in Crane's worlds, the possibility of abuse is strong. A stable position of superiority means that the threat of mockery or challenge that others usually present has been removed: there are no longer any checks on the workings of egotism, and without checks it can expand fantastically. The result might be not only arrogance but also abuse; great superiority implies that others are greatly inferior and thus worthy of less consideration and, in the extreme, contempt and mistreatment. In turn, the ability to act tyrannically toward another confirms and feeds the feeling of superiority.

As Maggie becomes dependent on Pete, his reaction goes through a couple of stages. First, "Pete's air of distinguished valor had grown upon him until it threatened to reach stupendous dimensions. He was infinitely gracious to the girl" (38). But soon his noblesse oblige turns to abuse. The "direct effect" of Maggie's "spaniel-like dependence" on her lover is, finally, "the peculiar off-handedness and ease of Pete's way towards her" (43). When Nell, the woman of "brilliance and audacity" (43), shows up, he simply abandons Maggie. And when she goes back to him out of desperation, he tells her to "go teh hell" (50).[60]

Similarly, as soon as George is "the acknowledged victor" in "the critical battle" against his mother, his egotism runs wild, and his cruelty is loosed: "He
brooded upon his mother's agony and felt a singular joy in it. As opportunity offered, he did little despicable things. He was going to make her abject. He was now
uncontrolled, ungoverned; he wished to be an emperor. Her suffering was all a sort
of compensation for his own dire pains."[61]

11. Episodes of Self-Forgetfulness

In certain situations, the usual struggle for self-esteem is superseded by curiosity
or viewing pleasure.[62] Characters can find temporary relief from the ongoing
struggle for self-esteem through casual observation. We have already seen how, in
Crane's slum writing, curiosity and spectatorship are often occasions of forgetfulness. The importance of spectatorship inheres partly in the fact that it offers the
single easy alternative to the world of egotistical positioning. While watching
something compelling, people can forget about themselves and their need for self-
assertion.[63] Here, if the game of self-esteem is not altogether canceled, then it is no
longer zero-sum. In the case of the theater, where the actors may be swelling to the
attention and applause, the audience does not deflate. Because the actors' performance is impersonal, ritual, and accepted, it is not perceived as a challenge by the
audience.

Though the desire for spectacle may be great, the tendency toward self-promotion is ultimately greater, so moments of forgetfulness do not last long. After a certain amount of time in the relatively passive position of a spectator, one experiences a renewed need for self-assertion. Thus, in *Maggie*, the people emerging
from the theater "who had been constrained to comparative silence for two hours
burst into a roar of conversation" (51). Or one begins, in the middle of the spectacle, to identify with the situation being dramatized and to fantasize. Maggie and the
rest of the audience of a sentimental melodrama begin to draw parallels between
their own lives and that of the hero. "Joy always within, and they, like the actor, in-
evitably without. Viewing it, they hugged themselves in ecstatic pity of their imagined or real condition" (27). At another point, the theater leads Maggie to fantasize
about her own situation: "She wondered if the culture and refinement she had seen
imitated, perhaps grotesquely, by the heroine on stage, could be acquired by a girl
who lived in a tenement house and worked in a shirt factory" (28).[64]

Self-Esteem and the Spectacle of the Self

The metaphor of universal competition—a battle of all against all in the zero-sum
game of superiority—roughly describes the logic of Crane's episodes, but only
roughly. This metaphor needs to be further honed, precisely because actual fighting, though common enough in Crane's slum novels, is only one strategy of self-
promotion. The image of universal war might be supplemented by that of general-

ized theater: Crane's characters are usually either performers (who swell as they boast and show off) or spectators (who deflate or forget themselves as they passively admire or watch or, alternatively, aggressively defend themselves as they mock). His slum figures often adopt conspicuously theatrical measures in their egotistical pursuits. In her final confrontation with her daughter, Maggie's "mother paced to and fro, addressing the doorful of eyes, expounding like a glib showman" (48). Likewise, Maggie acts the part of a set designer as she decorates her home in order to impress Pete. The fantasies of Crane's characters are regularly dreams of ideal audiences; George, for instance, imagines himself the king of a "people" who can "wonder" at him.[65] Similarly, Crane's downtrodden characters consistently imagine a sympathetic audience for their exquisite suffering.

It is no coincidence that the theater is at the center of the slum world of *Maggie* and that Crane devotes significant space to detailing the stage acts that are performed there. In *Maggie*, the theater has replaced the church as the popular source of community, the house of worship, and the special domain of the soul. Meanwhile, in Crane's other slum novel, the church becomes just another sort of theater. George feels on display as he enters; all he senses are "the multitudinous pairs of eyes" upon him; he even imagines that "little brass tacks . . . penetrated his soul with . . . pitiless glances."[66]

It is telling that Crane should bring up the stage performer Lillian Russell in discussing the issue of conceit. In a letter about *Maggie* and the slums, he writes, "I do not think that much can be done with the Bowery as long as the [blurred word] are in their present state of conceit. A person who thinks himself superior to the rest of us because he has no job and no pride and no clean clothes is as badly conceited as Lillian Russell."[67] Conceit and spectacle are, for Crane, usually related: conceit generally involves an audience, at least a fantastical one. Self-esteem normally depends on others' recognition or at least the fantasy of such recognition.

As we have seen, Crane's style mixes physical impressions and moral judgments, and this mixture too might be further characterized: often, his style deliberately juxtaposes the language of appearance with that of esteem, the language of theater with that of personal prowess. Nowhere is that coupling more concise than in the epithet that Crane applies to Nell, the successful prostitute in *Maggie*. She is repeatedly described as "a woman of brilliance [appearance] and audacity [self-esteem]"; her carefully crafted looks (she dresses in the "prevailing fashion" [43]) win her recognition and enable her confidence, which in turn makes her even more intimidating (both Maggie and Pete are thoroughly cowed by her).

Nell's epithet, while especially economical, is hardly a stylistic aberration. In a very curious metaphor, Pete's "patent-leather shoes" are said to look "like murder-fitted weapons." But in fact, Maggie's initial attraction to Pete is an irreducible alloy of awe for his personal power (and powerful defiance) and of admiration for his cultivated appearance. Just before Maggie recognizes Pete's superiority and bravery, she notices "his oiled bang," his "bristling mustache," "his blue double-

breasted coat," his "red puff tie, and his patent-leather shoes." Her very first impression of Pete is the way "he sat on a table in the Johnson home and dangled his
checked legs with an enticing nonchalance." Again and again, Maggie is enthralled
by Pete's "mannerisms":

> His *mannerisms* stamped him as a man who had a correct sense of his personal supe-
> riority. There was valor and contempt for circumstances in *the glance of his eye. He
> waved his hands* like a man of the world, who dismisses religion and philosophy, and
> says "Fudge." He had certainly seen everything and with each *curl of his lip*, he de-
> clared that it amounted to nothing. Maggie thought he must be a very elegant and
> graceful bartender. (17–18, my italics)

And later "Maggie was anxious for a friend to whom she could talk about Pete. She
would have liked to discuss his *admirable mannerisms* with a reliable mutual friend"
(26, my italics). This is an interesting assertion: the heroine of a moralistic tale
would want to discuss her beau's admirable character or achievements, not his admirable mannerisms.

Mannerisms have an interesting ontological status in Crane's novel. While obviously physical, they also convey a moral attitude. They could be said to be the
material representation of a philosophical perspective. In the world of Crane's fiction, as we have seen, philosophical perspectives do not come unattached to physical facts; the dance is never separate from the dancer. It is significant that what
Maggie falls for in Pete are his mannerisms and that she makes no attempt to separate his beliefs from his gestures, his facial expressions, and his clothes. For her,
they are of a piece.

But more than this, Maggie takes Pete's confident mannerisms, along with
his clothes, as signs or expressions of his personal superiority. Conversely,
the wealthy client rejects Maggie the prostitute because she is "neither . . .
Parisian, nor theatrical" (52). Dress and performance (gestures, poses, mannerisms) are the source of others' admiration and so usually of one's own self-esteem:
hence Crane's stylistic mixture of theatrical and psychological registers.

The issue of conceit, for Crane, immediately suggests Lillian Russell the actress
because the business of the self is often performance. And in the emerging culture
of mass entertainment, meanwhile, the star is an apotheosis, or an ultimate fantasy
of the self that strives for esteem. Spectacle is so important in Crane's work not
only because most of his characters are "anxious to see" but also because they are
desperate to show themselves off. Crane's ethnography of spectacle is continuous
with his psychology of self-respect.

In his *Principles of Psychology*, William James proposes that "Self-esteem =
Success/Pretensions."[68] According to this formula, since self-esteem depends on
success, and success in turn is a measure of social estimation, and social estimation,
finally, can only come out of social observation, self-esteem is based on a spectacle
of the self. This is the way things usually work in Crane's fiction. In his view, the
essence of the self is self-esteem, so most selves are essentially actors, performers.

But some selves are not. Though performance is generally the source of self-esteem in Crane's fiction, it is not the only source, and a competition for self-esteem is not an absolute rule (even outside the case of a ritual spectacle). There is an exceptional sort of episode of self-esteem in Crane's fiction (absent from *Maggie*) in which the struggle for self-promotion is put aside and acts of care and friendship—ethical actions, for Crane—become possibilities. Following up on the typology of eleven events of egotism from the previous section, we might add:

12. Episodes of Quiet Confidence

"The Open Boat" depicts comradeship of a sublime quality:

> It would be difficult to describe the subtle brotherhood of men that was established on the seas. No one said that it was so. No one mentioned it. But it dwelt in the boat, and each man felt it warm him. They were a captain, an oiler, a cook, and a correspondent, and they were friends—friends in a more curiously iron-bound degree than may be common. The hurt captain, lying against the water jar in the bow, spoke always in a low voice and calmly; but he could never command a more ready and swiftly obedient crew than the motley three of the dinghy. It was more than a mere recognition of what was best for the common safety. There was surely in it a quality that was personal and heartfelt. And after this devotion to the commander of the boat, there was this comradeship, that the correspondent, for instance, who been taught to be cynical of men, knew even at the time was the best experience of his life. But no one said that it was so. No one mentioned it.[69]

It is not that the men forget about their own safety, but they are able to feel something beyond their own self-concern. The obedience and also the reticence of the men attest to the lack of self-assertion. As we have seen, Crane describes plenty of noisy, self-congratulatory scenes of fraternity, but this case is not one of competitive or collective boasting. That this was "the best experience" of the correspondent's life clearly indicates an ethical judgment.

Similarly, in the *Red Badge of Courage*, the "loud soldier" who takes cares of Henry Fleming when he returns to the regiment with a wounded head is not without pride, but his egotism is contained. After the first day of fighting, when, as the once loud soldier puts it, "th' reg'ment lost over half th' men," this soldier has quieted down, shedding his boastfulness of the day before.

> He seemed no more to be continually regarding the proportions of his personal prowess. He was not furious at small words that pricked his conceits. He was no more a loud young soldier. There was about him now a fine reliance. He showed a quiet belief in his purposes and his abilities. And this inward confidence evidently enabled him to be indifferent to little words of other men aimed at him.[70]

Again, Crane's moral judgment is clear: this soldier has a self-reliance that is "fine."

In each of these cases, Crane sets up a contrast between a "loud" or boastful conceit and a "quiet" or "inward confidence"—and indicates his preference for the latter. For Crane, then, there are at least two different kinds of self-esteem, thus two different types of relationship to oneself and others, and one is better than the other: Crane imagines the possibility of a relation to others that is not based on performance or submission and a relation to oneself that is not predicated on social esteem. It is this exceptional episode of self-esteem which makes clear that Crane's radical psychological view of human experience is not, for him, amoral.

6 ⬱ Psychological Moralities of the Slum

At this point one is perhaps tempted to conclude that Riis and Crane reject harsh moralism and bring moral conceptions about the poor in line with psychological facts. This is how we often view these writers, and this is how we normally imagine psychology: as an amoral knowledge that allows us to lower our ethical demands to a realistic level. But in fact, psychology ceases to be amoral the moment it becomes either normative or prescriptive, and Riis and Crane do not simply lower or discard traditional moral expectations in light of psychology. Crane's psychology is normative, and Riis's is both normative and prescriptive: they both assert new ethical objectives. Riis finds in the tough the "hopeful symptom" of pride and imagines social programs built around its cultivation. Crane faults the Bowery for its "cowardice" and praises "inward confidence." And one does not have to have read Crane's letters to conclude that the characters in *Maggie* are too willing to "be knocked flat and accept the licking": the novel strongly implies that something is wrong with Maggie's extreme self-doubt, just as it indicates that Jimmie's and Pete's relentless self-promotion has something unseemly about it.

To be sure, self-esteem (or its equivalent) was a significant ethical substance for the prevailing Protestant morality: it was one of the passions or "propensities" that needed to be kept in check by conscience. In his standard *Elements of Mental Philosophy*, Upham concludes of each such propensity that it was "innocent and useful when restricted within . . . limits," and evil when it passed those limits.[1] In other words, the traditional moral problem in regard to self-esteem was one of restricting it; moreover, it was only one of many passions that needed controlling.

With Riis and Crane, self-esteem takes on a new centrality—it is so central that it begins to be talked about as "individuality" or the "engine of life"—and its new status involves a new ethical problem, which perhaps applies especially to the poor: nurturing it. For Riis, this new ethical aim must be balanced with the traditional objective of promoting good character, which it always threatens to controvert. For Crane, too, the issue is loosely the amount of self-esteem but, more precisely, the source: the problem is to insulate one's sense of self from outside influences.

Riis's Politics of Self-Esteem

Riis helps pioneer social programs within a new morality. And this new politics of self-esteem in which he participates, brings along with it an innovation in social technology or practices of power. Certainly, Riis's social prescription for tenement reform is largely traditional in its moral aims and the "disciplinary"[2] techniques to achieve them. His architectural solution, in the form of separate family units—with its explicit moral aims of modesty and decency as well as its hygienic objectives—is reminiscent of the instrumental use of space that one finds in such traditional moral reformatories as the juvenile asylum and the penitentiary.

But Riis's social projects also depart from the usual moral aims as well as the familiar disciplinary strategy. Though his plan of model tenements is an architectural politics, like that of the asylum or the penitentiary, Riis is careful to distinguish his blueprint from theirs. He insists that his model tenements must not have "anything of the 'institution character' that occasionally attaches to ventures of this sort, to their damage."[3] What he means is that the buildings must not be too drab or monotonous; in effect, issues besides those of separateness, privacy, decency, and health must be taken into account. Riis puts it bluntly: tenement houses need "aesthetic resources" (122).

Of course, in model tenements "there is light and air in abundance, steam heat in winter in the latest ones, fire-proof stairs, and deadened partitions to help on the privacy that is at once the most needed and hardest to get in a tenement." But that is not all. In addition, the model "houses do not look like barracks. Any one who has ever seen a row of factory tenements . . . will understand how much that means. I can think of some such rows now, with their ugly brick fronts, straight up and down without a break and without a vine or a window box of greens and flowers, and the mere thought of them gives me the blues for the rest of the day."[4] Accordingly, in the model tenement "every room . . . looks out either upon the street or the yard, that is nothing less than a great park with a play-ground set apart for the children, where they may dig in the sand to their heart's content. Weekly concerts are given in the park by a brass band" (225). In a chapter in *The Children of the Poor*, Riis spells out in some detail the child's need for playgrounds and parks.[5] The tenement must be "bright and gay" (that is part of the appeal of the saloon, with which it must compete); it must take into account "the love of youth for beautiful things" (123). The individuals who populate the tenements need more than walls and light and air; they need entertainment and beauty and play.

In fact, Riis levels a critique at the exemplary disciplinary institutions. Children's asylums, he explains elsewhere, can "become public tenements, with most of the bad features of the tenement left out, but the worst retained: the smothering of the tenant's individuality. [The boy] is saved from becoming a tough to become an automaton." The industrial school is preferable to the juvenile asylum because at the school, "the child's individuality is preserved at any cost. Even the clothes that are given to the poorest in exchange for their rags are of different cut and color, made so with this one end in view. The distressing 'institution look' is wholly absent from these schools, and one of the great stumbling-blocks of charity administered at wholesale is thus avoided."[6]

It is Riis's new ethical aim based on his new conception of subjectivity—his notion of individuality, in addition to character—that leads him to this critique and to what might be called a different politics of the body. For along with a modern soul comes a modern body through which to get at it. When character was considered the single principle of interiority, a purely disciplinary treatment of the body made sense: through repetition and regularity, correct habits could be ingrained, inappropriate passions could be ground out, and character could thus be improved.[7] But the perceived failure of the great disciplinary experiments—the failure of the penitentiary and the juvenile asylum to reform many of their inmates and, even in the best cases, to do any more than create passive automatons—this was in fact one of the historical forces that helped produce a reformed conception of the individual. And it should be added that this perception was in part shaped by the same masculinist reaction against a sentimentalized Protestantism that would legitimate interest and faith in the tough.

The National Congress of Penitentiary and Reformatory Discipline had found, as early as 1870, that the fixed sentence, silence, solitary confinement, and lockstep of the penitentiary deprived the prisoner of pride and initiative.[8] A couple of years later, in *The Dangerous Classes of New York*, Charles Loring Brace had leveled a similar, if more clearly masculine, attack on the children's asylum and had suggested, instead, resettling wayward boys in western homes. "Asylums . . . breed a species of character which is monastic," he had written, "indolent, unused to struggle; subordinate indeed, but with little independence and manly vigor."[9] Riis's writing is itself part of the account of the failure of the purely disciplinary institution. In *The Children of the Poor*, he approvingly quotes the managers of the Union Temporary Home in Philadelphia, who have come to the same conclusions: boys in the asylum "have been dulled in faculty, by not having been daily exercised in the use of themselves in small ways; have marched in platoons; have done everything in squads; have had all the particulars of life arranged for them; and, as a consequence, they wait for someone else to arrange every piece of work, and are never ready for emergencies, nor able to 'take hold.'"[10]

The new individual that emerges out of this institutional failure, with a self-esteem as well as a character to be cultivated, requires a new corporal technology. The new body needs more than regimented movements, regular routines, and separate space; too much of these can even be detrimental to individuality. This body also needs attractive things to look at and hear, places to play, and individualized clothing. This body does not simply need to be correctly trained; it also needs to be pleasantly surrounded and adorned. It is a body that social work will recognize in its pursuit of parks, playgrounds, home decorating, and American clothing for immigrants.

Against my argument, it might be objected that Riis's distinction between his own tenement plan and that of the juvenile asylum is in fact rather flimsy, and that it is naive to take his assertions at face value; Riis's concern with the "look" of the institution, it might be argued, betrays the strictly superficial nature of the difference. It might more generally be objected that the critique of the asylum was nothing more than an alibi for its continued operation. The proclaimed failure of the disciplinary institution did not, after all, lead to its dismantling. It might be asserted that it simply led to its aesthetic disguise.

This structure of disguise or mask is one common way in which the relationship between aesthetics and power is imagined: art is regularly seen to justify or to make palatable a system of control.[11] The overt ideology of art—be it resistance, reform, exoticism, or delight—is seen to mask a covert exercise of power. Riis's embellishments of the tenement might be construed in this way, as a pleasing packaging of a disciplinary architecture. In fact, Riis's aestheticism in general might be conceived as a benign mask for power: one might conclude that Riis's picturesque style, his exotic photography, and his concern with looks give his social intervention into the lives of the urban poor an aesthetic and thus an enticing, even acceptable form.

But to construe aesthetic considerations as a superficial phenomenon, nothing but a distracting veil beneath which function the real workings of power, is to miss a new ethics and a corresponding politics of self-esteem—a politics, principally, of "looks"[12]—that become so important around the turn of the century in America. I am not arguing that disciplinary techniques give way to some other form of power; the mere presence of old prisons and school buildings, the continuing use of cell blocks and rows of desks, attests to the healthy survival of disciplinary technology. Discipline has not been abandoned, but neither has it simply been dressed up and made palatable; it has been supplemented. A politics is being developed that recognizes the power of surfaces.

The child tough cannot be reformed by a purely disciplinary treatment: that is, in effect, what the critics of the asylum, including Riis, assert in the last decades of the century. If the subject refuses to follow the regimen except mechanically, mocking authority at every unsupervised turn, it will fail; if it succeeds, he will be nothing more than an automaton, robbed of individuality, manly vigor, and ambition. Some other techniques of power are necessary. Riis suggests clothes of different cut and color and views of the yard or street. These may seem like very petty innovations, but they are nonetheless qualitative. The soul of the child will be won not simply through a regimentation of habits but also through a mobilization of looks.

For many in Riis's time, including, it seems, the federal commissioner of education, individuality and self-respect come from independent and virtuous achievement, from good works, from labor. That is why, for the commissioner, the criminal lacks self-respect (or is born out of such a lack). For the commissioner and others, there is no real difference between individuality and character.

But for Riis, there is. In acknowledging the self-respect of the tough, Riis implicitly recognizes what Crane explicitly develops: namely, that self-respect need not have a Protestant moral correlative. The source of self-respect can vary incredibly: it might be a traditional moral behavior, such as productive industry; it might also be a clever burglary, or simply an intimidating look. Riis's belief that there is hope for the tough, outside the asylum—that there is a "a possible handle by which to catch him" (186), but not the pauper—could be formalized in the manner of a law of thermodynamics: self-respect cannot be created, once lost; it may be destroyed, and it can be converted into any number of forms. Self-respect, that is, can be transferred from one source to another: from gang violence and uniforms, say, to nice clothes and an honest job. Any reform program must take care to preserve and cultivate self-esteem.

Riis knows that people want spectacle; he has seen poor people forgo comfort, even health and food, in order to get it, so he provides it in abundance to his middle-class readers. He also understands that people want to be seen and recognized; he has seen the eagerness of children, as well as toughs, to take risks in order to pose for the camera.[13] All this Riis considers human, not scandalous. Thus another reason for his particular interest and faith in the tough. If Riis is so invested in the tough, to the extent of being strangely willing to encourage him with his camera, it is partly because the body of spectacle and the body of individuality overlap in him: in the importance of appearances. The tough's distinctive "uniform" and his bravado make him photogenic for Riis's middle-class audience; at the same time, they are the corporal signs that the tough's individuality is intact, that there is a handle by which to catch him. The case of the tough demonstrates something that was implicit in Crane's notion of identity: that self-respect is generally based on an ethics of spectacle, a spectacular relation to others and even oneself. The tough, Riis realizes, is eager to be photographed because notoriety and, specifically, the "embellishments" of the newspapers "fall in exactly with his tastes":[14] his self-respect is partly based on being seen—by others and himself—in the streets and in the press.

Daniel Levine has indicated that Riis's aesthetic approach to poverty reform was superficial; as we saw, he patronizes the photographer-reformer, explaining that Riis "found his cure in the most visible aspects of slum life" and "seemed to think that justice could be a product of the architect's drawing board" because he was merely "a visitor to rather than a resident amidst poverty."[15] Levine's assessment is important,[16] but it should also be acknowledged that in those visits to the slums with his camera, Riis found out just how profound the power of appearances could be. Riis discovered that people want *to look*: to look at others and to present a look themselves. Riis is hopeful about the power of appearances. While Crane has a problem with an ethics based on style and performance, on personal spectacle, Riis sees an opportunity there.[17] What Riis has hit upon is a politics of individuality based not, as in the disciplinary politics of moral character, on the body's receptivity, through repetition, to habits, but on the body's receptivity, especially through variety, to looks. And in fact, this aesthetic body is more tractable than the body of habits. The disciplinary politics of character sets out expressly to suppress the passions. The visual politics of individuality effects a reversal of disciplinary procedures: it exploits desire—desire for esteem and for entertainment.

Riis's aesthetics did not merely dress up essentially disciplinary institutions or distract from his basically Protestant aims. They complemented and challenged this traditional morality and form of power with another, fundamentally different ethics and corresponding tactics. Riis contributed to the development of new spectacular relations of power between the middle class and the poor, relations that supplemented the paternal relations of sympathy and control; he also contributed to the creation of new aesthetic techniques for guiding and rehabilitating individuals, techniques that supplemented disciplinary technologies.

Let us be clear about the moral transformations represented in Riis's reform programs. It is not simply that mores about dress and architecture have changed as a result of the industrialization of the building and clothing industries. What has changed is not only mores, but also morals. What would previously have been considered immodest and immoral, such as giving individualized clothes to juvenile delinquents or trying to decorate tenements so they can compete aesthetically with saloons—these are now not simply tolerated but programmatic. These practices become new standards, and behind them stands new values or a new ethical objective. The growing acceptability of the human science of psychology is giving legitimacy to styles of dress, architecture, and entertainment (including photography and film) that are still suspicious if not downright evil to traditional moralists—and is giving legitimacy to their mobilization in social programs.

We are today so accustomed to the role of photography in consumer culture and the mobilization of aesthetics in social programs that these realities seem natural or inevitable. But there is nothing essentially aesthetic about photography that undermines its disciplinary potential. Mug shots are the obvious instance of photos in the service of policing, and one might cite other examples around the turn of the century: Frederick Taylor's disciple Frank Gilbreth used photographic studies of workers' movements to sharpen the discipline of the factory.[18] Likewise, there is nothing essentially aesthetic about the body; the penitentiary of the early nineteenth century stands as a monument to a purely mechanical incarnation. The political discovery of looks is not the historical moment when faith in the mind first gives way to a larger faith in the body. Indeed, the great disciplinary institutions were predicated on the notion that reason alone could not reform a person; the body too would have to be enlisted and trained in the battle against the passions.[19] This deployment of looks is rather the moment when a faith develops in surfaces, precisely because surfaces—like movements in the disciplinary model—are discovered to have their own direct line to the human interior: in this case, to a self that requires individuality and entertainment. The new discovery of the power of looks comes out of fortuitous technical innovations (including photography, clothes manufacturing, and moving pictures). But their deployment in architectural reforms and plans for individualized clothing, parks, and entertainment programs is not accidental, nor deceitful, nor cynical. The politics of self-esteem, with its mobilization of looks, marks the moment when a new ethics—new values or a new ethical aim—has implicitly become standard for a whole population of social reformers.

Crane's Rebel Morality

To say, as Crane does, that Jimmie "clad his soul in armor by means of happening hilariously in at a mission church where a man composed his sermon of 'yous'": this is to imagine a different kind of soul. It is impossible for soul here to mean "moral character" or "conscience." First of all, Jimmie has walked into a church, a place where character or conscience thrives and so would have no reason to protect itself; Crane makes it absolutely clear that this soul is not at home here. More fundamentally, it makes no sense to say that character was clad in armor, because character is itself armor—against temptation—that either holds or corrodes and gives. Character is imagined in relation to the environment and the passions as something that withstands them, fends them off, or, through weakness, gives in. As John Dewey puts it in his *Psychology* (1886), "[C]haracter . . . is will which . . . has turned its force in one direction. The man with character, whether good or bad, is not easily daunted. He does not recognize obstacles. . . . Weakness means instability, and instability is lack of character."[20] And as we saw with Fawcett's Cora, conscience is hardly in need of armor: it is pictured as an offensive weapon, against which one arms oneself to protect oneself from the pain of remorse in case of wrongdoing.

What needs to be clad in armor is something soft, and here something vulnerable to a "sermon of 'yous'": the preacher is calling Jimmie and the others "sinners" and telling them, "You are damned." Soul here refers to something like deep or intimate feelings about oneself. Self-esteem, or even spirit, to use Nell's Bowery terminology: this is the sort of ethical substance that needs armor against this preacher's sermon.

What we are seeing in this passage is an instance of Jimmie's moral growth: he is toughening up. It is not that Crane gives us no moral account of his characters; it is rather that the accounting comes within a different ethics. We get another ethical dynamic. It seems to me that the statements "he developed a strong character" and "he clad his soul in armor" are of the same type: the first is considered moralistic or preachy simply because it is readily recognizable as praise; a strong character is traditionally valued.

Crane's statement, on the other hand, might seem to be just a factual statement of ethical transformation, but that is only because its moral significance is not yet clear. Crane is not indifferent to this change, just as he is not indifferent to Jimmie's subsequent betrayal of his ethics and of Maggie. By the time one finishes reading the novel, one has good reason to believe that a soul clad in armor is a valuable thing.

The alternative is a soul vulnerable to the judgments of others—many of which, like the priest's here, are hostile and potentially destructive. Maggie has never developed any armor for her soul, and the judgments of others beat her down and eventually destroy her. Likewise, Jimmie's sudden "nervousness" and his fearful denunciation of Maggie come about precisely because his armor deserts him or is not strong enough. Jimmie finds himself vulnerable to the judgments of the tenement crowd. In the mission church, his armor allows him "all the freedom of English gentlemen" (13). This freedom is conspicuously absent in the case of the attack on Maggie and the family: because he feels "queered," he is compelled to serve the mob and dissociate himself from his sister.

Though Jimmie's freedom in the mission church is depicted in somewhat comic terms, it is not simply a joke. Freedom may be fantastical in a slum world where the constraints of the environment are so conspicuous, hence the humor of this assertion, but submission is absolutely real and unmistakably contemptible for Crane, and something like freedom is valued. Like his younger Bowery characters, Crane thinks in terms of submission and its opposite. Maggie is dismayed to sense an "air of *submission* about her leonine Pete"; meanwhile, in his initial description of the tenement, Crane assesses the slum dwellers in the same terms. His Bowery is populated with "formidable women" and "withered persons, in curious postures of *submission* to something" (45, 6, my italics). It is not that these "formidable women" represent ethical paragons. They are engaged in "frantic quarrels"; in fact, like Maggie's formidable mother, for Crane they are instances of another sort of moral monster. But if Crane is not impressed by bravado, as Maggie is, he no doubt shares her opinion of submission. To say that "the root of Bowery life is a sort of cowardice" is to imply that submission is not a morally neutral act and that something else is possible. And though we know from other personal letters that Crane believes in an "inherent indolence and cowardice which is the lot of all men," he also speaks there of the need to "battle" these "colossal impulses."[21] This is an ethical project; indeed, at first glance it seems identical to the Protestant project of self-restraint.

Although *Maggie* finally contains no ethical characters by Crane's standards, Crane elsewhere imagines the hero who could stand up to someone or something formidable and refuse to be knocked flat. Interestingly, Crane wrote a letter in which he pictured the Bowery tough as such a hero. The letter concerns a matronly woman who is reminiscent of Maggie's mother in her unimpeachable power to terrorize others with her moral judgment:

> She has no more brain than a pig and all she does is to sit in her kitchen and grunt. But every when she grunts something dies howling. It may be a girl's reputation or a political party or the Baptist Church but it stops in its tracks and dies. . . . No man is strong enough to attack this mummy because she is a nice woman. She looks like a dried bean and she has no sense, but she is a nice woman. . . . Right now she is aiming all her artillery at Cornelia's [Crane's brother William's wife] new hat. . . . We rustle in terror because this maggot goes to and fro grunting about it. If this woman lived in Hester Street [in the Bowery] some son or brother of a hat would go bulging up to her and say, "Ah, wot deh hell!" and she would have no teeth any more, right there. . . . No man has power to contradict her. We are all cowards anyhow.[22]

Crane, like Riis, is infatuated with the tough, but for different reasons. For Riis, the tough has self-esteem and thus the making of something else in him; for Crane, the tough (ideally) has a toughness that insulates his self-esteem. He has the proper relation to others: he is dedicated to defiance, immune to their opinions of him, and thus capable of resistance. The problem with Jimmie and Pete is not that they are toughs but that ultimately they are not. Their toughness turns out to be a pose. In Crane's ethical terms, their souls are not thoroughly clad in armor.

Crane represents acts of resistance in some of his later tales as well. For example, Dr. Trescott defies an entire town in *The Monster* (1898), in spite of the virtual ruin of his medical practice and the ostracism of his family. He stands by Henry Johnson after Johnson's mutilation in a fire from which he saves Trescott's boy; though the town wants to get rid of the monster, Trescott refuses to let him die, be expelled from the community, or be put in a public institution.[23]

Crane imagined his own participation in the trial of Dora Clark, a woman accused of prostitution, in much the same terms. He recounted being warned that if he testified on behalf of the woman he would "come out with mud all over" him. In effect, Crane depicted himself as being put to the same test that the characters of *Maggie* fail. He wrote before the trial: "[A]ll that I value may be chanced in this affair. Shall I take this risk for the benefit of a girl of the streets?"

And after his testimony on behalf of the woman, he told reporters:

> Although I had never seen her before until last night, I made up my mind to find out what she was arrested for, and to see her through. The Sergeant at the desk . . .

told me the woman was just an ordinary streetwalker, and that I had better not get mixed up in the case, adding that it might do a great deal of harm if I did. What did I care for such talk? I'd do the same thing again, if I thought it necessary. By heaven, I'd do it, even if I lost any little reputation I may have strived to get. It would be well if others would follow my example.[24]

Crane holds up the Bowery tough, Trescott, and himself as examples; he clearly imagines ethical actions. Generalizing from these cases, an ethical action for Crane is the refusal to submit to a threatening power—especially on behalf of someone else; it is the facing down of tyranny in the interest of a potential victim. The men in "The Open Boat" should also be included in this group of Crane heroes: in the interest of themselves and the others, they battle the powerful sea, which is importantly imagined in moral terms as tyrannical (its "waves were most wrongfully and barbarously abrupt and tall"). There is clearly a moral question at issue in this story; the narration speaks of "the ethics of their condition," which "was decidedly against any open suggestion of hopelessness." The reason why Crane's ethics forbids such a suggestion—even though "any particular optimism at this time they felt to be childish and stupid"[25]—is that it would inspire submission to the waves, and as we have seen, submission for Crane is a wrong, even if the situation is hopeless.

Ethical behavior, for Crane, clearly involves resistance: the rebel becomes the hero. What is less clear is how one is to effect this resistance, how one is to relate to oneself. With what is one to battle the impulse of cowardice, to resist, and to follow Crane's examples, or, to put it in Crane's new ethical terms, with what is one to clad the soul—what is this armor made of—if not moral will? Where could such courage and resistance come from, if not from a moral character, conscience, will, or transcendental soul?

Indeed, Crane's allusions to courage (and his reference to a "battle" against "impulses") sound a good deal like those of conventional moral philosophers of the nineteenth century. Thomas Upham, in his *Elements of Mental Philosophy*, remarks that "it often requires no small degree of moral courage to deviate from the line of precedents. Whether right or wrong, we feel a degree of safety so long as we tread in the path of others."[26] In this regard Crane sounds even more like Emerson in "Self-Reliance": "Society everywhere is in conspiracy against the manhood of every one of its members. . . . Whoso would be a man, must be a nonconformist."[27] Crane's biographers meaningfully note that a quotation from Emerson was chalked in the artists' studio where Crane lived part of the time he was writing *Maggie*.[28] The contradiction between Crane's psychology and his ethical language can thus be resolved, but only, it would appear, if one acknowledges that Crane is finally a sort of moral elitist, that in the end he allows for the existence of moral character in some individuals.

But he never does: what is true of Crane's slum fiction is also true of his later tales. Unlike Upham or Emerson, Crane never posits a higher mental or spiritual

faculty which subordinates the appetites and propensities. There is no transcendental moment in Crane's oeuvre when, as Upham puts it, "an Enlightened Conscience . . . infallibly prescribes the limits of their just exercise"[29] or when, as
Emerson describes it, "all mean egotism vanishes. I become a transparent eyeball;
. . . I am part and parcel of God."[30] The judge in *The Monster* does posit "conscience" and "virtue" in explaining Trescott's support of the mutilated man, but
these terms are not sustained by the tale. Trescott himself implicitly rejects them.
He does not claim to be certain about what he is doing; he is not even sure that
Henry—who is mindless as well as faceless—is not better off dead. "Who
knows?" he says. All Dr. Trescott can say—and repeat—is, "He saved my boy's
life. . . . What am I to do?"[31] Trescott's course of action is not the result of a
moral choice; rather, the moral question ("What am I to do?") comes after the explanation ("He saved my boy's life") and hangs there, unresolved. (And this chapter of *The Monster* ends with the judge echoing Trescott's moral confusion: "It is
hard for a man to know what to do.") The doctor is acting not from conscience or
virtue but from feelings of gratitude, from emotional compulsion.[32]

But Crane's consistent denial of the existence of a transcendental moral will or
conscience is only half the story; the other half remains unanswered: namely, what
is the internal stuff that allows Trescott to resist the condemnation and rejection of
the community? What ethical substance protects his feelings (for Henry and for
himself) against the external onslaught? The answer becomes clear when one
looks closely at those moments when Trescott is being attacked for his stance: in
each case one finds him reacting not with conscience but with *anger*. When the
judge chastises Trescott for having committed "one of the blunders of virtue" and
"making . . . a monster, and with no mind," the doctor responds first with "eyes
suddenly lighting like an outburst from smouldering peat" and then with "sudden
polite fury." Trescott brushes aside the judge's label of "monster" and defends his
feelings for Henry: "'He will be what you like, Judge,' cried Trescott. . . . 'He
will be anything, but, by God! he saved my boy.'" The doctor goes on the counterattack "acidly," making "a perfectly childish allusion to the judge's bachelorhood.
Trescott knew that the remark was infantile, but he seemed to take desperate delight in it." Likewise, when someone named Winter goes "clean crazy over this
business" and Trescott is informed by the chief of police that this man wants to
have him arrested, he reacts angrily and calls Winter an "idiot." Finally, when a
man with whom Trescott hopes to lodge Henry becomes hysterical upon seeing
him, the doctor speaks "in the manner of a commander of a battalion." He
"roared: 'You old black chump! You old black—Shut up! Shut up!'"[33]

When Crane's most famous "hero," Henry Fleming in *The Red Badge of
Courage*, stops fleeing from battle and begins to fight courageously, it is not because
of character or will but out of anger at perceived insults, first from the opposing
army, then from his lieutenant, and finally from a Union general. As for the Rebel
army, "He felt that he and his companions were being taunted and derided from

sincere convictions that they were poor and puny. . . . The tormentors were
flies sucking insolently at his blood, and he thought that he would have given his
life for a revenge of seeing their faces in pitiful plights." When the soldiers stop
their forward progress, and their lieutenant goads them on, Fleming

> felt a sudden unspeakable indignation against this officer. . . .
> "Come on yerself, then," he yelled. There was a bitter challenge in his voice.

Henry's wildest fighting is a result of his fury against his own general. He takes up
the flag and drives the regiment on himself, spurred on by the hatred of insult.

> He had thought of a fine revenge upon the officer who had referred to him and his
> fellows as mule drivers. . . .
> A dagger-pointed gaze from without his blackened face was held toward the
> enemy, but his greater hatred was riveted upon the man, who, not knowing him, had
> called him a mule driver. . . .
> [T]he youth allowed . . . rage . . . to possess him. . . .
> *He presently wrapped his heart in the cloak of his pride* and kept the flag erect. . . .
> Between him and the lieutenant, scolding and near to losing his mind with rage,
> there was felt a subtle fellowship and equality.[34]

In order to allow for resistance, one need not suppose that Crane subscribed, in
a backhanded way, to a typical nineteenth-century Protestant belief in the individual's moral autonomy from the environment in the form of will, character, or
conscience. Resistance is not a reasoned choice with Crane; it is an emotional response to a hostile environment. Courage, or an unwillingness to be knocked flat,
then, is lodged not in will but in hatred, in an angry compulsion to fight back. (For
Protestant morality, hatred and anger were passions that needed to be controlled
by will; for Crane they are the internal stuff that allow for resistance and insulate
feelings of self-worth and compassion. Hatred and anger are not to be restrained
but, rather, allowed free reign.) In Crane's movement from Protestant morality to
an ethical psychology, something like anger replaces will, and resistance replaces
autonomy.

Interestingly, in the description of Henry Fleming's internal state we see another version of a soul clad in armor: a heart wrapped in the cloak of pride. The
armor that clads the soul, the cloak of pride that wraps the heart, it now becomes
clear, is not will: it is anger, hostility, stubborn pride, or, as Crane says of Jimmie,
"a belligerent attitude" (14).

At first glance, there seems to be a problem in our account of Crane's ethical
substance: deep or intimate or true feelings, including a sense of self (soul or
heart), are protected by feelings of anger (armor or pride). It is not surprising that
both the soul and the armor, heart and pride, are feelings; Crane does not posit any
other material in the mental makeup. But because in general usage self-esteem and
pride are interchangeable terms, both elements in these pairs seem to be of the
same sort of feeling. On closer inspection, it becomes clear that they are distinct:
according to Crane's lexicon, one can have self-esteem without pride. Soul and

heart here involve private, inward sensations; armor and pride here are social, outward reactions. In fact, this distinction explains the apparently paradoxical comment that Crane makes about the Bowery bum who is "badly conceited" and "thinks himself superior to the rest of us" partly "because he has . . . no pride." The bum has plenty of good feelings about himself, but he lacks anger: he will always allow himself to be knocked flat and accept the licking (while perhaps congratulating himself on his peacefulness). Pride here is roughly equivalent to the stubbornness or "pig-headedness" the community leaders attribute to Dr. Trescott.[35] This pride implies a belligerence; "heart" is a warm feeling.

In *Maggie*, Jimmie clads his soul, his feelings about himself, in the armor of a belligerent attitude; in *The Monster*, Trescott protects his self-esteem and his feelings for Henry with anger; in "The Open Boat," the men's "love" for themselves is protected by a desire "to throw bricks" in the direction of an indifferent nature;[36] in *The Red Badge*, Henry Fleming wraps his heart, his deep feelings of self, in the cloak of his pride or anger: these are all ethical moments, in which the characters have the proper relation to themselves and thus the ability to act ethically, to resist tyrannical forces (a mission preacher, an entire community, the sea, an opposing army).

Meanwhile, Crane's fiction presents a few types of unethical postures. There is the bum who has "no pride" or anger and thus accepts humiliations while he continues to generate self-esteem out of fantasy. There is Maggie, who does not use anger to protect herself either: she not only accepts abuse; she comes to believe what others think of her. Then there is a third case, the case of Jimmie and Pete.

For Crane, the ethical individual has a sense of self that is armed against outside judgments and thus predicated on something other than social esteem. This necessarily implies a rebellion against others' values.[37] Crane's ethics, like the tough's, is dependent on an adversary; it is rebel morality. Opposition is a prerequisite for ethical behavior and an ethical relation to oneself. Without an opponent, there is no anger; without anger, there is no insulated sense of self; without an "inward confidence," there can be no care for others. (Maggie and the bum are unethical because they submit to their opponents.) The silent, "personal and heartfelt" obedience and "comradeship" in "The Open Boat"—which Crane valorizes— would be impossible without the common enemy of the sea, and the anger directed against it. Likewise, the once "loud soldier" who helps Henry is no longer "furious at small words that pricked his conceits," not because he is not angry but because he has a real adversary in the enemy army.

The biggest ethical problem, for Crane, in his personal letters, was how to deal with praise, which suddenly started flooding in after the publication of *The Red Badge of Courage*. He wrote to Howells in early 1896:

> I am . . . afraid. Afraid that some small degree of the talk will turn me ever so slightly from what I believe to be [my] pursuit . . . , and that my blockhead will lose something of the resolution that carried me very comfortably though the ridicule. If they would only continue the abuse, I feel able to cope with that, but beyond I am in great doubt.[38]

Crane is afraid because he is about to lose his opposition: the condition of his ethics. It now becomes clear that Crane's morality involves a further twist: one is in danger not only of being beaten down by hostile opinions but also of being seduced by friendly ones. One needs not only anger directed outward but also anger directed at one's own desires for praise. In Crane's ethics, success makes one weak because one starts to depend on the good opinions of others—and no longer on one's hostility, one's "blockhead"—to assure one's self-esteem.

This, to be sure, is Jimmie's and Pete's problem: they do not accept humiliation as Maggie does; rather, they sidestep abuse. They have good reputations in the Bowery that they want to preserve, so they are no longer toughs. Their feelings of self-worth are now tied to other's opinions, and they fear rejection. This is perhaps even more clear in the case of George in *George's Mother*. He would like to rescue Maggie from her hostile environment, but he is too cowardly to acquaint himself with her. Each time out, "his courage flew away at the supreme moment. Perhaps the whole affair was humorous to her. Perhaps she was watching his mental contortions. She might laugh. He felt that he would then die or kill her." George's self-esteem is so dependent on others' opinions that he dreads making himself the least bit vulnerable to another's estimation, even for a moment.[39] Crane wrote in a letter after his success with *The Red Badge*: "I perceived that the fight was not going to be with the world but with myself. I had fought the world and had not bended nor moved an inch but this other battle—it is to last on up through the years to my grave." "When I speak of a battle," he went on, "I mean myself and the inherent indolence and cowardice which is the lot of all men. I mean, also, *applause*." He wrote to Howells on the success of the novel: "I have not elected to shout any shouts."[40]

In Protestant ethics, moral character or conscience is supposed to rule harshly over the passions, including self-esteem. (The individual is aided in this project of self-restraint by obeying authorities—parents, husband, clergymen, friendly visitors—who remind one of one's moral duty.) This morality requires conformity to moral dictates and is predominantly ascetic.

In Crane's ethics—which he largely reproduces in his imagined Bowery—the ethical substances are differently arrayed; in fact, his morality effects a partial reversal of Protestant ethics. To begin with, his mental philosophy posits nothing but feelings. There is no higher mental element that rules over them; rather, there are deeper feelings that are more "personal and heartfelt." A mental hierarchy is replaced by depths of feeling. The "heart" or deep feeling (for others and oneself) is now promoted to the status of soul. This soul is supposed to be protected by hostile feelings that are turned outward (partly against traditional morality and its representatives, which denigrate the substance of the new soul),[41] but it is also insulated by hostile feelings that are turned inward (against one's cowardice and desires for social acceptance or applause, which are generally two sides of the same coin). Crane's ethics is thus at once rebellious and ascetic, though its asceticism differs from that of Protestant morality in two ways: First, the battle against internal impulses is carried on with anger, not will. Second, the targeted impulses are different—one is not to control anger, clearly, and Crane evinces little concern about restraining sexual passion; rather, one must battle egotistical desires for praise that threaten to make one conform. One must fend off condemnations with anger; one must also forgo the pleasure of acclaim. One must exert hostility against any external force that would assault one's personal or true feelings and against any internal impulse that would make one vulnerable to outside opinion. In response to a world in which a tyrannical environment is frequently imagined to shape lives regardless, this rebel morality is a new ethics of independence, individuality, and authenticity.

Afterword

We began the book with a *Time* magazine article that is one of the many mainstream successors to Riis's morally schizophrenic slum reporting. Crane has descendants as well, though they are (initially) culturally marginal: they are first of all bohemian, mostly male authors who articulate a rebel morality, champion the slum dweller as an ethical paragon, and celebrate the life of the slums as a vital and virile antidote to a middle-class materialism, security, and caution, experienced as deadening and depersonalizing[1]—and unlike Crane, they do so explicitly, often in philosophical exposition, in their literary works. Whereas Crane's faith in the moral potential of a bohemian existence in the slums must be gleaned from his life and letters in conjunction with his fiction, and in his writing he represents bohemians only rarely and then largely comically,[2] his literary successors earnestly depict bohemian moral heroes who are often their alter egos.

It might be said that these twentieth-century bohemian writers spin out and elaborate an ethics that is implicit in Crane's life and writing. For writers such as Henry Miller, Jack Kerouac, William Burroughs, Norman Mailer, and Kathy Acker, as for Crane, the moral aim is no longer (as it is in Protestant ethics) to preserve one's character by controlling the passions; the aim for these writers is rather to develop an individuality by resisting restraints. The soul or valuable part of oneself has been redefined as something like individuality, passion, life, or deep feelings, which need to be discovered and developed despite all inhibitions, repressions, and social constraints. In essence, the bohemian literature of these authors effects an inversion of traditional Protestant morality, similar to the one we saw with Crane: passions, once the enemy within, are reconstituted as the source of individuality; what was moral character is refigured as internalized social constraints to be overcome.

But this is often only half the story, as Crane also indicates, for a total liberation of the passions could easily devolve into a fresh seduction or intimidation by the very forces of middle-class social conformity against which one is attempting to rebel, so the bohemian or counterculture ethic of these writers also includes a less obvious ascetic element, an element of self-restraint. This ascetic element is also familiar to us, though; it often comes under the rubric of "cool." This bohemian or countercultural ethics thus involves two complementary aims: on the one hand, one is encouraged to throw off external and internal restraints, come *alive*, and let blossom an anarchic individuality; on the other hand, one must exert *cool*, toughness, or self-restraint in the interest of safeguarding one's new vitality against certain "regressive" emotions (such as hope for a transcendent meaning, fear of loneliness, desire for security or—in the case of Crane—the enjoyment of praise or need for acceptance) that would suffocate this vital individuality and eventually return one to the lockstep of middle-class conformity.

On one side of this bohemian ethics, then, the relation one is supposed to establish with oneself is no longer control but aliveness, honesty, authenticity, and a liberation that results in joy. Protestant emotional control must be overthrown. In *Tropic of Cancer* (1934), Henry Miller claims that he is treading the "meridian that separates the hemispheres of life and death" and attempting "a resurrection of the emotions." He asks one of his comrades, "[W]hat is it you'd *really* like to do?" and counsels, "Do anything, but let it yield ecstasy."[3] For Kerouac's Sal Paradise the key question is not "what one should do" but, likewise, "[W]hat are we all aching to do? What do we want?" Dean Moriarty of *On the Road* (1957) advises that "the thing is not to get hung up," and despite Dean's apparent selfishness, Sal argues that he is really a true friend because he has brought to others "sexuality and . . . life."[4] William Burroughs speaks in *Junky* (1953) of "the life force . . . that we all have to score for all the time."[5] And Mailer says in "The White Negro: Superficial Reflections on the Hipster" (1957) that the Hip "ethic reduces to Know Thyself and Be Thyself": "to do what one feels whenever and wherever possible."[6]

This bohemian literature redefines Protestant goodness and middle-class security as conformity, along with blandness, repression, and death. As in *Maggie*, in which members of the traditional morality and culture are put down as "ciphers," of "no spirit," and as smacking of "pumpkin pie and virtue," middle-class "conformists" are the "square," "the unaware," "the unattuned," the "straight souls" in Tom Wolfe's *Electric Kool-Aid Acid Test* (1968);[7] they are "those who are dead" in Miller's *Tropic of Cancer*,[8] and in *Junky* they suffer from "death and rot."[9] The moral opposition is no longer between good and evil but between life and death, individuality and conformity, freedom and constraint, truth and repression, hip and square, real and unreal. As Kathy Acker bluntly puts it, "Evil versus good has become unreal versus real."[10]

On the other side of this ethics, one must exert a self-control that is reminiscent of Protestant asceticism but is aimed in part at a different set of emotions. Here again there is a sort of reversal, especially of the sentimentalized Protestant ethics of the nineteenth century. While passions are now to be unleashed, Victorian sentiments—such as awe for chastity, respect for parents, and pity for the poor—are to be reigned in. Perhaps it is more accurate to say that this bohemian asceticism is at once a complete rejection of a Victorian ethics perceived as "feminized" and a partial return to the masculine stoicism of pioneer or frontier Protestantism (partial because while bohemian cool does indeed call for courage, or the control of fear, it certainly does not call for the restraint of sexual desire, but just the opposite).

Miller's expatriation from the "treadmill" of American culture and escape from his charismatic wife are not simply a plunge into a sordid and cruel freedom in the Paris slums, a liberation of the sexual passions, and a lawless outbreak of a pornographic prose. His writing and his sexuality both are part of a movement into a self-imposed "loneliness,"[11] a painful but creative solitude that involves an ascetic resistance to longings for love and transcendent meaning and also to "fear[s] of living separate"[12] and being rejected as a bum or a failure. For Miller, the trick is giving up hope (for love or salvation) without despairing or giving in to dread. Mailer's ideas are analogous, and his language of asceticism is closer to Crane's. "In a bad world there is no love nor mercy nor charity nor justice unless a man can keep his courage," Mailer writes, paraphrasing Hemingway but inadvertently calling up, as well, Crane and his many stories (including *Maggie*) that present tests of loyalty. To have courage, "to be cool" is, for Mailer, to allow "to come to consciousness a pain, a guilt, a shame or a desire which the [Square] has not had the courage to face." This is precisely what the false toughs in *Maggie* fail to do; as we have seen, Jimmie squelches his one moment of incipient self-consciousness that would have meant facing the fact that in his relations with his sexual partners he is as guilty as Pete—and Maggie. When Jimmie and Pete suddenly wriggle with nervousness and abandon their toughness, they do what Mailer's Hipsters cannot do too often without ceasing to be Hip: they "flip."[13]

In this bohemian literature, the slum is the key place to find life and freedom and also the place to "find [one's] courage at the moment of violence"[14] or police arrest—in bars, clubs, shooting galleries, whorehouses—as one leaves behind the safe, bland, and inhibited world of the middle class. The new ethical hero—with his (and in some cases her) infectious aliveness and his cool and, as a result of the latter, his ability to stand up for himself and his friends—is the indigenous slum dweller or the bohemian exile in the slums.

As Crane flirts with the tough, Miller, Burroughs, and Acker present themselves (or their alter egos), along with certain prostitutes, junkies, and gang members, as inspiring or courageous low-life heroes. Miller presents himself, in his wanderings of the Paris streets, as a saint and evangelist of a "new religion" whose task is to restore the "dead" to life.[15] And Burroughs suggests that one of the things he finds more attractive about the junk subculture is its more stringent ethics of friendship or self-sacrifice, which grows out of necessity: "right" people never turn their friends in to the police,[16] and this sort of courageous loyalty is something he finds much more often outside the middle class.

Kerouac's Sal explicitly emulates the "Negro" (and the poor Mexican and the "poor overworked Jap") for the emotional intensity of his existence: Sal wishes he "were a Negro, feeling that the best the white world had offered was not enough ecstasy for me, not enough life, joy, kicks, darkness, music, not enough night."[17] Mailer declares simply that "the source of Hip is the Negro." And he explains why: because poor blacks in America have "been living on the margin between totalitarianism and democracy for two centuries," they have developed "a morality of the bottom,"[18] a code of toughness and indulgence that the Hipster or "White Negro" needs for psychological survival in a socially marginal bohemian existence. Faced with the threat of psychic "death by conformity" to a "partially totalitarian" postwar middle-class culture, the Hipster rebels and looks to "the Negro" as a model of defiance. Mailer's Hipster looks to the poor black man because "knowing in the cells of his existence that life was war, nothing but war, the Negro (all exceptions admitted) could rarely afford the sophisticated inhibitions of civilization, and so he kept for his survival the art of the primitive, he lived in the enormous present, he subsisted for his Saturday night kicks."[19]

Crane was one of the first to begin to frame this new moral view of the poor, especially the urban poor: their oppression makes them holy because it makes them courageous and nonconformist, and it makes them attractive because it makes them uninhibited and pleasure-seeking. Looking to the black urban poor for moral inspiration, the Hipster sees himself, Mailer says, as a sort of "frontiersman in the Wild West of American night life."[20] Part of this frontier night life means freedom and rebellion, dangerous adventure and toughness, and self-discovery; another part means new forms of sexual, narcotic, musical, and sartorial pleasure. And just as Riis and Crane were absorbing a slum style into their own middle-class representations (and so it could be said that it was the lower class that was converting the middle class to its aesthetics), likewise "in this wedding of the white and the black" that for Mailer results in the Hipster, "it was the Negro who brought the cultural diary."[21] The most obvious part of the aesthetic dowry inherited by the middle class from the black poor is of course musical: jazz, blues, rock-and-roll and, most recently, rap.

Mailer estimated in 1957 that there were perhaps 100,000 self-described Hipsters in America,[22] but the social phenomenon he was describing would soon blossom into something much more widespread. By this I mean not only the short-lived Hippie movement, which of course popularized Hip, but also, on the one hand, the persistence of bohemian enclaves in and around the slums in major American cities and, on the other, the steady rise of a middle-class youth culture that still takes its aesthetic cues from the slums, most blatantly in rap (and gangsta rap), even if its rebellion is largely imaginary and its toughness largely ersatz. Though the styles and argot have changed more than several times,[23] and though Mailer concentrates on the male bohemian, his Hipster phenomenon is still with us among what the media refers to as "slackers" or "Generation X-ers." And for some middle-class boys and girls, this journey through the slums continues to serve as a liberating rite of passage from a childhood perceived of as sheltered or effeminate into a vital manhood or a rugged, unsentimental womanhood—much as it was for Crane, who must be considered one of the pioneers or at least early popularizers of this route (though in Crane's day it was almost exclusively for males). Meanwhile, the difference between Mailer's Hipsters or today's bohemians and the faux-rebellious middle-class teenagers of today is not only the greater numbers and lower age of the average participant in the latter group but also the facts that for these youths the move to the slums is made mostly imaginatively and their imaginative leap is made almost exclusively through consumption.[24]

It should be underlined that this flirtation with an imagined slum ethos, though more recently open to women as well, has remained, as it was in Crane's and Riis's day, an anti-Victorian movement infatuated with masculinity and given to misogyny. The toughness of the slums is contrasted to the weakness of a middle-class culture that is associated with the pampered and the feminine. Mailer, for instance, makes clear the masculine bias of his Hipster revolt: to "flip" is to "lose your control, reveal the buried weaker more feminine part of your nature."[25]

Moreover, the sexual revolt against middle-class inhibitions often takes the form of the rank objectification of women and even violence against them. Miller's notorious, sustained sexual romp in the brothels and parlors of Paris serves as a means of weaning himself from his longings for love. Women are routinely referred to as and reduced to "cunts," as part of a strategy of immunization against sentiment. *Tropic of Cancer* is a book of sexual predation, and the reader cannot but sense in it Miller's long-suppressed rage and the violent, if also gleeful and comic, revenge for his perceived suffering at the hands of women. Mailer's *An American Dream* (1964) takes this misogyny to its extreme conclusion, suggesting that "all women were killers," and "women must murder us [men] unless we possess them altogether."[26] The main character's act of liberation, self-empowerment, and spiritual rebirth is the murder of his domineering, castrating, upper-class wife—followed by celebratory, forcible, and ultimately anal sex with the maid and then an auto-da-fé in the underworld of the slums, where he finds a woman who is his equal in toughness and where sex is restored to an act of creation and "bliss."[27] Even Kathy Acker's *Blood and Guts in High School* (1978), which generally critiques American sexuality as sadistic toward women and specifically denounces the sexual revolution as "glorification of S&M and slavery,"[28] adopts the traditionally masculine profanity that has been used to objectify women. More striking is the tough female protagonist's unstinting, if tragic, complicity with bohemian male misogyny and sexual violence against women. The main character again and again allows herself to be sexually abused because she feels that S&M is preferable to middle-class life, "our nicey-nicey-clean-ice-cream-TV-society."[29] Perhaps the art of today that most unmistakably combines a romanticization of the slums with misogyny would be rap music.[30]

Crane's escape from the respectable confines of middle-class society also had a misogynistic edge. For him, the most intolerable representatives of middle-class respectability were matronly women. As we have seen, in 1894 he angrily derided such a woman, in a letter from Port Jervis, New Jersey, and she would reverberate in his fiction for the rest of his career. R. W. Stallman notices that this gossip reappears in *The Third Violet* (1897), in Martha Goodwin of *The Monster*, and in *The O'Ruddy* (1903);[31] Wilson Follet claims that "Crane pilloried her over and over again, where she fitted the story and where she did not."[32] Crane's list of hypocritical and destructively overbearing matrons also includes Maggie's mother, George's mother in the book by that name, and the lady of the house in "An Experiment in Luxury."

Crane's vituperative letter is worth returning to in full because it is a fantasy that could be said to encapsulate, with a fairy-tale-like compression common in Crane's oeuvre, the cultural meaning of the bohemian and youth-culture romance with the slums.

> If you hear that I have been hanged by the neck till dead on the highest hill of Orange County you may as well know that it was for killing a man who is really a pug—No, by the legs of Jehovah! I will not insult any dog by comparing this damned woman to it. There is a feminine mule up here who has roused all the bloodthirst in me and I don't know where it will end. She has no more brain than a pig and all she does is to sit in her kitchen and grunt. But every when she grunts something dies howling. It may be a girl's reputation or a political party or the Baptist Church but it stops in its tracks and dies. Sunday I took a 13 yr. old out driving in a buggy. Monday this mule addresses me in front of the barber's and says, "You was drivin' Frances out yesterday" and grunted. At once all present knew that Frances and I should be hanged on twin gallows for red sins. No man is strong enough to attack this mummy because she is a nice woman. She looks like a dried bean and she has no sense, but she is a nice woman. Right now she is aiming all her artillery at Cornelia's [Crane's brother William's wife] new hat. . . . We rustle in terror because this maggot goes to and fro grunting about it. If this woman lived in Hester Street [in the Bowery] some son or brother of a hat would go bulging up to her and say, "Ah, wot deh hell!" and she would have no teeth any more, right there. She is just like those hunks of women who squat on porches of hotels in the summer and wherever their eye lights their blood rises. Now, my friend, there is a big joke in all this. This lady in her righteousness is just the grave of a stale lust and every boy in town knows it. She accepted ruin at the hands of a farmer when we were all 10 or 11. But she is a nice woman and all her views of all things belong on the tables of Moses. No man has power to contradict her. We are all cowards anyhow.[33]

In Crane's thumbnail sketch of the middle-class moral regime, it is the matron who rules, and middle-class men lack the strength and courage to stand up to her.

Crane imagines, meanwhile, that a man of the slums would have the requisite toughness to confront her. This is on the literal level.

On a mythic level, Crane's fantasy could be read not only as a demonstration that the romanticization of slum morality served as a remedy for a middle-class culture perceived as constricting and feminized but also that this invigorating embrace of the slums involved a revenge on women—as the police of Victorian mores, whose moral energy is understood by knowing boys to derive from nothing more than repressed sexuality ("grave of a stale lust"). Finally, what the masculine ethos of the slums makes possible, in its violent silencing of the middle-class matron, is a loosening of the strictures governing male and female interaction and, likewise, a liberation of the emerging consumer culture from the Victorian constraints of good taste. What the Bowery tough's intervention legitimates, in the letter, is Crane's brother's wife's apparently racy hat and Crane's own unchaperoned buggy ride with a young girl: both perfectly acceptable in the culture of the slums. Despite the bohemians' ostensible hostility to middle-class materialism, it can be claimed—as Crane's imagined scenario implies—that counterculture rebellion, though indeed hostile to middle-class concerns for security and propriety, is hardly against consumerism per se but, rather, against its circumscription by moralism or caution. The slums, then, according to Crane's fantasy, will violently free middle-class girls (and boys like Crane) from the burdensome obsession with feminine purity and allow women to express themselves (and men to enjoy them) sensually or erotically—especially through buying. Read as a sort of intuitive or visionary allegory, Crane's letter tells us that the middle-class flirtation with the slums will play a role in the backlash against a sentimentalism perceived as hypocritical and in the masculine regeneration of the values of toughness and pleasure; it will hasten the relaxation of sexual mores and the development of an unbridled consumer culture in society at large.

In 1917 John Dewey redefined human experience: whereas orthodox philosophy had conceived of experience as "primarily a knowledge-affair," Dewey recast it as "an affair of the intercourse of a living being with its physical and social environment."[34] We consider Dewey's philosophy to be Progressive par excellence. We generally associate the Progressive Era with the innovation of social thinking and engineering; if the discovery of the importance of the social environment in individual behavior came earlier, it was not until the Progressive Era that such thinking came to fruition, both intellectually and practically. So Crane's comment that "environment frequently shapes lives regardless" is vintage Progressive thought. And Riis's slum clearance and model tenement projects are prime examples of Progressive reforms. But what this characterization of Progressivism leaves out is the *type* of intercourse that a human being has with its environment, the *way* environment can shape lives, and thus the *sort* of model tenement that will reform people.

Progressivism is generally imagined to combine hygienic and traditional moral aims, pursued in part through new techniques of environmental improvement. Christopher Lasch has made the important distinction between traditional moral Progressivism and New Radicalism, which developed during the same era but was interested in the reform of education, American culture, and sexual relations and included an affinity for the lower classes and a critique of middle-class morality and its programs of moral "uplift" for the poor.[35]

But the problem with these accounts of the Progressive Era is that they are still too neat: they do not see that some of the most important reforms of the era—including Riis's—had mixed ethical agendas. Social thought or the environmental approach does not in itself imply a commitment to any particular morality. Though the reformers were not always aware of it, they imagined that harmful intercourse between the individual and the environment took place in two very different ways: according to a traditional Protestant model of moral corruption or infection, but also according to a new ethical model of psychological self-defense. It is easy to class Crane as a moral radical of some sort, but Riis presents a problem. Riis's environmental reforms would have to be called Progressivist, but that is not all: they were aimed in part at traditional moral uplift, but they also had new and opposing ethical objectives, namely, the cultivation of pleasure and self-esteem. And Riis's ethical schizophrenia is by no means singular: it was shared by the reform of the juvenile asylum and the penitentiary, the campaign for parks and playgrounds, and the institution of social work, which incorporated a psychological approach.

The Progressive Era popularized the environmental approach to social problems, but it did something else as well. It contributed to the beginnings of the (still continuing) shift from a sentimentalized Protestant ethics to a modern psychological morality. Looking back from today's vantage point, we can identify at least three separate ethical strains in the Progressive Era approach to the slums. There are the harsh traditional moralists, for whom Riis, let alone Crane, is vulgar and dangerous. But they are not new. What is new is first of all the mixed ethics of Riis and others, which sees in the common street tough no longer simply viciousness but also the virtue of self-esteem. Traditional Protestant moral aims for the poor remain, but they are supplemented by and in tension with new ethical aims (though they are not articulated as such) as well as new social programs (both environmental and individualized) to effect these aims.[36] What is also new is a purely counterethical strain launched by Crane and others, a rebel or bohemian morality, that holds up the tough and streetwise slum dweller as an ethical paragon.

While Crane's bohemian literature explicitly rejects traditional middle-class morality in favor of an ethics that is associated with the slums, Riis's mainstream reporting on the poor is not nearly so clear-cut, coherent, or self-aware. Crane's attack on the hypocrisy and dullness of middle-class culture and his romanticization of the tough is explicit. Meanwhile, Riis's critique of the middle class and his emulation of the tough is never more than implicit, in his search for excitement and ethic of adventure. Much the same might be said about their different responses to slum entertainment: Riis decries the cheap aesthetic of the streets while at the same time employing it (and paying lip service to high art), while Crane is open about his fascination with slum dives and his disdain for sentimental art and melodrama.

This mainstream discourse not only mixes its opposing moral aims with the traditional ones; it also fails to recognize this ethical tension. One might reasonably say that this discourse holds onto traditional morality and legitimates itself through its modern, humanitarian, masculine, and aesthetic commitments to psychological health and audience pleasure. To be sure, it saves from extinction and renovates a worn-out moral and social discourse perceived as effeminate, priggish, and self-righteous (the charity writing that has already lost some status by the time Riis is writing). But it must be acknowledged that in the process, these traditional moral and social aims are also substantially diluted by the new commitments.

The turn-of-the-century, middle-class stirrings of a therapeutic and entertainment morality is partly shaped in the examination of the slums, which itself takes two very different directions: a counterethical bohemian literature and a schizophrenic mainstream discourse. And today the middle-class imagination of the slums continues to exert an influence on middle-class moral conflict and transformation. If Riis's brand of Progressivism now finds its incarnation in a middle class that wants to reform the slums even as it enjoys their spectacle, Crane's furthest descendants are members of a youth culture that imagine they are rejecting the middle-class culture of their parents and partaking of the slum culture of the streets largely by buying an aesthetic that has originated there and whose cachet is precisely its slum pedigree.[37] It might even be said that today the moral confrontation between middle-class adults and children, or the generation gap, is shaped and mediated by our modern myths of the slums. In this confrontation, the slums function as a refracted mirror for both middle-class adults and children: adults see a dangerous and disordered wasteland that is the antithesis of their middle-class neighborhoods, and their children imagine a zone of freedom from parental control, an endless playground where tough kids rule themselves in gangs.

But it must be emphasized too that these different strands of slum mythology—the mainstream and the countercultural—nonetheless have much in common. What they share is a fascination with and investment in the tough, whether for his proud defiance or for his alarming but ultimately hopeful mix of violent irresponsibility and self-esteem. What they share is a devotion to an ethics of pleasure and excitement: even the popular photojournalist Riis is sympathetic to the slum dweller's "human" desire for spectacle, and he has no problem with the need to entertain his audience. What the mainstream and bohemian strains share is the deployment of an ethical relationship of spectacle between the middle class and the slums, and a commitment to the new ethical substance of individuality.

Notes

Introduction

1. The sentence continues: they are "often so much enfeebled as to be able only to move about in search of sustenance, or of the stimulus which they feel to be more important than food."

2. Joseph Tuckerman, *On the Elevation of the Poor: A Selection from His Reports as Minister at Large in Boston* (Boston: Roberts Brothers, 1874), pp. 64, 66, 67, 69, 168, 169–170, 178. I have chosen Tuckerman's book and specifically the quotations here as representative of the discourse on the urban poor from the 1820s to the 1850s. The observations I will be making in this chapter in regard to Tuckerman's writing could also be made by looking at a host of other authors from this period, and I will be referring to these authors in some detail in chapter 1.

3. The author concluded with the necessity of "encouraging incentive in the underclass."

4. "The American Underclass," *Time*, 29 Aug. 1977, pp. 14–27.

5. Tuckerman was writing about Anglo-Saxon slum dwellers, and *Time* focused on a black ghetto. Since the middle of the nineteenth century, certainly, with the increased immigration of the Irish and the Germans, the representation of the slums is both a class and an ethnic or racial issue. That is to say, the reporting on the slums is shaped by upper- and middle-class conceptions of the poor as well as by Anglo-Saxon and white conceptions of other ethnic or racial groups. (Late-nineteenth-century slum writing is mostly about southern and eastern Europeans, though Riis also writes about Chinese immigrants and African Americans, and Crane writes mainly about slum dwellers of Irish ancestry; today's slum literature is largely about African Americans and Hispanics.) For practical reasons, this study limits itself to the class issue and attempts to look at continuities and discontinuities in the representation of the slums that cut across ethnic or racial lines. Ethnic or racial is-

sues—in all their complexity—would have to be addressed in a complete study of slum literature; they are simply beyond the scope of this book.

6. It is not that the contemporary account appreciates economic, social, or environmental causes of poverty, while the earlier one finds its source in individual viciousness alone; though this individualistic view of poverty was more prevalent in the 1830s than it is today, Tuckerman's report addresses the problem of low wages and the material destitution into which the poor are born, and though it does not use the words "slum" or "ghetto," it recognizes that there are "abodes of poverty" that exert their particular "influences." "Who [then] are these idle and able-bodied, intemperate and improvident claimants of alms?" asks Tuckerman.

> Some of them, indeed, were reared under advantages, from which a better condition and character might have been hoped for. But they had not the moral strength to resist strong temptations to early vicious indulgence surrounded as they were with facilities and excitements to this indulgence. . . .
> A very great proportion, however, of these degraded fellow-beings drew their first breath in the abodes of poverty, were reared amidst improvidence and intemperance, had few or no advantages during their childhood for religious or any other useful instruction, and in the most susceptible season of life were exposed to all influences which can corrupt the mind in all its springs of thought and disposition and conduct.

The author goes on to say that not only in the case of the virtuous poor but even in regards to the "idle, intemperate, and improvident," "a tremendous responsibility" for "their poverty, their character, their moral exposures" "lies upon the society around the poor of this class; for the cause of the degradation of these unhappy fellow-beings are within the control of the society around them" (Tuckerman, *On the Elevation of the Poor*, pp. 168–171).

Still, to be sure, the *Time* article is separated from these reports of a Boston minister at large by a greater reliance on statistics, a larger consideration of the historical heritage of poverty, a more complex sense of economic relations, and even a powerfully expanded notion of the social causes of poverty.

7. That book was John Thomson's *Street Life in London* (London: Sampson Law, Marston Searle and Rovington, 1877).

8. Charles Loring Brace, *The Dangerous Classes of New York, and Twenty Years' Work among Them* (New York: Wynkoop and Hallenbeck, 1872).

9. As with Tuckerman's book, the 1977 *Time* cover story "The American Underclass" is by no means an isolated event; I have chosen it as representative of our current discourse on the urban poor because it is a significant and notable appearance of the slums in the mainstream press (it created a certain sensation) and is relatively extensive. Since its publication, there have appeared many magazine pieces, newspaper articles, and television shows that indulge in a fascination with slum life and explore the subject psychologically and anthropologically. The situation of the slums recurs from time to time in the mainstream press, and again and again in these representations of the urban poor, there is talk of other values, a lack of motivation, low self-esteem, a separate culture.

Instead of the *Time* piece, I might have equally well have chosen the CBS network's televised report called "The Vanishing Family: Crisis in Black America" that appeared almost a decade later (it aired 25 Jan. 1986). In this telecast, CBS broadcast conversations between Bill Moyers and a several young ghetto blacks, including a man named Timothy, intercut with commentary and shots of the Newark, N.J., slums where the conversations took place: densely crowded streets, rows of tenement apartments and burned-out buildings, police cars and sirens, a boy beating on an assortment of makeshift drums (made of cans of all shapes and sizes) in front of a weedy vacant lot, other boys sitting on a stoop listening to rap music on a boom box.

Moyers asked Timothy, "How many children do you have?" "Six," replied Timothy, with a big smile and a laugh. Moyers's voice-over explained that Timothy had "fathered those six children by four women."

> Moyers: So many women, so many children. Do you ever think that maybe you shouldn't do it? Unless you can be sure you don't have a kid?
> Timothy: Not really. 'Cause I'm highly sexed. But I have ways of cooling myself down. You know. 'Cause . . . when you've done it with one female and you're not doing it with another female, having sex with her too much is bad, so you have to . . . set a schedule. . . . When you should do it and when you should not.
> Moyers: You seem to break your schedule sometimes.
> Timothy: Well . . . Most women say, 'You a baby maker." I just got strong sperm, that's all. (Laughs.)
> Moyers: Would you have had these kids if you had thought about them in advance?
> Timothy: No.
> Moyers: They were an accident?
> Timothy: Yeah, you could say that.
> Moyers: Were you just having a good time?
> Timothy: (Smiles and laughs) Yeah, a real good time. I enjoyed myself.

At the beginning of the show, Moyers stood in front of an abandoned building and explained that for Timothy and others like him "in cities all over America, the traditional family no longer exists. It has vanished and something new is taking its place. Single women and the children they're rearing alone are the fastest growing part of the black population. What becomes of the black family in a world where the values are being turned upside down?" During the broadcast and in a panel discussion afterward, Moyers turned to blacks involved in social service to their communities and blacks in politics or academia to explain the nature of the problem and what might be done. A woman from the International Youth Organization said, "If the parent is seventeen or eighteen, uneducated, unmotivated, fooling around, wandering around, what's the child gonna learn? Who's to teach him? . . . It's not racism that I'm fighting now. It's the lack of motivation." A young man who organized recreation, including boxing, for kids, commented, "Self-control and self-esteem are far more important than a good left hook." A psychologist said that in a ghetto like Newark's, having six kids is "the only badge of honor that you intend to get." And a professor of political economy at Harvard's John F. Kennedy School of Government noted that "we can see in this [CBS] film . . . the importance of what might be called the local culture, the values and the interactions between people that were happening in that particular context."

In short, according to the CBS report, Moyers's Timothy is living in a world where "values are being turned upside down," where "the local culture" is suffering from a "lack of motivation," and where having a lot of children is the only badge of self-esteem one can hope for ("The Vanishing Family: Crisis in Black America," *CBS Reports*, narr. Bill Moyers, CBS, 25 Jan. 1986).

To take some other recent examples of reporting on the slums: A 1988 *San Francisco Chronicle* special report called "Black America Today" finds more blacks than ever "without jobs, without schooling, and without aspirations," a welfare system that ends up "sapping [the] independence and self-esteem" of black mothers ("Black America Today," *San Francisco Chronicle*, 28 Mar. 1988, p. A6) and "a drug culture" that influences young people Black Hard-Liners in the War on Drugs," *San Francisco Chronicle*, 28 Mar. 1988, p. A7). In a discussion of street gang violence on ABC's *Nightline* in 1988, the Los Angeles district attorney refers to "gang culture" and "the violent culture of street gangs" ("Street Gang Violence," *Nightline*, narr. Ted Koppel, ABC, 11 Oct., 1988). "A lot of youngsters join a gang because . . . it helps their self-esteem," a neighborhood counselor tells the *San Francisco Chronicle* in a 1989 piece titled "New Ways to Battle Gang Violence" (*San Francisco Chronicle*, 1 May 1989, p. A6).

In April of the same year, thirty teenagers went on what the press called a "wilding" rampage in Central Park, and a group of eight of them—not on drugs, most without criminal records, and "some . . . from families that cared and watched over them"—raped and assaulted a woman jogger until she was comatose; and anthropologists and sociologists were called in by the *New York Times* to explain the "baffl[ing]" attack. These experts on East Harlem explained "how the street culture could have fostered a rampage that otherwise appears senseless"; they spoke of "an element of lawlessness . . . hanging over the community." The "drug culture" had produced "a new model of teen-age behavior" even for teenagers who are not part of the drug trade: "[T]o be respected in the community, a young man has to prove he can be brutal." "Crack permeates East Harlem. . . . And with it comes a new model of teen-age behavior, social scientists say. 'To be successful in the underground economy, you have to be ruthless and you have to be violent,'" said Philippe Bourgois, a professor of anthropology living in East Harlem. "Even though the teen-agers in the Central Park attack were apparently not using drugs . . . , 'the models come from the drug world,'" said Ansley Hamid, another anthropology professor living in East Harlem (Gina Kolata, "Grim Seeds of Park Rampage Found in East Harlem Streets," *New York Times*, 2 May 1989, p. B5).

In some contemporary descriptions of the urban poor, psychological and cultural facts seem as important as the raw economic facts of poverty. A 1987 article in *Fortune* claims that what defines the underclass is "not so much their poverty as their behavior—their chronic lawlessness, drug use, welfare dependency, and school failure. 'Underclass' describes a state of mind and a way of life. It is at least as much a cultural as an economic condition" (Myron Magnet, "America's Underclass: What to Do?," *Fortune*, 11 May 1987, p. 130). A *Chicago Tribune* piece the year before declares that members of the underclass "don't share traditional values of work, money, education, home and perhaps even life. . . . Over the last quarter-century in America, this subculture has become self-perpetuating. It devours every effort aimed at solving its problems, resists solutions both simple and complicated" (quoted in William Julius Wilson, "The American Underclass: Inner-City Ghettos and the Norms of Citizenship," *The Godkin Lecture*, John F. Kennedy School of Government, Harvard University, 26 Apr. 1988, pp. 39–40). An *Esquire* article in 1988 asserts:

> The heart of the matter is the continued existence and expansion of what has
> come to be called the Underclass . . . : that group of five million black

> Americans . . . who are trapped in cycles of welfare dependency, drugs, al-
> cohol, crime, illiteracy, and disease, living in anarchic and murderous isola-
> tion in some of the richest cities on the earth. . . . [T]his ferocious subcul-
> ture . . . [is] the single most dangerous fact of ordinary life in the United
> States. (Pete Hamill, "Breaking the Silence," *Esquire*, Mar. 1988, p. 92)

In 1988, the California Task Force to Promote Self-Esteem and Personal and Social Responsibility was created; it interviewed street-gang members and single mothers (as well as
people from other walks of life) to discover, as their mandate says, "whether healthy self-
esteem relates to the development of personal responsibility and social problems (like
crime and alcoholism and violence) and how healthy self-esteem is nurtured, harmed or reduced, and rehabilitated." The creator of the program explained: "I've seen the cost of
prisons . . . and dropouts and drugs. . . . We have to get at the root cause; self-esteem
informs everything. Nancy Reagan tells people to just say no, but they can't do that until
they [say] yes to themselves." (Quoted in Anne Taylor Fleming, "Will the Real Self-Esteem Please Stand Up?" *New York Times*, 9 Nov. 1988, c10).

   10. Sigmund Freud, *Civilization and Its Discontents*, trans. James Strachey (New York:
Norton, 1961), pp. 108–109.

   11. The magazine also does not explain how else the social service expert might give
people a better image of themselves, but the implication is that there are other ways to gain
self-esteem besides working.

   12. The *Time* piece, which is by no means an exception within the genre, hides this tension: it wants to maintain that psychologically, the culture of the streets does nothing but
produce low self-esteem because it must denounce that culture at the same that it wants to
come down unequivocally in favor of high self-esteem.

   13. "Black Hard-Liners in the War on Drugs." Another example comes from sociologists writing in the *New York Times* after the seemingly senseless "wilding" incident in
Central Park. They explain that the "drug culture" has produced "a new model of teen-
age behavior": "[T]o be respected . . . , a young man has to be prove he can be brutal"
(Kolata, "Grim Seeds of Park Rampage"). Self-esteem, which most everybody wants to
encourage because it is considered to be the foundation of psychological health, can be
generated by the same street-gang values that most everybody wants to dispose of.

   14. To take a few examples: Robert Wiebe's *The Search for Order, 1877–1920* (New
York: Hill and Wang, 1967) has traced the disappearance of locally autonomous moral
communities and the eventual rise of a new bureaucratic order that no longer governs
men's essences but simply rules their actions. Alan Trachtenberg's *The Incorporation of
America: Culture and Society in the Gilded Age* (New York: Hill and Wang, 1982) has argued
that the corporation and the city had their own logic of consumption and spectacle that undermined the morality of the traditional village. Christopher Lasch's *Haven in a Heartless
World: The Family Besieged* (New York: Basic Books, 1977) has chronicled the assertion of
managerial and professional control over activities once left to individuals and families, a
social control that has made people dependent and incapable of real initiative. Robert Bellah's *Habits of the Heart* (Berkeley: U of California P, 1985) has talked about the marginalization and privatization of moral discourse and the popularization of management and
psychology, as ways of ordering our lives. Henry May's *The End of American Innocence: A
Study of the First Years of Our Own Times, 1912–1917* (New York: Knopf, 1959) has looked
to new intellectual developments, such as skepticism, pragmatism, relativism, and literary
naturalism and realism, to understand the loss of faith in a universal morality and culture.

15. T. J. Jackson Lears, *No Place of Grace: Antimodernism and the Transformation of American Culture, 1880–1920* (New York: Pantheon, 1981), pp. xiii–xviii.

16. See, for instance, Lasch, *Haven in a Heartless World*, pp. xiii–xxiv.

17. Lasch, *The Culture of Narcissism* (New York: Norton, 1978), p. 21.

18. Michel Foucault, *The Use of Pleasure*, trans. Robert Hurley (New York: Pantheon, 1985), pp. 25–32. "For a rule of conduct is one thing; the conduct that may be measured by this rule is another. But another thing still is the manner in which one ought to 'conduct oneself'—that is, the manner in which one ought to form oneself as an ethical subject acting in reference to the prescriptive elements that make up the code." Foucault calls the ethically relevant part of oneself "*the ethical substance*; . . . the individual has to constitute this or that part of himself as the prime material of moral conduct" (p. 26).

19. I want to underline that this book is concerned with the upper- and middle-class representation of the slums, along with changes in upper- and middle-class ethics. I am considering literature that (explicitly or implicitly) conceives of urban poor neighborhoods as other, as different from upper- or middle-class communities (thus, for example, its use of such terms as "slums" and "tenements"). There is another entire literature of urban poor communities (which should not, perhaps, properly be called "slum" literature) which is indigenous to the neighborhoods it describes—and which this book does not address. This often ethnic or minority literature no doubt shares some thematic features with upper- and middle-class slum literature, but it also has its own distinct concerns. Riis's immigrant status and initial poverty in America should not cloud the issue here: by the time he produced his books, he was no longer part of the lower-class socioethnic community which he passed through in New York but, rather, a member of the professional middle class. (A stylistic note: rather than repeating the ungainly phrase "upper and middle classes," I will in general, from here on out, discuss the middle class, though what I am claiming will often be applicable to both the middle and upper classes.)

20. Walter Taylor makes a different and stronger claim about Riis's importance. "In 1890 appeared the key-book of the entire anti-slum movement, Jacob Riis' *How the Other Half Lives*. . . . Thenceforward—and especially for the next five years—the slum was in effect a fresh literary field, strange to the readers of the eighteen-nineties as the solitary forests and great lakes of interior America had been to the reader of Fenimore Cooper's time; and both writers and readers appear to have explored that new area with an intense curiosity" (Walter Fuller Taylor, *The Economic Novel in America* [Chapel Hill: U of North Carolina P, 1942], pp. 79–80). Taylor is certainly correct about the general interest in the slums in the 1890s, and he is also correct that Riis was very influential. Perhaps Riis's was "the key-book of the entire anti-slum movement," but it would be hard to argue that it was the first antislum book, even of the turn-of-the-century period.

21. Until recently, very little had been written about Crane's slum representations in relation to other practices besides literary ones, in relation to other events besides the production of fiction and poetry—even though, for instance, he wrote a good number of documentary sketches for newspapers. Marcus Cunliffe noted in 1955 that *Maggie* is a fictional retelling of previous sociological and religious reports on the slums; Charles Loring Brace's *The Dangerous Classes of New York* (1872), Thomas De Witt Talmage's sermons, collected in such works as *The Abominations of Modern Society* (New York: Adams and Victor, 1872), and Riis's *How the Other Half Lives* all have material on more or less innocent slum girls who have ended up as prostitutes; Brace and Talmage both imagined scenes in which a prostitute is on the brink of suicide (Marcus Cunliff, "Stephen Crane and the

American Background of *Maggie*," in *Maggie: A Girl of the Streets*, ed. Thomas A. Gullason [New York: Norton, 1979], pp. 94–103).

Thomas Gullason, in 1959, found sources, including Riis, for Crane's "pessimistic bias" and some of his ideas about "psychology" (Thomas Gullason, "The Sources of Stephen Crane's *Maggie*," in Gullason, *Maggie: A Girl of the Streets*, pp. 103–108).

More recently, Alan Trachtenberg discusses Crane's city sketches in the context of documentary writing about the slums, in "Experiments in Another Country," in *American Realism: New Essays*, ed. Eric J. Sundquist (Baltimore: Johns Hopkins UP, 1982), pp. 138–154. (The article was first published in 1974.)

Allan Gardner Smith compares Crane's impressionism to the psychological concepts of William James in "Stephen Crane, Impressionism and William James," *Revue Francaise d'Etudes Americaines* 17 (May 1983), pp. 237–248.

Michael Fried discusses Crane's writing in conjunction with Thomas Eakins's painting in *Realism, Writing, Disfiguration* (Chicago: U of Chicago P, 1987).

Mark Seltzer discusses Crane along with Riis in "Statistical Persons," *Diacritics* 17.3 (Fall 1987), pp. 84–85.

Riis, meanwhile, is still almost always examined without exploration of the slum fiction of his day. One exception is Seltzer's article. Another is Maren Stange's *Symbols of Ideal Life* (New York: Cambridge UP, 1989).

22. David Leviatin, "Framing the Poor," Introduction to *How the Other Half Lives*, by Jacob Riis (Boston: Bedford Books, 1996), p. 17.

23. It is tempting to claim that Riis found models for his photojournalism across the Atlantic, in the English investigative tradition of the previous half century. Henry Mayhew, whose *London Labour and the London Poor* began weekly publication in 1850, and John Thomson and Adolphe Smith, whose *Street Life in London* came out in serial form in 1877 and 1878, were spectators of the lower-class urban world in general. They were limited neither to moral and social issues nor to crime stories; theirs were inquiries, as Mayhew put it, "into the state of the people." Mayhew aimed to give "a literal description of their labour, their earnings, their trials, and their sufferings, in their own 'unvarnished' language; and to pourtray the conditions of their homes and their families" (Henry Mayhew, *London Labour and the London Poor* [New York: Dover, 1968], p. i). Smith and Thomson wanted to provide "a vivid account of the various means by which our unfortunate fellow-creatures endeavour to earn, beg, or steal their daily bread" (John Thomson and Adolphe Smith, *Street Life in London* [New York: B. Blom, 1969], preface). Both works included descriptions and photographs (or, in Mayhew's case, engravings made from photographs or daguerreotypes) of street types and representative members of urban occupations and entertainments, such as "The London Costermonger," "The Baked Potato Man," "The Jew Old-Clothes Man," "The London Sweep," "Rat-Killer to Her Majesty," "Street-Conjuror" (Mayhew), and "London Nomads," "Covent Garden Flower Women," "The Dramatic Shoe-Black," "The London Boardmen," and "Italian Street Musicians" (Thomson). But while these Englishmen are in certain respects Riis's predecessors, there is no evidence that Riis learned his outlook from them; in fact, it seems that he knew very little about their work. Peter Hales reports that Riis "did not immediately hit on the camera as the instrument ideally suited" to his project, and someone familiar with the books of Mayhew or Thomson could hardly have avoided thinking of the camera immediately (Peter Hales, *Silver Cities: The Photography of American Urbanization, 1839–1915* [Philadelphia: Temple UP, 1984], p. 169).

24. In using this term, I do not mean to identify Riis's project with the "ethnography" of Indian life in the second half of the nineteenth century. Susan Sontag has noted the similarity between amateur photographers of the Indians and social-reform photographers:

> After the opening of the West in 1869 by the completion of the transcontinental railroad came the colonization through photography. The case of the American Indians is the most brutal. Discreet, serious amateurs like [Adam Clark] Vroman had been operating since the end of the Civil War. They were the vanguard of an army of tourists who arrived by the end of the century, eager for "a good shot" of Indian life. The tourists invaded the Indians' privacy, photographing holy objects and the sacred dances and places, if necessary paying the Indians to pose and getting them to revise their ceremonies to provide more photogenic material.
>
> But the native ceremony that is changed when the tourist hordes come sweeping down is not so different from a scandal in the inner city that is corrected after someone photographs it. Insofar as the muckrakers got results, they too altered what they photographed; indeed, photographing something became a routine part of the procedure for altering it. (Susan Sontag, *On Photography* [New York: Dell, 1977], p. 64)

It is not likely, though, that Riis's project comes out of the ethnographic tradition of the American Indian. Riis was apparently aware of this tradition, for he does refer to it in passing: in a story in *Out of Mulberry Street* about an old squaw and an Indian girl lost in New York, he finds that the doll of the child "was a real ethnological study. It was a faithful rendering of the Indian papoose" (Riis, *Out of Mulberry Street, Stories of Tenement Life in New York City* [New York: Century, 1898], p. 75). But it is precisely the incidental manner in which Riis alludes to this practice that indicates the limited nature of its meaning for him. Riis is never too proud to note the sources for his notions: in setting out his moral and social argument in the introduction to *How the Other Half Lives*, he quotes liberally from testimony of the secretary of the Prison Association of New York, and in his autobiography he credits men of the Health Department with having given him "pretty much all the understanding I have ever had of the problems I have battled with." Indian ethnology, on the other hand, gets nothing more than a curious glance (Riis, *How the Other Half Lives: Studies among the Tenements of New York* [New York: Hill and Wang, 1957], pp. 1–2; *The Making of an American* [New York: Macmillan, 1901], p. 242).

The origin of Riis's ethnography is discussed later in the introduction.

25. Crane, *Stephen Crane: Letters*, ed. Robert Wooster Stallman and Lillian Gilkes (New York: New York UP, 1960), p. 14.

26. This is not to suggest that there is a critical consensus about Riis; rather, a composite view can be formed by combining the two basic critical positions.

Riis has traditionally been championed as a hero of social justice. Theodore Roosevelt was one of the first to eulogize his humanity, calling him "one of those men who by his writings contributed most to raising the standard of unselfishness, of disinterestedness . . . in this country." Sam Bass Warner has emphasized Riis's sympathy above all his other qualities; Alexander Alland has called his work "a crusade for human decency"; Ansel Adams has spoken of his "humanistic photography," and his biographer, James B. Lane, has referred to him as "a humanitarian reformer" (Theodore Roosevelt, "Jacob Riis," *The Outlook* 57 [June 1914], p. 284; Alexander Alland Sr., *Jacob A. Riis, Photographer and Citizen*

[Millerton, N.Y.: Aperture, 1974], p. 5; Ansel Adams, Preface to Alland, *Jacob A. Riis*, p. 6; James B. Lane, *Jacob A. Riis and the American City* [Port Washington, N.Y.: Kennikat, 1974], p. x).

Meanwhile, some recent criticism of Riis takes issue with the myth of the single-minded reformer and notices that he was, in fact, of two minds on the subject of the poor. Daniel Levine, for instance, finds that Riis partakes of the harsher, moralistic view of poverty, the idea that the poor came in two kinds, the worthy poor and the pauper. And he concludes that "for the 'pauper,' Riis had no sympathy." Meanwhile, Thomas Leonard, while acknowledging that poverty was Riis's "obsession," notices that he was also concerned about urban crime: "Riis' camera frequently strayed from the pathos of the tenement to show thuggery"; his collection of photographs include murder scenes, theft reenacted for the camera, gangs in hideouts, a rogues' gallery, and police in pursuit of criminals. Similarly, Alan Trachtenberg finds that Riis's writings appeal to "middle-class worries over safety and security." According to Trachtenberg, Riis "represented the slum as the antithesis of the home, a breeding ground of menacing ignorance and discontent . . . an offense to all notions of the clean, the sanitary and the civilized." Where Riis's admirers have wanted to see nothing but humanitarian sympathy, recent critics have discovered also the assertion of stern morality, middle-class values, and social defense (Daniel Levine, *Jane Addams and the Liberal Tradition* [Westport, Conn.: State Historical Society of Wisconsin, 1971], p. 132; Thomas Leonard, *The Power of the Press: The Birth of American Political Reporting* [New York: Oxford UP, 1986], p. 154; Trachtenberg, *The Incorporation of America*, pp. 124–128).

And in this regard, it is relevant to note that in his own day, Riis was sometimes cited by immigration restrictionists, who felt that his work provided evidence for their cause. Francis A. Walker, for example, the famous administrator of Indian affairs who was also an immigration restrictionist, referred to the "habits of life" of the urban poor as of "the most revolting kind" and simply counseled, "Read . . . Mr. Riis" (Francis A. Walker, "Restriction of Immigration," *Atlantic Monthly* 77 [June 1896], pp. 822–829).

27. For *Maggie* as naturalistic or deterministic, see Vernon L. Parrington, "The Beginnings of Critical Realism in America," *Main Currents in American Thought* (New York: Harcourt, Brace, 1930), vol. 3, pp. 323–329; Charles Child Walcutt, "Stephen Crane: Naturalist and Impressionist," in *American Literary Naturalism: A Divided Stream* (Minneapolis: U of Minnesota P, 1956), pp. 67–72; Lars Ahnebrink, *The Beginnings of Naturalism in American Fiction* (New York: Russell and Russell, 1961), pp. 250–264; David Fitelson, "Stephen Crane's *Maggie* and Darwinism," *American Quarterly* 16 (Summer 1964), pp. 182–186.

Other critics have found in *Maggie* a moral stance, and some have specifically tried to demolish Crane's reputation as a naturalist: James Colvert finds that the theme of the novel is "that human incompetency . . . finds its source in vanity, delusion, and ignorance of self"; he has described the novel as an "ironic study of vanity and conceit" in "Structure and Theme in Stephen Crane's Fiction," *Modern Fiction Studies* 5 (Autumn 1959), pp. 199–208. Edwin H. Cady has drawn attention to "the moral vitality of its irony" in *Stephen Crane* (New York: Twayne, 1962). Marston LaFrance has tried to demonstrate that "Maggie's fate . . . results primarily from . . . moral cowardice and personal dishonesty" and that "none of Crane's characters can be legitimately excused by any appeal to philosophic determinism" in "*George's Mother* and the Other Half of *Maggie*," in *Stephen Crane in Transition: Centenary Essays*, ed. Joseph Katz (Dekalb: Northern Illinois UP, 1972), pp. 35–53; he also develops the idea in *A Reading of Stephen Crane* (Oxford:

Clarendon, 1971), pp. 37–94. Milne Holton finds that "*Maggie* is . . . about an incapacity of vision," and if the characters are "trapped in their environment," it is not merely because of "their poverty" but also "their delusions," in *Cylinder of Vision: The Fiction and Journalistic Writing of Stephen Crane* (Baton Rouge: Louisiana State UP, 1972), pp. 35–54. James Nagel has concluded that "Maggie's death is the result of the epistemological problems of perception and interpretation and not of deterministic forces beyond the control of the characters" in *Stephen Crane and Literary Impressionism* (University Park: Pennsylvania State UP, 1980), pp. 94–100. David Halliburton has attributed to Crane a classical ethical "standard of measure" in *Maggie*; he claims that "the victimizers of Maggie are wanting in virtue," because "virtue entails self-control," in *The Color of the Sky* (New York: Cambridge UP, 1989), pp. 54–56.

Other critics, though not specifically commenting on *Maggie*, have talked about Crane's existentialism in reference to his concern with illusion and vision. One commentator has suggested that in Crane's works, "man does have will, and . . . the ability to reflect, and though these do not guarantee that he can effect his own destiny they do enable him to become responsible to some degree for the honesty of his personal vision" (Stanley B. Greenfield, "The Unmistakable Stephen Crane," quoted in James T. Cox, "The Imagery of 'The Red Badge of Courage,'" *Modern Fiction Studies* 5 [Autumn 1959], p. 209). Peter Buitenhuis takes a similar view in "The Essentials of Life: 'The Open Boat' as Existentialist Fiction," *Modern Fiction Studies* 5 (Autumn 1959), pp. 243–250.

Some critics have aimed for a compromise between Crane's naturalism and what might be called his ethicism; R. W. Stallman has called the novel a "paradox" in "Crane's 'Maggie': A Reassessment," *Modern Fiction Studies* 5 (Autumn 1959), pp. 251–259. Donald Pizer has said it is both an affirmation of determinism and a critique of those human values that deny determinism in "Stephen Crane's *Maggie* and American Naturalism," *Criticism, a Quarterly for Literature and the Arts* 7 (Spring 1965), pp. 168–175.

28. See Sam Bass Warner, Editor's Introduction to *How the Other Half Lives*, by Jacob Riis (Cambridge, Mass.: Belknap P of Harvard UP, 1970), pp. xv, xix.

29. The tenements of Mulberry Bend, which Riis condemns in *How the Other Half Lives*, were subsequently demolished and replaced with a park, and their residents were relocated, by order of Governor Theodore Roosevelt. Then there is the influential New York Tenement House Commission of 1894, and the New York Tenement House Acts of 1895 (outlawing rear tenements) and 1901 (concerning light, ventilation, building height, room space, fire safety), which Riis did a good deal to inspire (Lawrence Veiller, *Tenement House Reform in New York, 1834–1900* [New York: The Evening Post Job Printing House, 1900], pp. 32–36; Robert Weeks DeForest and Lawrence Veiller, eds., *The Tenement House Problem . . . by Various Writers* [New York: Macmillan, 1903], pp. 165–201). Riis has been appraised in terms of his call for reform because he got results there. Compared to his spectacular and concrete achievements—the antimonument of a razed Mulberry Bend, for one—the picturesque style of his writing and his typical racist notions seem rather petty distractions.

The next step, in the critical apotheosis of Riis, has been to give him nearly full credit for these particular tenement reforms; see, for example, Francesco Cordasco: "In large measure, the Law of 1901 was due to the efforts of Jacob Riis" (Introduction to *The Children of the Poor*, by Jacob Riis [New York: Garrett, 1970], p. viii). This law, not surprisingly, had been in the making for at least two decades of social investigation. Riis himself documents the struggle that precedes him in *The Battle with the Slum* (New York: Macmillan, 1902), chapters 1–4.

30. Robert Wooster Stallman, *Stephen Crane: A Biography* (New York: G. Braziller, 1968), p. 215.

31. Realists and naturalists, such as Crane, have often been extended a privileged place, outside the moral fray; his realism is often described as amoral. It seems to me fallacious to imagine a site outside of all moral questions and positions. What these critics have done, in exempting Crane, is to imply that traditional or religious morality *is* morality, the only morality.

32. Crane, *Stephen Crane: Letters*, p. 133.

33. Warren Susman, *Culture as History: The Transformation of the American Society in the Twentieth Century* (New York: Pantheon, 1984), p. xx. As Susman puts it, "The older culture . . . demanded something it called 'character,' which stressed moral qualities, whereas the newer culture insisted on 'personality,' which emphasized being liked and admired" (p. xxii). Where Susman talks of "a culture of personality" (pp. 271–285), I talk about an ethics of self-esteem. I might have used other words, such as self-respect, egotism, conceit, vanity (all words Crane and Riis also use); I choose "self-esteem" because I want to indicate the link between Crane's and Riis's ideas and our own contemporary moral-psychological perspective.

Some scholars, indeed, trace today's "self-esteem movement" back to the 1890s—and especially to the figure of William James. See Martin E. Seligman, *The Optimistic Child* (Boston: Houghton, Mifflin, 1995), pp. 30–33, "A Brief History of Self-Esteem": "[T]he notion of self-esteem lay dormant for almost seventy-five years after James proposed it, as America was consumed with fighting wars and overcoming economic depression. Given the specter of such powerful real-world problems creating such misery, American psychology was dominated by theories that had people pushed or pulled by the powerful forces beyond their control. . . . A sea change occurred in the social sciences of the 1960s. Individual choice became a legitimate explanation of human action" (31).

34. John Higham, "The Re-orientation of American Culture in the 1890s," in *The Origins of Modern Consciousness*, ed. John Weiss (Detroit: Wayne State UP, 1965), p. 46.

35. See, for example, Paul Boyer, *Urban Masses and Moral Order in America, 1820–1920* (Cambridge, Mass.: Harvard UP, 1978), chapters 11 and 12.

36. Ann Douglas, *The Feminization of American Culture* (New York: Knopf, 1977).

37. See Lears, *No Place of Grace*, p. xiii.

38. Higham, "The Re-orientation of American Culture in the 1890s," pp. 35, 40.

39. Theodore Roosevelt, *The Strenuous Life: Essays and Addresses* (New York: Century, 1901), pp. 8, 20–21.

40. Higham, "The Re-orientation of American Culture in the 1890s," p. 27.

41. Douglas, *The Feminization of American Culture*, p. 327. During the late 1880s and early 1890s, "many men, and women, were becoming deeply concerned about the 'feminization' of American culture and the closing of the frontier, actual and metaphorical, which it suggested."

42. Lears, *No Place of Grace*, p. xiii. Lears himself includes Progressive social reform when he discusses the "much broader quest for intense experience which ranged from militarism and 'Progressive' social reform to popular occultism and the early fascination with depth psychology" (xiii). While Lears associates Progressive social reform with "efforts to regenerate a bourgeois morality of self-control" (143), I will see within it, specifically in the case of Riis, a secondary and contradictory effort to pursue excitement and vitality in and of themselves.

43. Stallman, *Stephen Crane*, p. 35.

44. Crane quoted in ibid., p. 36.

45. Stanley Wertheim and Paul M. Sorrentino, *The Crane Log: A Documentary Life of Stephen Crane* (New York: Maxwell Macmillan International, 1994), pp. 15–16.

46. Joseph Conrad quoted in Stallman, *Stephen Crane*, p. 347: "Nothing could have held him back."

47. J. C. Levenson, quoted in Christopher Benfey, *The Double Life of Stephen Crane* (New York: Knopf, 1992), p. 4.

48. Stallman, *Stephen Crane*, pp. 73, 79.

49. Crane participated in the mythologizing of the West as a masculine utopia even as he debunked aspects of the myth in such stories as "The Blue Hotel" and "The Bride Comes to Yellow Sky." In a letter of 1895 to a friend, he expressed an opinion about the West that was consonant with Roosevelt's, for example:

> I have always believed the western people to be much truer than the eastern people. We in the east are overcome a good deal by a detestable superficial culture which I think is the real barbarism. Culture in its true sense, I take it, is a comprehension of the man at one's shoulder. It has nothing to do with an adoration for effete jugs and old kettles. This latter is merely an amusement and we live for amusement in the east. Damn the east! I fell in love with the straight out-and-out, sometimes hideous, often braggart westerners because I thought them to be the truer men. . . . They are serious, those fellows. When they are born they take one big gulp of wind and then they live. . . . What I contend for is the atmosphere of the west which really is frank and honest and is bound to make eleven honest men for one pessimistic thief. More glory be with them. (Crane, *Stephen Crane: An Omnibus*, ed. Robert Wooster Stallman [New York: Knopf, 1961], pp. 629–630)

50. Stallman, *Stephen Crane*, p. 59.

51. Van Wyck Brooks, *The Confident Years, 1885–1915* (New York: Dutton, 1952), p. 218; see Higham, "The Re-orientation of American Culture in the 1890s," p. 39.

52. Quoted in Leviatin, "Framing the Poor," p. 25.

53. Riis, *The Making of an American*, p. 132.

54. Ibid., chapter 10, "My Dog Is Avenged."

55. *Indianapolis News*, in review of Riis's *The Making of an American*.

56. Theodore Roosevelt, Introduction to Riis's *Making of an American*, p. xi (from "Jacob Riis," an obituary published in *The Outlook*).

57. Josephine Shaw Lowell founded the New York chapter of the Charity Organization Society (COS) in 1881. As Maren Stange explains:

> [T]he COS held [that] poverty resulted chiefly from the moral flaws and personal failings of poor people [and thus that] the cure for such moral illness was not a charitable dole but rather honest work, wise advice, and moral leadership. Supervised public relief given within poorhouses and hospitals must be restricted to the "chronically homeless and unemployed," and only after all efforts at rehabitation have failed. "Friendly visiting" by the COS worker to needy families who had asked for relief was the agency's chosen method to strengthen the values of family, thrift, and work to prevent the demoralizing

effects of too easily obtained charity. "Not alms, but a friend," the COS vowed, and the friendly visitor attempted to set an inspiring example within the tenement home. (Stange, *Symbols of Ideal Life*, p. 32)

Stange is quoting from William R. Stewart, ed., *The Philanthropic Work of Josephine Shaw Lowell* (New York: Macmillan, 1911), pp. 123–124. On friendly visiting, see also Paul Boyer, *Urban Masses and Moral Order*, chapter 10.

58. It is also evident in his early life. As David Leviatin points out, he was a "youth weaned on the works of Charles Dickens and James Fenimore Cooper and touched by a spirit of reform and adventure" (Leviatin, "Framing the Poor," p. 12).

59. Riis, *The Making of an American*, p. 20.

60. Jacob Riis, *Theodore Roosevelt: The Citizen* (New York: Outlook, 1903). In discussing Roosevelt the urban reformer, Riis wrote of "the strong hand he lent in the battle with the slum, as a member of the Health Board. . . . We had all the ammunition for the fight, the law and all, but there was no one who dared begin it till he came. Then the batteries opened fire at once, and it is largely due to him and his unhesitating courage that we have got as far as we have" (p. 151). In describing Roosevelt the western hunter, Riis quoted Roosevelt's *Ranch Life and the Hunting Trail*:

> To appreciate properly his fine, manly qualities, the wild rough-rider of the plains should be seen in his own home. There he passes his days; there he does his life-work; there, when he meets death, he faces it as he faces many other evils, with quiet, uncomplaining fortitude. Brave, hospitable, hardy and adventurous, he is the grim pioneer of the race; he prepares the way for the civilization from before whose face he must himself disappear. Hard and dangerous though his existence is, it has yet a wild attraction that strongly draws to it his bold, free spirit. (pp. 95–96)

Riis also described Roosevelt the Rough Rider: "So the army came home, his Rough-Riders with it, ragged, sore, famished, enfeebled, with yawning gaps in its ranks, but saved; they to tell of his courage and unwearying patience; how in the fight he was always where the bullets flew thickest" (p. 198).

61. Riis, *Hero Tales of the Far North* (New York: Macmillan, 1913), pp. 11, 15. This is the swashbuckling story of Peter Tordenskjold (Thunder Shield, a name given to him by the king), an eighteenth-century, Norwegian-born sailor who rises to the rank of admiral on the strength of his daring exploits. The following quote is a sample of Riis's romantic narration: Peder "halted them with the threat that every man Jack in the fleet should be made to walk the plank. . . . [He] took ship and prize with a rush, killing and throwing overboard such as resisted. In Sweden, mothers hushed their children with his dreaded name; on the sea they came near to thinking him a troll, so sudden and unexpected were his onslaughts" (pp. 9–10). "When on board, pistol and cutlass hung loose" (p. 10). Outnumbered by enemy dragoons on shore, Peder "suddenly dashed among them, cut one down, and, diving through the surf, swam out to the boat, his sword between his teeth. Their bullets churned the sea all about him" (pp. 10–11). "When things were at their worst in storm or battle, he was wont to shout to his men, 'Hi, *now* we are having a fine time!'" (p. 30).

62. Riis's description of a street flirtation in the slums will be discussed in chapters 1 and 4. In *Hero Tales of the Far North*, Riis writes that his hero Peder, while risking his life in enemy territory, "took notice, along with the position of the guns and the strength of the

garrison, of the fact that the commandant had two pretty daughters. He was a sailor, sure enough" (pp. 10–11).

63. Writing of the 1890s, John Higham observes that "for decades the popular novel had concentrated on domestic or rococo subjects rather than wilderness adventures. Above the level of the dime novel, the wild West had played very little part in fiction since the 1850s. Now it came back with a rush" (Higham, "The Re-orientation of American Culture in the 1890s," p. 30).

64. Lears, *No Place of Grace*, p. xiii.

65. Crane's turn-of-the-century Bowery is a more advanced culture of consumption, obviously not because it is wealthier than middle-class neighborhoods but because it has far less interest in production—very little belief in hard work paying off—and fewer qualms about pleasure and indulgence, and, of crucial importance, has access to a new world of mass-market goods.

66. The quotation in the head for this section comes from Riis, *The Making of an American*, quoted in Hales, *Silver Cities*, p. 167.

67. Brace, *The Dangerous Classes of New York*, p. 100.

68. Stephen Crane, *Maggie: A Girl of the Streets*, ed. Thomas Gullason (New York: Norton, 1979), p. 13.

69. In this regard of new vantage points, the settlement house movement should be mentioned. Jane Addams, for instance, had moved into Hull House in the immigrant slums of Chicago in 1889, the year before Riis's book appeared, and would live among and attempt to understand the people there for the rest of her life (Jane Addams, *Twenty Years at Hull House* [New York: Macmillan, 1961]). For more on the settlement house movement and Jane Addams, see note 5 to chapter 5. See also Boyer, *Urban Masses and Moral Order*, chapter 10; Allen F. Davis, *American Heroine: The Life and Legend of Jane Addams* (New York: Oxford UP, 1973); Levine, *Jane Addams and the Liberal Tradition*.

70. "[D]ry-plate materials [were] ten to twenty times as fast as wet-collodion [the old method], [and] they were designed to be used on or off a tripod, at speeds as fast as $\frac{1}{30}$ second or less." The dry-plate thus obviated the need for long-held poses. As for the flash, "it was *Blitzlichtpulver*, an explosive combination of powdered magnesium and two other substances." Riis read about it in the newspaper one morning in 1887 (Hales, *Silver Cities*, pp. 170–171).

71. Dianne Arbus, quoted in Susan Sontag, *On Photography*, p. 41.

72. Riis, *The Children of the Poor* (New York: Scribner's, 1892), pp. 77, 82.

73. I am borrowing the language of Thomas Kuhn's *The Structure of Scientific Revolutions* (Chicago: U of Chicago P, 1962).

74. Crane's concern with psychology is certainly part of a larger cultural movement: American universities were starting to offer separate courses in the subject in the 1880s and 1890s, and William James had just come out with his landmark *Principles of Psychology* in 1890; beginning in the late 1880s psychology was becoming a scientific discipline in its own right, separate from philosophy, ethics, and theology. In 1886, John Dewey's *Psychology* announced that "it is only recently that psychology has attained any independent standing. . . . [P]sychology was largely a compound of logic, ethics, and metaphysics" (John Dewey, *Psychology* [New York: Harper and Brothers, 1898], preface). Meanwhile, in the 1890s, psychiatry was starting to liberate itself from the mental asylum and to blur the line between the mentally ill and the mentally well ("Psychology in American Colleges and Universities," *American Journal of Psychology* 3 [April 1890], pp. 275–286; Abraham Aaron Roback, *History of American Psychology* [New York: Library Publishers, 1952],

pp. 121–128). By the end of the nineteenth century, "modern psychiatry was born. Leaders like Adolf Meyer . . . understood that there was no sharp line between the mentally ill and the mentally well" (Charles Edward Armory Winslow, *Twenty Years of Mental Hygiene, 1901–1929* [New York: American Foundation for Mental Hygiene, Inc., 1929], p. 183).

75. See the short discussion of Pragmatism in chapter 1.

76. Many critics have placed Crane squarely in a "realist" tradition that begins with William Dean Howells and Hamlin Garland. Crane himself allied his artistic practice with the "realism" of Howells and the "veritism" of Garland, though he did not claim to have copied their methods: "I developed all alone a little creed of art. . . . Later I discovered that my creed was identical with the one of Howells and Garland" (John Berryman, *Stephen Crane* [Cleveland: Meridian, 1950], pp. 52–53). Howells advocated a novelistic pursuit of "real life" (quoted in Trachtenberg, *The Incorporation of America*, p. 184) and suggested that novelists go "into the dark places of the soul, the filthy and squalid places of society, high and low" (quoted in Daniel Aaron, "Howells' 'Maggie,'" in Gullason, *Maggie: A Girl of the Streets*, p. 116); Garland asserted that the novelist should "insist on sincerity" and truth (Garland, *Crumbling Idols*, quoted in Stallman, *Stephen Crane*, p. 215).

But the intellectual revolution of *Maggie* is not the result of a simple transposition of Howells's and Garland's literary methods to the territory of the slums. Howells's Victorian realism put great stake in the Protestant notion of moral character; the realist text was, for Howells, supposed to present itself as a model of middle-class values (Trachtenberg, *The Incorporation of America*, pp. 184–186). *The Rise of Silas Lapham* (1885; New York: Signet NAL, 1980) contains a salute to "character" and incorporates a veritable critique of "immoral" novels (Howells, *The Rise of Silas Lapham*, p. 270, 184). For this reading, I am indebted to a lecture Walter Michaels gave at the University of California at Berkeley in fall 1985. "The novelist has a grave duty to his reader," Howells wrote elsewhere; he attacked "innutritious" novels "that merely tickle our prejudices and lull our judgment, or that coddle our sensibilities, or pamper our gross appetites for the marvelous . . . [and] clog our soul with unwholesome vapors of all kinds" (quoted in Trachtenberg, *The Incorporation of America*, p. 185). Though he praised Crane's novel, when Howells himself turned to the representation of the slums in "New York Streets," in *Impressions and Experiences* (New York: Harper, 1909), he adopted the moral and social themes of charity writing and the aesthetic of the picturesque. (Much the same could be said of Howells's earlier representation in "Suburban Sketches" [1871]). Howells identifies a "terrible picturesque fact" in the suicide of a "Fallen Woman"; he imagines her "wickeder" and "simply horrible" lovers (quoted in Aaron, "Howells' 'Maggie,'" pp. 112–114). And though Crane often praised Howells in turn, he also criticized him for failing to live up to his own realist creed. Howells himself admitted his own polite limits. "The novelist," he wrote, "must endeavor to give exactly the effect of life. . . . I can never do it, for I was bred in a false school whose trammels I have never been quite able to burst" (Crane's and Howells's comments in Aaron, "Howells' 'Maggie,'" p. 116). As for Garland, though he too praised *Maggie*, he understood it in moralistic terms. "It creates the atmosphere of jungles," he wrote in review, "where vice festers and crime passes gloomily by." He went on to criticize the story for being "only a fragment. It is typical only of the worst elements of the alley." He suggested that Crane "should delineate the families living on the next street, who live lives of heroic purity and hopeless hardship" (Hamlin Garland, "An Ambitious French Novel and a Modest American Story," in Gullason, *Maggie: A Girl of the Streets*, p. 144).

Various literary critics have located Crane's sources in French novels of the slums;

specifically, they have noticed extensive similarities between Crane's *Maggie* and Zola's *L'Assommoir*, which appeared in an American translation in 1879. Lars Ahnebrink, for instance, finds that "Crane was indebted to *L'Assommoir* . . . as to plot, characterization, technique, episodes and particulars." But Crane's ethnography goes beyond Zola's, just as it goes beyond that of most of his American contemporaries. Zola has by no means dispensed with moralism, as Crane has: the Frenchman's protagonist, Nana, "était dans le vice comme un poisson dans l'eau" ("was in vice like a fish in water"), and his description of Nana's coworkers focuses particularly on their moral decay. As Ahnebrink admits, on the subject of moral decay, "Crane showed more restraint" than Zola (Lars Ahnebrink, "Zola as Literary Model for *Maggie*," in Gullason, *Maggie: A Girl of the Streets*, pp. 92–93).

77. These intellectual resources do not include modern sociology and anthropology. Though Riis's notion of immigrant "ways" and Crane's conception of "social forms" are similar to the modern sociological and anthropological notions of ethnicity and culture, it is not the case that their ethnographic perspectives have been borrowed from these disciplines. To begin with, it was not until after 1900 that the anthropologist Franz Boas formulated the relativist notion of culture (as opposed to the humanist notion of the progressive accumulation of human creativity—culture as art, science, government, refinement). And it was not until after the appearance of Riis's and Crane's books that sociologists began to develop the concept of social, as opposed to physical, heredity—that James M. Baldwin wrote about imitation, E. A. Ross about "social control," and William Graham Sumner about "folkways" and "mores" (George Stocking, *Race, Culture, and Evolution: Essays in the History of Anthropology* [New York: Free Press, 1968], pp. 195–269; James M. Baldwin, *Mental Development in the Child and the Race*, 2nd ed. [New York: Macmillan, 1895]; Edward Alsworth Ross, *Social Control: A Survey of the Foundations of Order* [New York: Macmillan, 1901]; William Graham Sumner, *Folkways: A Study of the Sociological Importance of Usages, Manners, Customs, Mores, and Morals* [Boston: Ginn, 1906]). Before the 1890s, sociologists had not begun to divide racial influence from the forces of culture and environment; they had not questioned the popular Lamarckian and Spencerian ideas that acquired traits could be inherited. And Riis at least, like almost everyone else at the time, clearly takes these older ideas for granted. The "mendacity" (88) of his Jews, for instance, is both social and racial. They have a "strong commercial instinct" (99) and are naturals at "mental arithmetic" (84), while their thrift also grew out of particular conditions in the Old Country: "Become an overmastering passion with these people who come here in droves from Eastern Europe to escape persecution, from which freedom could be bought only with gold, it has enslaved them in bondage worse than that from which they fled" (78–79). In the same way, Riis's Chinese men are characterized as essentially stealthy and secretive, even though he speculates that perhaps they learned these traits from the "attitude of American civilization toward the stranger" (69). Riis can provide ethnographic details without ever doubting his racialism. (Numbers in parentheses refer to pages in *How the Other Half Lives*.)

78. "During the season to which the present chronicle belongs," writes H. H. Boyesen in the early 1890s, "it was a favorite diversion in fashionable circles to make up what were called 'slumming parties'" (Hjalmer Hjorth Boyesen, *Social Strugglers: A Novel* [New York: Scribner's, 1893], p. 259).

79. *New York Times*, Jan. 1858, quoted in Albert Parry, *Garrets and Pretenders: A History of Bohemianism in America* (New York: Dover, 1960), p. 57.

80. This general pursuit of the picturesque that Riis comes to practice as a newspaper-

man marks a break with the American tradition of picturesque criminal reporting, which began in the 1830s and gave birth to muckraking at the turn of the century. *How the Other Half Lives* did grow directly out of Riis's police reports for New York newspapers, and Thomas Leonard has noticed that "his work honors conventions of beat reporting. Much of his documentary is told as an exciting chronicle of what Riis called 'raiding parties'" (Leonard, *The Power of the Press*, p. 154). But while police reporting was, like Riis's tenement study, highly invested in the spectacle of the urban underworld, it was obviously confined to the subject of crime. And while many muckraking reporters were, like Riis, eager tour guides of the slums, their connoisseurship was, again, mostly limited to the criminal; for Lincoln Steffens, Upton Sinclair, Josiah Flynt Willard, Charles E. Russel, and *McClure's Magazine*, the urban scandal and spectacle was primarily the collusion between government officials and crooks (Leonard, *The Power of the Press*, chapter 5; Upton Sinclair, *The Jungle* [1906; New York: Penguin, 1965]). Riis touches on this subject in *How the Other Half Lives* but does not dwell on it. For instance, he refers in passing to government corruption in New York as an earlier problem that confronted the city. He alludes to Boss Tweed and his Tammany cohorts as a "band of political cutthroats, the legitimate outgrowth of life on the tenement-house level" (3). In *The Battle with the Slum*, Riis does dwell on the subject of political corruption at much greater length.

Riis inherited a touristic tradition from the large daily American newspaper, with its expanded definition of journalism. The large daily, meanwhile, owed a significant debt for its picturesque style to Charles Dickens, and it may be that Riis borrowed some of his style from Dickens directly. Sam Bass Warner finds that "Riis, like most journalists of day, imitated the style of Charles Dickens" (Warner, Editor's Introduction, pp. xv–xvi). And, as David Leviatin points out, Riis was a "youth weaned on the works of Charles Dickens" (Leviatin, "Framing the Poor," p. 12).

81. "William Randolph Hearst's *New York Journal* created the modern sports page in 1896, just when its front pages filled with atrocity stories of Spanish brutes in Cuba" (Higham, "The Re-orientation of American Culture in the 1890s," p. 32).

82. Lane, *Jacob A. Riis and the American City*, p. 30–31.

83. Joseph Pulitzer, quoted in Trachtenberg, *The Incorporation of America*, p. 124.

84. Pulitzer quoted in Lane, *Jacob A. Riis and the American City*, p. 31.

85. Trachenburg, *The Incorporation of America*, pp. 124–126.

86. Lane, *Jacob A. Riis and the American City*, pp. 29, 34.

87. Riis, *The Making of an American*, quoted in Hales, *Silver Cities*, p. 167.

88. Crane's inability to find a publisher for *Maggie* is a good indication of the scandal—especially when one considers that at the time there was a slum fiction fad, and certain books about the poor were becoming veritable bestsellers (for example, Edward Townsend's *Chimmie Fadden* [New York: Lovell, Coryell, 1895]).

89. For an example of this latter view, see Alfred Kazin, *On Native Grounds: An Interpretation of Modern American Prose Literature* (New York: Reynal and Hitchcock, 1942), pp. 15–19.

90. Amy Kaplan, *The Social Construction of American Realism* (Chicago: U of Chicago P, 1988), p. 7, my italics.

91. Michel Foucault, *Discipline and Punish: The Birth of the Prison*, trans. Alan Sheridan (New York: Vintage, 1977).

92. Kaplan, *The Social Construction of American Realism*, p. 7.

93. It is interesting to note, in this regard, that Guy Debord "recanted" his *Society*

of the Spectacle (Detroit: Black and Red, 1970) after reading Foucault's *Discipline and Punish*.

94. Mark Seltzer, *Henry James and the Art of Power* (Ithaca: Cornell UP, 1984), pp. 41, 151, 140, 131.

95. Seltzer, "Statistical Persons," pp. 84, 85.

96. Leviatin, "Framing the Poor," p. 4.

97. Riis, *How the Other Half Lives*, p. 169.

98. Riis, *The Children of the Poor*, p. 84.

99. Riis, *How the Other Half Lives*, p. 168.

100. One could certainly claim that Crane and Riis are *like* policemen in certain ways; one could likewise compare them to other supervisory agents. One could argue that Crane is *like* a social worker in *Maggie* and that Riis is *like* a social worker in *How the Other Half Lives*: they are concerned with some of the same issues as social workers (the ways, aims, and home conditions of the poor) and use some of the same methods (careful and repeated investigations of the poor, case-by-case treatment, attention to the family life of problem children); they sometimes have a similar outlook (environmentalist, nonmoralistic). An analogy could certainly be made. In literary criticism, written works are most often related to social practices in the form of analogy: literature is seen to absorb and reproduce the logic of society. As Seltzer puts it, there is an "aesthetic duplication and formalizing . . . of social practices."

I would not argue that Riis's and Crane's written works followed and developed the logic of disciplinary techniques. Nor would I make an analogy. Rather, I would make a historical argument: Riis and Crane and many others (notably settlement house workers) were mining the material (constituting it, really) that social work would build itself around and treat, not only more rigorously, but in a different, and partially disciplinary, way. (Crane uses it to challenge moralism, to present spectacle, to develop an aesthetic; Riis also uses it to win sympathy, to encourage environmental reform, to substantiate ethical judgment; social work will use it to oversee and classify individuals, to mark them out for different treatments, to attempt to provide instruction and therapy for them.) And through the agency of social work, Riis's and Crane's and others' discoveries would be annexed and colonized by large-scale social institutions—such as the asylum, the hospital, and the justice system—which also employ, in part, disciplinary practices. The texts themselves are not duplications or institutionalizations of existing disciplinary technologies; rather, through the creation of new categories of perception, they help make possible new reform practices, some of which are disciplinary.

And some of which are not. There is a final problem to construing Riis's and Crane's texts as extensions of disciplinary power. Crane's and Riis's social ethnography and their psychology, Crane's residence in the slums and Riis's slum tourism and social reform projects involve technical breakthroughs in the realm of power; they do not simply make possible innovations of existing forms. These practices of knowledge and programs of power involve a new politics of the body, which will be discussed in chapter 6. (For histories of social work, see James Leiby, *A History of Social Welfare and Social Work in the United States* [New York: Columbia UP, 1978] and Ray Lubove, *The Professional Altruist: Social Work as a Career, 1880–1930* [Cambridge, Mass.: Harvard UP, 1965].)

101. I will discuss this change in political technology in chapter 6. While Seltzer does observe that "Crane insists on the ways in which the power of seeing is quickly disrupted by the pleasures of seeing" ("Statistical Persons," p. 85), and thus broaches a fundamental

tension in realist texts, he does not acknowledge that these pleasures of seeing are themselves connected to another sort of power relation, a politics of spectacle that is becoming tremendously influential in American life.

102. Stange, *Symbols of Ideal Life*, pp. xv, 13.

103. Leviatin, "Framing the Poor," pp. 29–30.

104. Lears, *No Place of Grace*, p. xv.

105. Leviatin, "Framing the Poor," p. 30.

106. Trachtenberg, *The Incorporation of America*, p. 141.

107. Stange, *Symbols of Ideal Life*, p. 18.

108. Kaplan, *The Social Construction of American Realism*, p. 51.

109. Crane placed an inscription on some of his original copies of the novel: "It is probable that the reader of this small thing may consider the Author to be a bad man, but, obviously, this is a matter of small consequence to The Author" (Crane, *Stephen Crane: Letters*, p. 14).

110. Kaplan, *The Social Construction of American Realism*, pp. 8, 55.

111. Leviatin, "Framing the Poor," p. 29.

112. Looking beyond the literature on urban realism to more general accounts of the development of modern American society, one does encounter a popular critical tradition that recognizes two opposing cultures at the turn of the century. But this criticism tends to privilege Protestant and disciplinary culture and to denigrate the culture of consumption and spectacle. If I address the question of ethics in this book, it is partly because this "oppositional" criticism maintains that the rise of consumer capitalism has led to an absolute decline in morality. It decries the moral devastation of consumer capitalism and sometimes attempts to identify literary works that stand in opposition to this devastation. (Walter Michaels has called this criticism "oppositional" and discussed it in his *The Gold Standard and the Logic of Naturalism* [Berkeley: U of California P, 1987], p. 14, note 16.)

Christopher Lasch's *The Culture of Narcissism* (1978) and Jackson Lears's *No Place of Grace* (1981) are examples of this sort of critical work; aligning himself with Philip Rieff and Daniel Bell as well as Lasch, Lears declares that he is "disturbed by the signs of spiritual sterility which surround us in the late twentieth century." Lears coins the term "antimodernists" to describe cultural players, among them certain imperialists, Orientalists, and naturalist writers, who opposed the dawning consumer culture. Lears contends that though "the accommodation was never complete," antimodernists in effect reinforced "the shift from a Protestant to a therapeutic world view," easing "their own and others' adjustments to a streamlined culture of consumption." Reasonably, it seems to me, he sees antimodernist activities as a mix of "accommodation and protest." In fact, I find Lears's analysis indispensable and see my slum aficionados as cousins to his antimodernists.

But I part company with him when he goes on to valorize the antimodernists' protest, to denigrate their accommodation, and to characterize the "therapeutic world view" as "self-absorbed nihilism" and a "nonmorality." He writes: "The older morality embodied the 'producer culture' of an industrializing, entrepreneurial society; the newer nonmorality embodied the 'consumer culture' of a bureaucratic corporate state" (Lears, *No Place of Grace*, pp. xiii–xviii). I find two related problems with Lears's critique. First, Lears is not always clear that some of his antimodernists not only opposed the nascent consumer culture but also (and sometimes principally) the well-entrenched Victorian respectability. Second, spiritual aspects of antimodernism such as the value placed on intense experience and struggle, which Lears seems to validate as protest, inform the "therapeutic world view" he attacks.

More generally, Lears's label of "nonmorality" to describe this newer worldview, along with his valorization of producer culture, strike me as arbitrary and nostalgic. I suggest instead that industrialization—and the accompanying cultural movements of the 1890s, including the fascination with the slums—have led to a decline in an already sentimentalized Protestant morality and the rise of an alternative psychological morality. (On sentimentalized Protestant morality, see Douglas, *The Feminization of American Culture*, for example, pp. 6–10. Douglas talks about "the process of sentimentalization" that, between 1820 and 1875, "did so much to gut Calvinist orthodoxy." This process was driven by northeastern clergymen and middle-class women, who were becoming "the prime consumers of American culture," including religious culture. It should be noted that Douglas's work has been seen as problematic by American feminists, beginning with Jane Tompkins. Much of the controversy centers on the value of sentimentalism, which many feminists do not see as categorically debilitating for women. See Jane Tompkins, *Sensational Designs: The Cultural Work of American Fiction, 1790–1860* [New York: Oxford UP, 1985], chapter 5, especially p. 217, note 3. On the debate between Tompkins and Douglas, see also Laura Wexler, "Tender Violence: Literary Eavesdropping, Domestic Fiction, and Educational Reform" in *The Culture of Sentiment*, ed. Shirley Samuels [New York: Oxford UP, 1992], pp. 9–38, especially pp. 9–15.)

I would argue that this alternative morality, of which therapeutic practices form a part, does not, as Lears asserts, "lack any but the vaguest ethical . . . commitments" (*No Place of Grace*, p. 306); rather, these ethical commitments are different from those of mid-nineteenth-century Protestant ethics. This alternative morality may indeed be vague in terms of a code of conduct, but it is quite clear about ethical commitments and, to use Foucault's terms, the "*ethical work* that one performs on oneself" in order to "transform oneself into the ethical subject of one's behavior" (Foucault, *The Use of Pleasure*, p. 27). To begin with, if this sentimentalized Protestant ethics put a premium on one's ethical commitment to others, specifically one's family, this psychological morality stresses the ethical commitment to oneself and one's peers and often involves a further commitment to resist repressive authority. The commitment to oneself involves exploring and developing one's self or individuality, often with peers, and often despite the constraints of authority. This sort of commitment and practice, then, may be "self-absorbed" and may dovetail with consumerism, but it is hardly "nihilistic" or "nonmoral."

(In Lears's account, as in Lasch's, therapeutic activity, self-exploration, and personal growth are not only demeaned as selfish and thus nonmoral; they are characterized as fraudulent, thin, unproductive, or failed. For example, Lasch writes: "[T]his 'massive self-examination' has produced few indications of self-understanding, personal or collective" [Lasch, *The Culture of Narcissism*, p. 15]. Thus Lears asserts that "calls for personal liberation have begun to ring hollow" and "the quest for alternative values gradually has become a casual choice," while self-exploration is "fated to frustration." These activities of self-development are seen to be failing—but for whom? It is hard to imagine that gays, lesbians, and feminists, for example, would concur with his perception. It seems to me that Lears simply judges this new moral activity in terms of traditional ethics, which valorizes relations to family members and a stable, "coherent sense of selfhood." When Lears does seem to entertain the idea that instead of a failure to develop a stable self, there is an alternative vision of the self—what I would call a new ethical aim—he switches the ground of his attack and finds that "a self in endless development is perfectly attuned to an economy based on pointless growth and ceaseless destruction." But this maneuver seems to me glib. It could just as easily be claimed that a self dedicated to a work ethic and a respect for authority is "perfectly attuned" to such an economy. The relationship between the American economy of "pointless growth and ceaseless destruction" and this alternative vision of the self is simply more complicated [Lears, *No Place of Grace*, pp. 305–307].)

Moreover, a general ethical commitment to others, an ethical relationship to strangers—for example, to the poor—does not disappear; it takes a different form. Riis's social programs constitute a mixed ethical bag, but to be sure, some of them are aimed at the new ethical substance of self-esteem or individuality. And though this book does not argue in general for (or against) this new morality, it is worth noting that some of its values seem quite an improvement on those of the older Protestant culture. It is hard to argue, I think, that the harsh moralism that characterized much of the approach to the urban poor in the 1820s (with its blanket dismissals of the "vicious poor"), say, is preferable to the social work of the 1920s. Lears's critique is more incisive when he claims that our therapeutic culture seems to lack commitments outside the self. But he essentially dismisses important exceptions, including such institutions of this culture as social work. Lears may reasonably find institutions of "welfare capitalism" suspect and criticize social engineers for "devalu[ing] public life . . . by insulating government from the electorate . . . [and] reducing political issues to psychological issues" (*No Place of Grace*, p. 304), but first of all, many of these social engineers nonetheless had commitments beyond the self, and second, the "value" of public life for the urban poor in the middle of the nineteenth century, and the extent of their representation in government, can likewise hardly be called encouraging.

(Lears's account of Crane's bohemian and "liberationist" successors, including the Greenwich Village intellectuals, the expatriate writers of the 1920s, and the Beat writer Jack Kerouac, is likewise reductionist and unsatisfying. For example, he claims that Kerouac "unwittingly caricatured the proliferating, insatiable wants of consumer capitalism" [Lears, *No Place of Grace*, p. 306] in the famous passage in "On the Road" in which Kerouac's narrator is walking "in the Denver colored section, wishing I were Negro, feeling that the best the white world had offered me was not enough ecstasy for me, not enough life, joys, kicks, darkness, music, not enough night." To say that Kerouac's yearning here is a caricature of consumerism is to miss a middle-class young man's flirtation with the slums which is anticorporate, anticareerist, and antiluxury—if also arguably consumerist as well as classist and racist. We will return to Crane's successors, including Kerouac, in chapter 6.

My overarching point is that the social-welfare descendants of Riis and the bohemian successors to Crane—in short, the middle-class relations to the slums—are *not* nonmoral and *not* without commitments beyond the self, even if this morality and these commitments are in part consumerist and objectionable.

Lears's attempt to separate out moral social protest and nonmoral individual fulfillment seems to be fundamentally misguided; it misses the fact that "the dominant ethos of individual fulfillment" generally involves, as I have suggested, a concomitant resistance to authority precisely because authority is seen to prevent the development of true individuality. For example, I think Lears is romanticizing the peace movement when he applauds "the principled opposition to the bureaucratic 'rationality' of the Vietnam War" but finds that this movement "lost moral force and faltered" when it "succumbed to the dominant ethos of individual fulfillment"; he fails to acknowledge that this opposition would have been impossible without the existence of an anti-authoritarian ethics of self-development and personal liberation, from which it largely sprang [Lears, *No Place of Grace*, pp. 305–307]. For an account of the coexistence of individual fulfillment and social commitment from the very start of 1960s political protest, see Bill Heath's thoroughly researched historical fiction about Freedom Summer, *The Children Bob Moses Led* [Minneapolis: Milkweed, 1995].)

Though I am indebted to Lears, Douglas, Trachtenberg, and Higham in my treatment of cultural shifts in the 1890s, the work that is perhaps closest to mine in theme is Warren Susman's history of identity in *Culture as History* (1984). Like Lasch and Lears, Susman identifies two cultures: "the original tradition" of "hard work, self-denial, and even sacrifice" in opposition to a "culture of abundance," "with its emphasis on pleasure and self-fulfillment and play"—what oppositional critics call "'consumer culture' and the 'therapeutic society.'" But he faults "the critic of the culture of abundance" for using terms that "deliberately limit the dimensions of that culture in ways designed to denigrate and criticize it." Susman goes on to say, "Let me make my position clear. . . . Buying things (consumption) and getting professional help (therapy) do not, I think, represent things that are intrinsically wrong. Nor does entertainment enjoyed by huge numbers of people (mass culture). . . . [I]t would be a serious methodological error not to attempt to understand the culture on its own terms" (*Culture as History*, pp. xxviii–xxix).

In his well-known essay called "'Personality' and the Making of Twentieth-Century Culture," Susman observes a change in the nature of American identity that accompanies the rise of the new corporate and consumer society. He describes the demise of the old "culture of character": the idea of character, he argues, with its premium on self-mastery and obedience, fit the world of production and entrepreneurship, but the notion of personality proved to be more suited to a world that encouraged the self-fulfillment of consumption and required "likability" for corporate promotion and success. By examining artifacts from high, middle, and low culture—self-development manuals and the motion picture industry as well as novels—Susman charts the construction, just after the turn of the century, of a new "culture of personality" (Susman, *Culture as History*, pp. 271–285).

Where Susman talks about a culture of personality, I talk about an ethics of entertainment and self-esteem (that informs not only representations but also social programs or politics). While Susman describes the change to a new consumer and corporate culture of personality that prizes unique personal qualities and a performing self that attracts others, I outline, through the media of Riis and Crane and their forays into the slums, a portion of the beginnings of a transformation from an ethics of character, self-control, and achievement to one of self-esteem, excitement, and spectacle: a transformation that I associate not only with the rise of consumer culture but also with Higham's, Douglas's, and Lears's fin de siècle "quest for intense experience" and masculine vitality in reaction to a culture perceived as "overcivilized" and "feminized." My study attempts to expand on Susman's alteration in forms of American identity, but while Susman tries to describe a general transformation in American identity, I focus on changes in the conception of the urban American poor.

While Susman locates the beginning of his cultural transformation in the middle of the first decade of the twentieth century, I find harbingers of this change in the previous decade. While Susman provides an overview and touches on numerous figures, I concentrate on just two writers, both of whom published their important works in the 1890s.

It seems to me, then, that something was stirring in regard to identity a decade before the starting date Susman sets for "another vision of self." Susman himself recognizes a number of antecedent "symptoms" of the change; he writes that "there is a clear and growing evidence of an awareness of significant change in the social order, especially after

1880." In consensus with a number of other contemporary American historians, he finds that the social order was changing "from a producer to a consumer society, an order of economic accumulation to one of disaccumulation, industrial capitalism to finance capitalism, scarcity to abundance, disorganization to high organization." And in regard to the awareness of these changes at the time,

> symptoms are easily suggested: what was called "American nervousness" and the various efforts at its diagnosis; the rash of utopian writings; the development of systematic sociological and economic analysis in the academic world; the development in government and public journals of a view of the need for "objective" and "scientific" gathering of data and treatment of social ills; and, even more important, the development of psychological and psychiatric studies. (Susman, *Culture as History*, p. 274–275)

I would like to add to Susman's list of changes in the social order the burgeoning of a culture of spectacle, whose career had special ties to the slums. Previous to the development of motion pictures, which Susman does note, there was the expansion of photography (in books and newspapers), the creation of the large daily newspaper, the sophistication and proliferation of advertising, and the growth of live theater. Significantly, these new media found large audiences, as well as sensational subject matter, in the slums. And to Susman's list of "symptoms," I would like to add a growing literature on the slums, and, specifically, writings that challenged the generally accepted moral evaluation of the poor (which leaned heavily on the idea of moral character) and that proposed an alternative or supplementary notion of identity.

My theoretical twist is to see this alteration as ethical transformation. If this book makes a methodological contribution to American Studies or the study of realism, it is to rethink morality and to reintroduce this term into the discussion. Again, this book centers on a photojournalist and a fiction writer, but it is neither a meditation on the relationship between images and writing nor an investigation of the interpenetration of documentary and fictional language and tropes. (For a brilliant example of the first, see Michael Fried's *Realism, Writing, Disfiguration*, on Crane and the painter Thomas Eakins. For an important example of the second, see Stange's *Symbols of Ideal Life* on Riis and the literary developments of his period.) Rather, this book is concerned with making aesthetic assessments of works in various media—photographs, documentary prose, *and* fiction—in terms of their ethical valence.

Chapter 1

1. Page numbers in parentheses refer to Jacob Riis, *How the Other Half Lives*.
2. Brace, *The Dangerous Classes of New York*, pp. 147–164.
3. For a sampling of writings that take up these issues in regard to the urban poor, see also Tuckerman, *On the Elevation of the Poor* (1874); Walter Channing, "An Address on the Prevention of Pauperism" (Boston: Office of the Christian World, 1843); Reverend Edwin Hubbell Chapin, *Humanity in the City* (New York: DeWitt and Davenport, 1854); Helen Campbell, *Prisoners of Poverty: Women Wage-Workers, Their Trades and Their Lives* (Boston: Roberts, 1887); and William T. Elsing, "Life in New York Tenement Houses as Seen by a City Missionary," in *The Poor in Great Cities: The Problems and What Is Going to Solve Them* (New York: Scribner's and Sons, 1895).

For instance, Campbell's book devotes most of its pages to exposing unjust working conditions and wages. But it also addresses the host of other themes native to the genre. In the course of a few pages in her chapter called "Under the Bridge and Beyond," she touches on most of them: she refers to crime ("little by little . . . the percentage of crime ceased to represent the largest portion of the inhabitants"), to vice and overcrowding ("the myriad who pass up and down . . . have small conception what thousands are packed away in the great tenements . . . or what depth of vileness flaunts itself openly when day is done"), to the lack of sunlight and the prevalence of filth ("sunshine has no place in these rooms . . . , the unspeakable filth ruling in tangible and intangible forms, sink and sewer and closet uniting in a common and all-pervading stench"), to disease ("the death rate has come within normal limits"), to forms of employment and habits of intemperance ("the men are chiefly 'longshoremen . . . varying this occupation with long seasons of drinking. . . . [T]he women scrub offices, peddle fruit . . . , take in washing, share, many of them, in the drinking bouts"), to immigrant groups and their different relations to their surroundings ("each nationality in the swarming tenements representing a distinct type of dirt and a distinct method of dealing with it and in it"), to the corruption of children ("hiding behind doors or in corners, or, grown bolder, seeking no concealment, children hardly more than babies teach one another . . . new facts of foulness"), and to the agencies dedicated to the amelioration of the slums and the need for further reform ("no Board of Health or of Sanitary Inspectors has yet been able to alter, save here and there, the facts that are a portion of the tenement-house system") (*Prisoners of Poverty*, pp. 126–130).

See also the legislative and health department reports for the city of New York that Riis cites in his work: for example, *Report of Select Committee of Assembly* (New York, 1857); *New York Health Department Report* (New York, 1866); *Citizen's Council of Hygiene's Report* (New York, 1866); *Report of Board of Health* (New York, 1869); *New York Health Department Report* (New York, 1870).

4. Chapin, *Humanity in the City*, pp. 190–191.

5. Brace, *The Dangerous Classes of New York*, pp. 26, 55–56. The quoted portion is from a report by Mr. Dupuy, Visitor of the Children's Aid Society of the First Ward.

6. Channing, "An Address on the Prevention of Pauperism," pp. 44–45. Of physical suffering and poverty, he remarks: "These all have an end. Death comes to end all bodily misery."

7. Brace, *The Dangerous Classes of New York*, p. 29.

8. Riis, *The Battle with the Slum*, p. 322.

9. Robert S. Corrigan, *An Introduction to C. S. Peirce* (Lanham, Md.: Rowman and Littlefield, 1993), pp. 52, 28–30.

10. John Dewey, *Human Nature* (New York: Henry Holt, 1922), pp. 16–17, 75, quoted in Edward C. Moore, *American Pragmatism: Peirce, James, and Dewey* (New York: Columbia UP, 1961), p. 220.

11. Charles Loring Brace even included drawings of slum figures in his *Dangerous Classes of New York*.

12. Ibid., p. 194.

13. The menace of order is reflected in the uncharacteristic deterioration of Brace's syntax. As if the bedlam of the scene has infected his prose style, the descriptive sentence quoted earlier grows to enormous length and takes on a monstrous form by the addition of ungrammatical sentence fragments. It is no coincidence that Brace restores the written

order with a statement of definitive moral condemnation: "They were . . . the dirtiest." While this statement does not adequately condemn the Italians for their implied sins against propriety (they are also overcrowded and disorderly), it has an emotional force (due to the superlative) and, most important, it has a simple orderliness that would be lacking in a catalogue of violations.

14. Signor A. E. Cerqua in Brace, *The Dangerous Classes of New York*, pp. 195–197.

15. Here is Chapin, at length: "And here, too, through the brilliant street, and the broad light of day, walks Purity, enshrined in the loveliest form of womanhood. And along the same street by night, attended by fitting shadows, strolls womanhood discrowned, clothed with painted shame." And: "Here sits the beggar, sick and pinched with cold; and there goes a man of no better flesh and blood, and no more authentic charter of soul, wrapped in comfort, and actually bloated with luxury. There issues the whine of distress, beside the glittering carriage wheels."

These were all popular figures in the depiction of the slums. Helen Campbell employs that of civilization and barbarism: "Not Africa in its most pestilential and savage form holds . . . more determined barbarians than nest together under many a roof within hearing of the rush and roar of the busy streets" (*Prisoners of Poverty*, pp. 160–161). Charles Loring Brace provides descriptions and an illustration of the "fallen woman" (*The Dangerous Classes of New York*, pp. 116–121). Walter Channing contrasts the rich and the poor and their sufferings ("An Address on the Prevention of Pauperism," p. 42).

16. Walter Channing makes a similar rhetorical move. "The saddest feature of poverty," wrote Walter Channing, "is not in its physical or mental suffering,—its hunger, its cold, its nakedness." It is not in the physical realm that he looks for

> the great, the leading calamity, and claim of pauperism. Much of all this is incident to every condition of man. Wealth has its sicknesses, and its acute pains. Its table is often spread in vain; and fevered limbs toss upon its downy beds. It has its full share of mental and moral sufferings in its apprehensions of changes of fortune . . . and then there is the heart-bitterness which the intemperance, the vice, and the profligacy of children, bring to the table of the rich, when they do come there, and which have their place at their luxurious firesides. It is not in its outward bearing, its physical suffering, that the deep misery of poverty lies. No. It is in its extreme, its dreadful helplessness, which shuts from its very soul the whole means of generous culture, and leaves the intellect a barren waste.

As Channing searches out the saddest feature of pauperism, physical suffering becomes but an "outward bearing" of poverty, a kind of dress or representation for an inner reality. By the time he compares the poor man to the rich man, the particular physical conditions of the poor man have been discarded, as if his nakedness or his rags are a superficial covering, like a rich man's gaudy clothes. Wealth has "its sicknesses" and "its full share of mental and moral sufferings," Channing intones, ignoring at this point that poverty has, in addition, the unique forms of physical discomfort he has just cited: "its hunger, its cold, its nakedness" ("An Address on the Prevention of Pauperism," p. 42).

17. Chapin, *Humanity in the City*, pp. 13–36.

18. In Riis, *The Children of the Poor*, back pages.

19. Brace, *The Dangerous Classes of New York*, p. 212, my italics.

20. This is not to imply that Riis's study among the tenements singlehandedly stakes

out a new genre. First of all, it is impossible to precisely date the beginning of an urban ethnographic literature, to locate the original text, because it is virtually impossible—and certainly fruitless—to establish an exact criteria for the genre. In this matter of a break-through in the discourse, one can only speak of significant differences between texts, not of absolute characteristics of a single text. One cannot speak of the first definitively ethno-graphic text, only, perhaps, of certain degrees of ethnographic saturation and ethno-graphic thoroughness. One can only point, for instance, to significant differences between *The Dangerous Classes of New York* and *How the Other Half Lives*, while admitting on the one hand that Brace's book contains certain ethnographic moments (its drawings of slum figures, its recording of curiosities) and on the other hand that Riis's book is still in large part traditional charitable writing. An argument could perhaps be made, then, that Brace's book actually inaugurates a genre that Riis's book more fully realizes. In any case, my point is that with the appearance of *How the Other Half Lives* there has been an identifiable change from the mid-nineteenth-century discourse on the poor, that something new has definitely entered the field of charitable writing.

Second, even if one decides to draw a somewhat arbitrary dividing line *after* Brace's book, the choice of Riis's book as the exemplary text of the new genre is perhaps even more arbitrary. Riis is by no means the only practitioner of urban travel literature around the turn of the century; nor does *How the Other Half Lives* make a clean break with tradi-tional charity writing. For many around the turn of the century, the boundaries of writing about poverty are being redrawn, and less tradition-bound and more purely aesthetic and ethnographic treatments of the poor are soon being produced by others, as well as Riis.

William Dean Howells's "New York Streets" (1896) in *Impressions and Experiences*, for example, is basically a travel piece in which the poor make up one of the sights. Though Alvan Francis Sanborn does indulge in some moral and social commentary about tene-ment-house life in *Moody's Lodging House and Other Tenement Sketches* (Boston: Copeland and Day, 1895), he explicitly distances himself from the charity writing and social-reform tradition. In his preface, he flatly declares that "the chapters that follow are not essays in sociology. . . . They are mere transcripts from life." And Sanborn does indeed push his ethnography further than Riis or Howells by characterizing not only the exotic appear-ances and strange ways of the poor but also their separate values. What leads him to this deeper ethnographic level is his general indifference toward the issue of social welfare: this detachment makes it possible for him to appreciate a portion of the slum population—the beggars—that everyone else agrees is a hazard. Hutchins Hapgood, in *Types of City Streets* (1910; New York: Garrett Press, 1970), and Josiah Flint Willard (who wrote under the pseudonym Josiah Flynt), in *Tramping with Tramps: Studies and Sketches of Vagabond Life* (New York: Century, 1899), had bohemian interests in "tramps" and "bums" that were comparable to Sanborn's.

Riis himself would go on to develop a travel writing of the slums that is nearly purified of charitable and reformist remnants; *Out of Mulberry Street, Stories of Tenement Life in New York City* (1898), and *Children of the Tenements* (New York: Macmillan, 1903), two of his later collections (which contain many of the same sketches) mostly do away with moral judgment and social sermonizing. But he would never come to appreciate slum dwellers the way Sanborn does the tramps. Though he was aware that the poor had their own ways and customs, he was unquestioningly committed to the notion that there was only one (proper) value system. There was no such thing for Riis as an entirely alternative set of ethics; what appeared to Sanborn as an alternative ethics would have appeared to Riis as immorality.

Chapter 2

1. Townsend, *Chimmie Fadden* (1895).

2. I am leaving Abraham Cahan's *Yekl and the Imported Bridegroom and Other Stories of the New York Ghetto* (New York: Dover, 1970) out of the following list because although it takes its reader to the streets of the Jewish ghetto (and even uses the word "ghetto" in its title), this short novel is arguably not slum literature as I have defined it but, rather, ethnic literature. See my introduction, note 19.

3. The whole passage reads:

> The Bowery, down in this crowded part of it, clamored to-day with hobgob-
> lin noises. Ragged boys were yelling "extra," in voices of unusual keenness,
> for that morning, at the Tombs near by, a quaking little Italian wife-murderer
> had been legally choked to death after four years' imprisonment and three
> elaborate trials. The broad street itself was crammed with vehicles, whose
> various wheels jarred upon its cobble-stones with every species of disso-
> nance, and across these, in a kind of vocal sword-thrust, darted the cry of the
> orange-and-banana vendors, with their laden carts trundled along the curb.
> (Edgar Fawcett, *The Evil That Men Do* [New York: Belford, 1889], p. 12)

4. "[I]n Minerva Court . . . there were frowzy, sleepy-looking women hanging out of their windows, gossiping with their equally unkempt and haggard neighbors; apathetic men sitting on the doorsteps, in their shirt-sleeves, smoking; a dull, dirty baby or two disporting itself in the gutter; while the sound of a melancholy accordion (the chosen instrument of poverty and misery) floated from an upper chamber" (Kate Douglas Wiggin, *Timothy's Quest: A Story for Anybody, Young or Old, Who Cares to Read It* [Boston: Houghton Mifflin, 1890], pp. 9–10).

5. The whole passage reads:

> They drove accidentally through one street that seemed gayer in perspective
> than an L road. The fire-escapes, with their light iron balconies and ladders of
> iron, decorated the lofty house fronts; the roadway and sidewalks and door-
> steps swarmed with children; women's heads seemed to show at every win-
> dow. In the basements, over which flights of high stone steps led to the tene-
> ments, were green-grocers' shops abounding in cabbages, and provision
> stores running chiefly to bacon and sausages, and cobblers' and tinners' shops,
> and the like, in proportion to the small needs of a poor neighborhood. Ash
> barrels lined the sidewalks, and garbage heaps filled the gutters; teams of all
> trades stood idly about; a peddler of cheap fruit urged his cart through the
> street, and mixed his cry with the joyous screams and shouts of the children
> and the scolding and gossiping voices of the women; the burly blue bulk of a
> policeman defined itself at the corner; a drunkard zigzagged down the side-
> walk toward him. . . .
>   . . . [I]t was as picturesque as a street in Naples or Florence . . . and
> . . . nobody came to paint it. (William Dean Howells, *A Hazard of New
> Fortunes* [New York: Dutton, 1952], pp. 197–200; 66–67).

6. "Women bare-headed, or wearing brass jewelry and gay-colored kerchiefs on their black hair, garnished the doorsteps, chattering like magpies, spending their lives in the

midst of an alien race in their amiable, out-of-door, Italian fashion. . . . [T]hese sun-browned children of the south . . . in their friendly gregariousness strove to counterfeit the life which they had left behind them in Naples and Palermo" (Boyeson, *Social Strugglers*, pp. 259, 263).

7. "In the street . . . , Sunday-dressed working people sauntered by; and on the corner . . . , a group of half-grown boys wearily killed the holiday, skylarking when the policeman was out of sight, and dispersing when he drew near. Within the house echoed the domestic noises of twenty families—doors slamming, children wailing, women scolding, boys hallooing, all mingling with the endless clatter of kitchen labors" (James W. Sullivan, *Tenement Tales of New York* [New York: Holt, 1895], pp. 48, 46–47).

8. This is the same man who wrote *Moody's Lodging House*, and his fascination with bums is also evident in this book. "Gawk is a genuine hobo, honestly proud of his profession, as genuine hoboes usually are. Judged by the standards of that profession, Gawk's orbit is circumscribed. Unlike the majority of his ilk, he makes no *villegiature* in the summer and no southern pilgrimage in the winter. . . . 'The city's good enough for me,' he says" (Alvan Francis Sanborn, *Meg McIntyre's Raffle and Other Stories* [Boston: Copeland and Day, 1896], p. 201).

Isaac Kahn Friedman, in his fictional *The Autobiography of a Beggar* (Boston: Small, Maynard, 1903), provides a first-person, vernacular "histree" of a beggar (p. 152).

9. The whole passage reads:

> On the fourth floor there is a suite of two rooms facing the street; from the window hangs a sign, "Madame Van Meer, Fortune-Teller." Poverty-stricken neighborhoods always abound with tellers of fortune. It is one of the ways the poor have of getting rich.
>
> The madame is a short, fat, coarse-featured woman who, when she is visible at all, is seen in a greasy wrapper. She has a parrot and three black cats. She is the kind of woman who goes with a parrot. . . .
>
> Across the street is another tenement just like ours—the one building might constantly be mistaken for another did not Malachy's saloon occupy its first floor and mark the difference.
>
> Vogel is over at Malachy's, half maddened by the vile liquor. He dances about and screams like an ecstatic dervish. He harangues incoherently against an unjust social system that will not let a willing man work. Even if his harangue were coherent few could understand him; for at such times he prefers his good German to his broken English. (Isaac Kahn Friedman, *Poor People: A Novel* [Boston and New York: Houghton Mifflin, 1900], pp. 90, 10–11)

10. Dreiser describes the nightly labor of a "religionist" who tries to secure lodging funds for every homeless man who approaches him for help:

> The motley company had increased to ten. . . . They were peevish, crusty, silent, eyeing nothing in particular and moving their feet. . . .
>
> They fell into a sort of broken, ragged line. One might see, now, some of the chief characteristics by contrast. There was a wooden leg in the line. Hats were all drooping, a group that would ill become a second-hand Hester Street basement collection. Trousers were all warped and frayed at the bottom and coats worn and faded. . . .

[Among] those . . . whose beds were safe, a relaxed air was apparent. The strain of uncertainty being removed, [they were] talking with moderate freedom and some leaning toward sociability. Politics, religion, the state of the government, some newspaper sensations, and the more notorious facts the world over, found mouthpieces and auditors there. Cracked and husky voices pronounced forcibly upon odd matters. (Theodore Dreiser, *Sister Carrie* [Boston: Houghton Mifflin, 1959], pp. 390–392)

11. The whole passage reads:

It was one of the laws of the *veselija* that no one goes hungry. . . . A charming informality was one of the characteristics of this celebration. The men wore their hats, or, if they wished, they took them off, and their coats with them; they ate when and where they pleased, and moved as often as they pleased. There were to be speeches and singing, but no one had to listen who did not care to; if he wished, meantime, to speak or sing himself, he was perfectly free. The resulting medley of sound distracted no one. (Upton Sinclair, *The Jungle*. p. 7)

12. The whole passage reads:

There is no swarming like that of Israel when once Israel has got a start, and the scene here bristled, at every step, with the signs and sounds, immitigable, unmistakable, of a Jewry that had burst all bonds. . . .

The children swarmed above all—here was multiplication with a vengeance; and the number of very old persons, of either sex, was almost equally remarkable; the very old persons being in equal vague occupation of the doorstep, pavement, curbstone, gutter, roadway, and every one alike using the street for overflow. As overflow, in the whole quarter, is the main fact of life. (Henry James, *The American Scene* [London: Harper, 1907], pp. 130–132)

13. We will explore this tension in Riis's text (a tension which Riis is apparently unconscious of) in chapter 3. We will also explore Riis's analogous concern with color and colorfulness, as well as Crane's different obsession with color.

14. Edward Waterman Townsend, *A Daughter of the Tenements* (New York: Coryell and Company, 1895), pp. 58–61, my italics.

15. James, *The American Scene*, pp. 123–129.

16. For some of these writers (as well as others not mentioned), the representation of the slums (in any form) is itself a sideline. For the most part, *Timothy's Quest, Social Strugglers*, and *Sister Carrie* are not set in the slums. Likewise, Josiah Gilbert Holland's *Nicholas Minturn* (New York: Scribner, Armstrong, 1877), Charles Joseph Bellamy's *The Breton Mills: A Romance* (New York: G. P. Putnam and Sons, 1879), and Helen Campbell's *Mrs. Herndon's Income: A Novel* (Boston: Roberts Brothers, 1886), among other novels, treat the slums in passing.

17. Rebecca Harding Davis, *Life in the Iron Mills* (1861; New York: Feminist, 1972), pp. 45–50.

18. Quoted in Eric Solomon, *Stephen Crane: From Parody to Realism* (Cambridge, Mass.: Harvard UP, 1966), p. 25.

19. Friedman, *Poor People*, pp. 161, 37.

20. Fawcett, *The Evil That Men Do*, p. 70.

21. Fawcett describes her experience of conscience at great length, and I provide more of this passage to give a sense of the moralistic hammering the reader often receives:

> That [conscience] cried to her in every brilliant she strung about her throat, every crimson or purple in which she clad her shape. Her outraged moral sense demanded some narcotic; love had no part in her new mode of life; or, if its influence entered there, the effect was one of reminded massacre and on-slaught. She had murdered sentiment, but she could lay its haunting ghost. Wine brought her peace, and the hands that paid her the wage of self-abase-ment lifted to her lips the cup that deadened remorse. . . . Horrible mo-ments of fatigue and self-disgust would be banished with draughts of stimu-lant. . . . There were times when she felt like shrinking from the very ardors that she aroused, as though they had been leprous and pestilent. (Fawcett, *The Evil That Men Do*, pp. 263, 268, 255–256, 295–297, 306–309)

Even in a novel as antimoralistic as Sinclair's *The Jungle*, there is a critical moral episode for the protagonist. The author regularly interrupts his narrative to preach about the social (and not moral) determinants of vices such as uncleanliness, lack of thrift, vagabondage, intemperance, and even prostitution (prostitutes, for instance, are seen as a "surplus labour army," "struggling for life under the stern system of Nature" [Sinclair, *The Jungle*, p. 262]). Nonetheless, the immigrant hero, who has been driven, out of an epic misery, to drink and illicit sex, undergoes remorse.

> Jurgis could not help but being made miserable by his conscience. It was the ghost that would not down. . . .
>
> Ah, what agony was that, what despair, when the tomb of memory was rent open and the ghosts of his life came forth to scourge him! What terror to see what he had been, and now could never be . . . he writhing and suffo-cating in the mire of his own vileness! (Sinclair, *The Jungle*, pp. 263–265)

22. Horatio Alger, *Ragged Dick; or, Street Life in New York* (New York: Collier, 1962), pp. 215, 129.

23. The author reports that "his Irish blue eyes were bright with a light new to them" (Sullivan, *Tenement Tales of New York*, pp. 18–19).

The artistic hero in *Poor People* succeeds in mastering his addiction to alcohol and thus in earning the hand in marriage of the narrator's noble daughter. The narrator celebrates both the victory and the moral struggle in an epilogue: "In the tenement, art battled poverty and came forth proud and triumphant from the combat, blessing its enemy for the strength that the struggle gave, perceiving that in luxury and sloth the shield tarnishes, and rust dulls the edge of the sword locked in idleness" (Friedman, *Poor People*, pp. 161, 37, 243).

24. The paragraph quoted earlier continues:

> Men staggered past, their bodies bent almost double under what seemed im-possible loads of clothing they were carrying to and from the sweaters' and the workshop-homes; women carrying similar bundles on their heads . . . hurried along . . . ; the children . . . were silent too, and had no games.

. . . In the dress of none was any bright color seen, and the only sounds were the occasional cry of a hurt child, the snarling of low-browed men who solicited trade for the clothing stores . . . ; and always, as the grinding ocean surf mutters an accompaniment to all other shore sounds—always, always, always!—was heard the whirring monotone of the sewing machine. (Townsend, *A Daughter of the Tenements*, pp. 61–70)

25. Ibid., p. 90.

26. Howells, *A Hazard of New Fortunes*, pp. 199–200.

27. Boyeson, *Social Strugglers*, p. 265.

28. Fawcett, *The Evil That Men Do*, pp. 87–88.

29. Sometimes the moral commentary is hopeful: the "nuggets of pure gold" that Friedman attempts to excavate from the "mine" of the tenement are not distinctive colors and actions but moral joys; it is with the "Angel of Charity and Mercy" that he descends into the depths of the slums.

30. Davis, *Life in the Iron Mills*, pp. 11–12.

31. James seems so intent, in fact, on remaining untroubled—or unsullied—by his visit to the slums that he refuses to see the (well-known) social evil in the tenements. On viewing a "'tenement-house,'" James finds it a "charming little structure" and has to ask his local guide "to what latent vice it owed its stigma." The guide replies that it pays "for its name by harbouring some five-and-twenty families." James then simply skirts the conventional social issue of overcrowding (and its attendant ills), claiming, "but this, exactly, was the way it testified—this circumstance of simultaneous enjoyment by five-and-twenty families on 'tenement' lines, of conditions so little sordid, so highly 'evolved'" (James, *The American Scene*, pp. 133–137).

32. Townsend, *A Daughter of the Tenements*, pp. 59, 284, 115, 51.

33. Ibid., pp. 82–84, 42, 47, 210, 32, 37.

34. Wiggin, *Timothy's Quest*, pp. 27, 29.

35. Townsend, *"Chimmie Fadden," Major Max, and Other Stories* (New York: Garrett, 1969), pp. 3–11.

36. The girl-vagrant "feels homelessness and friendlessness more; she has more of the feminine dependence on affection; the street-trades, too, are harder for her, and the return at night to some lonely cellar or tenement-room, crowded with dirty people of all ages and sexes, is more dreary. She develops body and mind earlier than the boy, and the habits of vagabondism stamped on her in childhood are more difficult to wear off."
Moreover, "there is no reality in the sentimental assertion that the sexual sins of the lad are as degrading as those of the girl. The instinct of the female is more toward the preservation of purity, and therefore her fall is deeper. . . . The crime, with the girl, seems to sap and rot the whole nature" (Brace, *The Dangerous Classes of New York*, pp. 114–117; see also pp. 55–56).

37. Sullivan, *Tenement Tales of New York*, pp. 87–88.

38. Fawcett, *The Evil That Men Do*, pp. 70, 9, 306, 334–335.

39. Ibid., pp. 304–305.

40. Quoted in Solomon, *Stephen Crane*, p. 26n.

41. Fawcett, *The Evil That Men Do*, p. 189, my italics.

42. For further discussion of this mental philosophy, see chapter 5.

43. There are arguably a few other fiction writers of the 1890s who are committed to

the slums' "distinctive color and action," but only a few, and their books appeared at least a couple of years after Crane's. I would include Sanborn in this group.

44. Stallman, *Stephen Crane*, pp. 73, 79. "My good friend Edward Townsend—have you read his 'Daughter of the Tenements'?—has another opinion of the Bowery and it is certain to be better than mine" (Crane, *Stephen Crane: Letters*, p. 133).

45. Crane, *Stephen Crane: Letters*, p. 14.

46. Frank Norris, "Stephen Crane's Stories of Life in the Slums: *Maggie* and *George's Mother*," in Gullason, *Maggie: A Girl of the Streets*, p. 151.

47. The reference to Talmage is in Halliburton, *The Color of the Sky*, p. 68.

48. See Douglas, *The Feminization of American Culture*, pp. 5–6. The Victorian literary themes were "feminine purity; the sanctity of the childish heart; . . . the meaning of religious conformity." "The virgin, the child, and the home" have the "status of cult objects."

49. Maggie's death has been a source of contention in Crane criticism, and some critics have insisted on murder. Hershel Parker and Brian Higgins have maintained that the text to which most critics refer, the 1896 edition, a second published version of the book put out by a commercial company called Appleton, is unintelligible on the issue. In fact, they claim that it is only confusions in the somewhat expurgated 1896 version that have led readers to suspect that Maggie commits suicide, whereas she is actually murdered by "a huge fat man in torn and greasy garments" who appears only in the 1893 edition. "The idea that she is meaning to commit suicide is not authorial but adventitious," claim these critics, "projected by some sense-making readers onto the unintelligible 1896 text" (Hershel Parker and Brian Higgins, "Maggie's 'Last Night': Authorial Design and Editorial Patching," in Gullason, *Maggie: A Girl of the Streets*, p. 239).

But homicide is merely implied in the 1893 version; it is no more definite than the suicide of the 1896 text: the reader sees no murder and is only told that "chuckling and leering, he [the fat man] followed the girl of crimson legions" (53). An argument could reasonably be made, even from the 1893 edition, that Maggie is a suicide: she does, after all, walk on into increasingly bad parts of town, while her garments suggest that she is not driven by urgent financial need. The text is simply not explicit about how she dies.

My sense is that Crane is purposely combining both variants of this stereotypical story of the slums. In an increasingly dejected mood, Maggie is heading toward the river where the slum girl drowns herself, according to the conventional story. Meanwhile, she is being stalked by a huge, gruesome, drunken man, a potential killer, in a deserted area. Crane has purposefully arranged things so that Maggie looks at once like a suicide and a murder victim. In the 1893 text, I would say she is a suicidal murder victim: by walking into this bad part of town (and, on a symbolic level, toward the river of suicides), she is showing that she is so despondent she no longer cares what happens to her.

For reasons that have to do with his conception of subjectivity, as we shall see in chapter 5, it is essential to Crane that Maggie is shown to be dejected here, so it does not surprise me that he was willing to sacrifice the "huge fat man" for the squeamish editors of the 1896 text. The 1896 version of Maggie's implied death does not strike me as "unintelligible" when one considers Crane's tendency for elision and his distaste for melodrama.

50. Page numbers in parentheses refer to the *Maggie: A Girl of the Streets* edited by Thomas Gullason.

51. Stephen Crane, "An Experiment in Luxury," in *The Complete Short Stories and*

Sketches of Stephen Crane, ed. Thomas Gullason (Garden City, N.Y.: Doubleday, 1963), pp. 152–153.

52. From "In the 'Tenderloin'" (1896), quoted in Solomon, *Stephen Crane*, p. 198n.

53. Crane, *Maggie: A Girl of the Streets*, p. 17, note 9.

54. To appreciate the scandalous nature of Maggie's feelings, one needn't search through contemporary reviews of Crane's novel. Faced with the passages in which Maggie idealizes an "uncouth bartender," one modern critic concludes that their relationship is "too heavily" ironic, a "parody [that] gets out of hand." In effect, Eric Solomon classifies these passages as instances of irony for its own sake and thus does not consider them true examples of interiority: they don't properly belong to any character because no character could possibly think this way; no woman could possibly listen to a man "describe his brawls in filthy language" and then conclude that he was the ideal man (Solomon, *Stephen Crane*, p. 37). Many readers of Crane subscribe to this sort of view, but it is nonetheless a prejudice of a middle class that still values modesty, restraint, and proper language, especially for women. It was precisely this type of prejudice that Crane assaulted in writing *Maggie*; some middle-class critics in his own time found the book horrible, morbid, and unhealthful; some middle-class critics in our time find it, with more worldliness, too heavily ironic.

The fact is that Crane provides rather good reasons to believe in Maggie's idealization of Pete. Why would she be impressed with Pete's tough language and his fights? Crane gives us a reason that is immediately compelling: "To her the earth was composed of hardships and insults. She felt instant admiration for a man who openly defied it." And again, a few pages later, after Pete describes a fight with an obviously middle-class man who has called him an "insolen' ruffin" and a "contempt'ble scoun'el" and threatened him with "everlastin pe'dition," Maggie concludes: "Here was a formidable man who disdained the strength of a world full of fists. Here was one who had contempt for brass-clothed power; one whose knuckles could ring defiantly against the granite of the law. He was a knight" (20). For a woman who must quietly endure the monotonous labor of a sweatshop, the criticisms of an authoritarian boss, the ravings and insults of a drunken mother, the domestic violence of her household, and the regular police arrests of her family members, in short, for a woman whose entire life is composed of passive acceptance of arbitrary hardships and insults, Pete's general defiance and contempt must indeed seem ideal. Lacking the confidence or the daring to be defiant herself, she finds Pete all the more admirable. When Maggie's environment and her emotional reactions are taken into consideration, her romanticizing of Pete is not "perverse," as Solomon refers to it, but quite reasonable. She does not "quixotically convert . . . him from a brute into a knight"; for her, a brute (if a brute is understood to be a man of contempt and defiance) is a knight.

55. *George's Mother*, in Stephen Crane, *The Red Badge of Courage and Other Writings*, ed. Richard Chase (Cambridge, Mass.: Houghton Mifflin, 1960), pp. 100–102.

56. For a similar account of Jimmie's interesting decision to work, see Halliburton, *The Color of the Sky*, pp. 52–53.

57. Sullivan, *Tenement Tales of New York*, pp. 109–111.

58. For a discussion of this conundrum, see, for example, Halliburton, *The Color of the Sky*, pp. 66–67.

59. We will return to the issue of her inner state here in chapter 5.

60. Her interior experience will be examined in chapter 5.

Chapter 3

1. This advertisement appeared in the back pages of Jacob Riis, *The Children of the Poor* (1892).

2. Crane, *Stephen Crane: Letters*, p. 133.

3. When Crane published *Maggie* himself in 1893, he sent a batch of copies to a number of ministers who were enthusiasts of social reform, but he got no response from any of them. "You'd think the book came straight from hell and they smelled the smoke," commented the author to his friend C. K. Linson (Stallman, *Stephen Crane*, p. 79). John D. Berry, the editor of the *Forum*, wrote to Crane in 1893, "[I]t is pitilessly real. . . . To be frank with you, I doubt if such literature is good. . . . I know that one might say that the truth was black and that you tried to describe it just as it was; but, one ought always to bear in mind that literature is an art, that effect, the effect upon the reader, must always be kept in view by the artist and as soon as that effect approaches the morbid, the unhealthful, the art becomes diseased" (quoted in James Colvert, *Stephen Crane* [San Diego: Harcourt, 1984], p. 51).

4. This accounts for the lack of critical consensus about Riis. See note 26 of the introduction for a sampling of critical differences.

5. Crane's reader would most likely have pitied the Johnson children when they are beaten by their drunken and belligerent parents. She would perhaps have felt sorry for Maggie as she is "strangled" by the sweatshop and for "the grizzled women in the room, mere mechanical contrivances sewing seams and grinding out" (25). She may even have sympathized with Maggie when the girl steals a flower from an Italian to place in her baby brother's hand as he is taken away "in a white, insignificant coffin" (13).

Meanwhile, Crane's drunken child-beaters and insensitive sweatshop bosses might very well have inspired anger and condemnation from his readers. His pauper woman, likewise, would probably have elicited scorn, despite the fact that he never passes judgment on her actions or her character:

> The old woman was a gnarled and leathery personage who could don, at will, an expression of great virtue. . . . Each day she took a position upon the stone of Fifth Avenue, where she crooked her legs under her and crouched immovable and hideous, like an idol. . . .
>
> Once, when a lady had dropped her purse on the sidewalk, the gnarled woman had grabbed it and smuggled it with great dexterity beneath her cloak. When she was arrested she had cursed the lady into a partial swoon, and with her aged limbs, twisted from rheumatism, had almost kicked the stomach out of huge policeman whose conduct upon that occasion she referred to when she said: "The police, damn 'em." (10)

Late-nineteenth-century readers were used to the figure of the dishonest beggar, who pretended to be spiritually better and materially worse off than he or she was. Crane's irony here is fairly heavy, which is to say, readily comprehensible: an "expression of great virtue" quickly betrays itself with thievery and vehement curses; "gnarled" limbs turn out to be capable of "dexterity" and powerful kicks.

Crane's reader was also likely to react with a typical fear of the slums to some of his images. Again, though Crane does not moralize on the threat of crime and riot from the slums, he certainly conjures it up. The man who last encounters Maggie (at the end of the

1893 edition) is a sinister incarnation of the menace of the urban underworld. Their encounter is gruesome:

> When almost to the river the girl saw a great figure. On going forward she
> perceived it to be a huge fat man in torn and greasy garments. . . . His
> small, bleared eyes, sparkling from amidst great rolls of red fat, swept eagerly
> over the girl's upturned face. He laughed, his brown, disordered teeth gleam-
> ing under a grey, grizzled moustache from which beer-drops dripped. His
> whole body gently quivered and shook like that of a dead jelly fish. Chuck-
> ling and leering, he followed the girl of crimson legions. (53)

And the violence or potential violence that Crane depicts is not always internecine, not
always contained among slum dwellers. Jimmie, for instance, "maintained a belligerent attitude toward all well-dressed men. . . . He and his order were kings, to a certain extent,
over the men of untarnished clothes, because these latter dreaded, perhaps, to be either
killed or laughed at" (14). Finally, Crane even calls up an image of class violence that was
stock in charity writing. Riis draws a frightening picture of social apocalypse; in *George's
Mother*, Crane lodges such a scene in the imagination of gang members:

> The vast machinery of the popular law indicated to them that there were peo-
> ple in the world who wished to remain quiet. They awaited the moment when
> they could prove to them that a riotous upheaval, a cloudburst of destruction,
> would be a delicious thing. They thought of their fingers buried in the lives of
> these people. They longed dimly for a time when they could run through
> decorous streets with crash and roar of war, an army of revenge for pleasures
> long possessed by others, a wild sweeping compensation for their years with-
> out crystal and gilt, women and wine. This thought slumbered in them, as the
> image of Rome might have lain small in the hearts of the barbarians. (p. 102)

Though Crane does not guide his late-nineteenth-century reader with a running commentary on the action, he creates images, characters, and actions that readily inspired her to occupy the traditional positions in relation to the poor.

It should be underlined that Crane does not directly condemn the poor for their sins;
nor does he express a concern about violence; nor does he take conspicuous pity on them
for their suffering. Editors to whom young Crane initially took the book found it problematic and refused to publish it. No sentiment, no pity, "too cruel," one of them said. What
must have first shocked readers of the 1890s, notes contemporary critic Frank Bergon, was
that the novel "totally lacked the condescension with which crusaders of the times ap-
proached such characters." John Berryman notes Crane's irony and attributes to him a
"nearly perfect detachment." One of Crane's biographers, R. W. Stallman, concluded that
"the lack of preaching in *Maggie* undoubtedly accounts for its neglect." For some editors,
the problem with Crane's book about residents of the Bowery was that it did not obviously
occupy any of the traditional postures toward the poor (Crane, *Stephen Crane: Letters*, p.
15; Richard Watson Gilder of *The Century*, quoted in Joseph Katz, Introduction to *Maggie:
A Girl of the Streets: A Facsimile Reproduction of the First Edition of 1893* [Gainesville, Fla.:
Scholars' Facsimiles and Reprints, 1966], p. xiii; Frank Bergon, *Stephen Crane's Artistry*
[New York: Columbia UP, 1975], p. 75; Berryman, *Stephen Crane*, p. 50; Stallman, *Stephen
Crane*, p. 78).

Still, in the course of reading the novel, the reader had plenty of opportunities to react with pity, contempt, and fear. Though Crane does not sermonize—and the nineteenth-century reader would certainly have found that disorienting—it is hard to argue that his novel generates indifference.

And, indeed, in our own day, critics have attributed to Crane both sympathy and hatred for the poor; they have called him a social reformer and accused him of asserting social control. Thomas Gullason finds him compassionate, as well as critical of the poor, and Donald Gibson feels that his irony about his characters, far from giving him a detachment, indicates not only a condescension toward them but a complete scorn and disgust. Gullason calls him a social reformer; Alfred Kazin insists that he was not a reformer but, rather, knew the world was bad and hated it; and Walter Michaels discovers in his novel impulses toward social control (Gullason, "Tragedy and Melodrama in *Maggie*," pp. 245–253; Donald Gibson, "The Flawed *Maggie*," in Gullason, *Maggie: A Girl of the Streets*, pp. 212–215; Alfred Kazin, *On Native Grounds*, p. 69; Walter Michaels, lecture at the University of California at Berkeley, fall 1985).

6. See Leonard, *The Power of the Press*, chapter 5. The midcentury novelist George Lippard might be included here; his famous book is *The Quaker City* or *The Monks of Monk Hall* (1844; New York: Odyssey P, 1970).

7. See chapter 4.

8. The use of this term is itself an ethnic joke. Riis explains: "The name was given to it probably in derision, for pork is the one ware that is not on sale in the Pig-market" (85).

9. "An Experiment in Misery," in Crane, *The Complete Short Stories and Sketches of Stephen Crane*, pp. 141, 146, my italics.

10. Alexander Alland claims that "photographically, *How the Other Half Lives* was a landmark—the first account of social conditions to be documented with action pictures" (Alland, *Jacob A. Riis*, p. 30).

Peter B. Hales writes that

> evidence suggests that before Riis published *How the Other Half Lives*, only three other photographers had worked the streets and slums of major cities with the intent of publishing their photographs, and none of them had worked in the United States. The first was daguerreotypist Richard Beard of London, who worked in the late 1840s to produce a collection of "street types" and typical members of social and occupation groups for Henry Mayhew's landmark study, *London Labour and the London Poor*, published in 1851. By the time they were published, however, the illustrations bore little resemblance to photographs. They were engravings which only accentuated Beard's stiffly conventional portrait style. . . . The second major publication of slum photographs was . . . *Photographs of Old Closes, Streets, Etc., Taken 1868–77*. . . . The Glasgow City Improvement Trust had ordered destruction of a part of the city's Old Town and had hired photographer Thomas Annan to document areas before wrecking began. . . . The dwellers of those areas did not appear prominently in the pictures. . . . [The third] was John Thomson and Adolphe Smith's *Street Life in London*. . . . Published in twelve monthly installments beginning in January 1877, the work was printed by . . . one of the very first printers to perfect a means of accurately reproducing photographs. *Street Life in London* was the first study of urban life to combine photographs and text. (Hales, *Silver Cities*, pp. 179–180)

11. Alland, *Jacob A. Riis*, p. 30.

12. The first halftones appeared in a daily in 1880, but they were found unsuitable for high-speed presses and were not used again until 1891 (Hales, *Silver Cities*, p. 169).

13. Leonard, *The Power of the Press*, pp. 98–104.

14. Hales writes:

> Until that decade, the genre seemed immutably bonded by technology and tradition to a celebratory, monumental style, whereby the outer surface of the city became a metaphor for its inner strength and civilized grandeur. But those years brought about a revolution in photographic technology which exploded the tight holism of the urban grand-style taxonomy and introduced an entirely new vision of the city. Acceptance of supersensitive dry-plate technology, the introduction of flexible film into the professional and amateur marketplace, the development of a new artificial light technology for photography, the advent of cheap, simple cameras that made use of these innovations—all served to break down the old strictures of professionalism and the outdated conceptions of urban style. (Hales, *Silver Cities*, p. 163)

What Leonard says of Thomas Nast, in accounting for the impact of his political cartoons, is also true of Riis: he "broke away from a whole gallery of benign urban types" (Leonard, *The Power of the Press*, p. 102).

15. As to the success of Riis's book, Hales writes:

> Its combination of terse, angry prose, voyeuristic sensationalism, straightforward statement of cause and cure, and vivid, high-quality illustrations yielded an unprecedented work. Few books have addressed the subject with such verve: Booth's *In Darkest England* and Helen Campbell's *Prisoners of Poverty* had the commitment and a measure of the writing, but lacked the force of illustrative fact that Riis had gained as a police reporter, lecturer, and writer. They also lacked the photographs, and it was the photographs that provided the real revolutionary impact to that first publication of *How the Other Half Lives*. (Hales, *Silver Cities*, p. 179)

16. Ibid., p. 163.

17. Ibid., p. 179.

18. On the domestic ideology of the late nineteenth century, see Trachtenberg, *The Incorporation of America*, and Lasch, *Haven in a Heartless World*. A well-known contemporary book on the home is Catharine Beecher and Harriet Beecher Stowe, *The American Woman's Home, or, Principles of Domestic Science* (New York: J. B. Ford, 1869).

19. Riis, *The Children of the Poor*, chapter 6, "The Little Toilers." There was a large movement against child labor by the time Riis was writing; see Walter I. Trattner, *Crusade for the Children: A History of the National Child Labor Committee and Child Labor Reform in America* (Chicago: Quadrangle Books, 1970).

20. Trachtenberg, *The Incorporation of America*, p. 127.

21. In 1882, Congress had passed the Chinese Exclusion Act, establishing a ten-year moratorium on Chinese immigration.

22. Riis, *The Children of the Poor*, p. 6.

23. Ibid., back pages, advertisement for *How the Other Half Lives*.

24. Trachtenberg, *The Incorporation of America*, p. 125.

25. Walter Benjamin, quoted in ibid., p. 125.

26. Debord, *The Society of the Spectacle*, paragraph 10.

27. Meanwhile, "to be in it, and not have the distance, is to inhale the stenches of the neglected street, and to catch that fouler and dreadfuller poverty-smell which breathes from the open doorways. It is to see the children quarreling in their games, and beating one another in the face, and rolling one another in the gutter, like the little savage outlaws they are. . . . All this makes you hasten your pace down to the river" (Howells, "New York Streets," p. 186).

28. Riis, *The Children of the Poor*, pp. 4–6.

29. Roland Barthes, *Mythologies* (New York: Hill and Wang, 1972), p. 152.

30. See note 5 in this chapter.

31. "As they went out, Maggie perceived two women seated at a table with some men. They were painted and their cheeks had lost their roundness. As she passed them the girl, with a shrinking movement, drew back her skirts" (39).

32. Some critics have claimed that Crane put the reader of *Maggie* in a double bind: both pity and condemnation had become untenable positions by the time he or she finished the book. If the reader was inclined to damn Maggie for her immorality, he had to ally himself with Maggie's thoroughly hypocritical and despicable mother. If, on the other hand, he wanted to see Maggie as an innocent victim of her cruel environment—as Crane suggests in his inscription to the original edition—he also had to acknowledge that she is guilty of the same moral indiscrimination and visceral prejudice as her fellows. Crane even has her draw back her skirts when she passes prostitutes in the bars she goes to with Pete: she herself observes the taboo that is the reason for her eventual ostracism. If the reader was inclined to forgive her her errors because she never had the chance to know any better, then this forgiveness should have in turn been extended to the other slum characters, but they would have seemed too self-righteous and downright vicious to be forgiven. The reader of *Maggie*, it is argued, found himself or herself disarmed. See Donald Gibson, who concludes that this is a flaw of the book, in "The Flawed *Maggie*," pp. 212–213. See also Frank Bergon, who finds that "the forgiving reader is caught in a moral contradiction, or like Maggie's mother, becomes bound to noble sentiments that are in themselves self-serving deceptions. Denied a normal response to events and characters, the reader is also refused the comfort of those values that he may most deeply cherish" (*Stephen Crane's Artistry*, pp. 73–74). I would follow Bergon and argue that this is part of Crane's assault on traditional morality.

By the end of the novel, then, it could be argued, the thorough reader found herself stripped of the comfort of her familiar morality.

Chapter 4

1. John D. Berry, the editor of the *Forum*, quoted in Colvert, *Stephen Crane*, p. 51.

2. Crane, *Stephen Crane: Letters*, p. 14.

3. Riis, *The Children of the Poor*, pp. 138, 180.

4. Some of this profanity was edited out in the 1896 version. As for the acts in the Bowery theater:

> The orchestra of yellow silk women and bald-headed men gave vent to a few
> short bars of anticipatory music and a girl, in a pink dress with short skirt
> galloped upon the stage. . . . When she broke into the swift rattling mea-

sures of a chorus some half-tipsy men near the stage joined in the rollicking refrain and glasses were pounded rhythmically upon the tables. . . .

An occasional man bent forward, intent upon the pink stockings. . . .

A ventriloquist followed the dancer. He held two fantastic dolls on his knees. He made them sing mournful ditties and say funny things about geography and Ireland. . . .

Two girls, on the bills as sisters, came forth and sang a duet that is heard occasionally at concerts given under church auspices. They supplemented it with a dance which of course can never be seen at concerts given under church auspices.

After the duettists had retired, a woman of debatable age sang a negro melody. The chorus necessitated some grotesque waddlings supposed to be an imitation of a plantation darkey, under the influence, probably of music and the moon. . . .

As a final effort, the singer rendered some verses which described a vision of Britain being annihilated by America, and Ireland bursting her bonds. A carefully prepared crisis was reached in the last line of the last verse, where the singer threw out her arms and cried, "The star-spangled banner." Instantly a great cheer swelled from the throats of the assemblage of the masses. . . .

After a few moments' rest, the orchestra played crashingly, and a small fat man burst out upon the stage. . . . He made his face into fantastic grimaces until he looked like a pictured devil on a Japanese kite. The crowd laughed gleefully. (23–24)

5. Stallman, *Stephen Crane*, p. 73.

6. Despite his reputation for "a single-minded pursuit of social justice," he is actually of two minds, each with its own criteria (Alland, *Jacob A. Riis*, p. 15). Riis may have been attracted to photography because of its spectacular (in addition to its reform) potential; he may also have fallen to some degree under the thrall of his camera. In any case, Riis's aesthetic concern and his interest in sights are not always accessories to his social and moral messages; they are not always subordinated to his call for reform.

7. Warner, Editor's Introduction, p. xvi.

8. Riis is again quoting from the first legislative committee, which met in 1856, according to Lawrence Veiller, *Tenement House Reform in New York*, p. 8, my italics.

9. We have seen the suspicion of the streets operating in Edward Townsend's fiction. See chapter 2.

10. Riis, *The Children of the Poor*, pp. 134, 175.

11. Higham, "The Re-orientation of American Culture in the 1890s," p. 27.

12. Berryman, *Stephen Crane*, pp. 297–298.

13. Stallman, *Stephen Crane*, p. 393.

14. Fried, *Realism, Writing, Disfiguration*, p. 121; Fried, "Realism, Writing, and Disfiguration in Thomas Eakins's Gross Clinic," *Representations 9* (Winter 1985), p. 95.

15. Berryman, *Stephen Crane*, p. 268.

16. Crane quoted in Stallman, *Stephen Crane*, p. 45.

17. Warner, Editor's Introduction, p. xvi.

18. Brace, *The Dangerous Classes of New York*, pp. 163–164.

19. Howells, "New York Streets," p. 186.

20. Riis, *The Children of the Poor*, pp. 76, 224.

21. Scenes of spectatorship in *Maggie* are extremely prevalent, as LaFrance has noticed. LaFrance, "*George's Mother* and the Other Half of *Maggie*," pp. 35–53.

22. "The Men in the Storm," in Crane, *The Complete Short Stories and Sketches of Stephen Crane*, p. 179.

23. "When a Man Falls a Crowd Gathers," in Crane, *The Complete Short Stories and Sketches of Stephen Crane*, p. 204.

24. *George's Mother*, in Crane, *The Red Badge of Courage and Other Writings*, p. 102.

25. For this observation, I am indebted to William Heath.

26. Helen Trent, with whom Crane was infatuated, quoted in Stallman, *Stephen Crane*, p. 45.

27. Settlement house work differed from friendly visiting in important ways. See note 5 to chapter 5.

28. Brace, *The Dangerous Classes of New York*, p. 302.

29. It was the heyday of live entertainment. See Robert C. Toll, *On with the Show!: The First Century of Show Business in America* (New York: Oxford UP, 1976).

30. Larry May, *Screening out the Past* (New York: Oxford UP, 1980), p. 63. Griffith is quoted on p. 60.

31. Trachtenberg, *The Incorporation of America*, p. 124.

32. These developments in the film industry started in the 1910s. Motion pictures began in the 1890s (May, *Screening out the Past*, p. 66).

33. Ibid., pp. 43–59. Reformer is quoted on p. 53; Griffith is quoted on p. 60.

34. Daniel J. Boorstin, *The Americans: The Democratic Experience* (New York: Vintage Books, 1974), pp. 89–90 and part 2.

35. Levine, *Jane Addams and the Liberal Tradition*, p. 133.

36. Riis's editors give a somewhat different account; they are eager to show that his particular reform message was unique. Warner, in his introduction, acknowledges a long tradition of charitable writing but claims that previous works were merely calls for more private effort. "They did not urge public effort of a magnitude that could give the public confidence in the city's ability to cope with the tide of the immigrant poor" (Warner, Editor's Introduction, p. vii). Likewise, Francesco Cordasco, in his introduction to Riis's *The Children of the Poor*, writes that "the ugly pictures which Riis sketched in his vignettes of the slum and the tenement poor were not new; they had been done before, but what was new was the book's raucous cry for reform, the vividness of its description and the prescription for change" (Cordasco, Introduction, p. vi).

37. Consider again the 1977 *Time* piece "The American Underclass," with which we began: the article described the bulk of the people of the slums as "socially alien." The members of the underclass "are victims and victimizers in the culture of the street hustle, the quick fix, the rip-off and, not least, violent crime. Their bleak environment nurtures values that are often radically at odds with those of the majority—even the majority of the poor." What distinguishes the American underclass, "this subculture," even from other poor populations "is the weakness of family structure, the presence of competing street values, and the lack of hope amidst affluence all around." "The underclass [is] a nucleus of psychological [as well as] material destitution" ("The American Underclass," pp. 14–27).

38. See William Julius Wilson, "The Cost of Racial and Class Exclusion in the Inner

City," *The Ghetto Underclass: Social Science Perspectives*, special issue of *The Annals of the American Academy of Political and Social Science* 501 (January 1989), pp. 9, 25.

Wilson criticizes the use of "moral-cultural or individualistic-behavioral" terms: he attacks "descriptions and explanations of the current predicament of inner-city blacks [that] put the emphasis on individual attributes and the alleged grip of the so-called culture of poverty"—instead of concentrating on "joblessness and economic exclusion." According to Wilson, these descriptions and analyses have not only diverted attention from the very real problems of "forcible socioeconomic marginalization"; they have also been employed by conservative theorists and policy makers to justify cutbacks in social programs and critiques of welfare since the beginning of the Reagan era. Wilson takes special aim at "popular magazines and . . . televised programs"—including the CBS report, with its focus on Timothy (see my introduction, note 9)—for giving "this vision of poverty . . . its most vivid expression." He calls their "descriptions of ghetto residents" as well as their descriptions of a culture of poverty "lurid." And for Wilson, these descriptions involve serious political stakes; they provide ammunition for conservative ideologues and marshall public opinion against programs of social amelioration (Wilson, "The Cost of Racial and Class Exclusion in the Inner City," pp. 9, 25; Wilson, "The American Underclass," pp. 33–35, 39).

Wilson's critical strategy does not mean condemning "any writer who focuses on traits and behavior of the ghetto underclass." He wants "to challenge the dominant themes on the underclass as reflected in the popular media and in the writings of conservative intellectuals, not by shying away from using the concept 'underclass,' not by avoiding a description and explanation of unflattering behavior, but by attempting, as did . . . liberal field researchers of the 1960s, to relate the practices and experiences of the truly disadvantaged to the structure of opportunities and constraints in American society." And in order to undermine "cultural transmission explanations of underclass behavior" and "underline the structural underpinnings of behavior," he is attempting to develop new terms of description and analysis. He would replace the concept of a "culture of poverty" with a notion of "social isolation": that is, ghetto-specific modes of behavior can be transmitted through role modeling in large part because "contact between groups of different class and/or racial backgrounds is either lacking or has become increasingly intermittent" (Wilson, "The American Underclass," pp. 41–47).

39. Our own tunnel vision of the slums might prove much harder to eradicate than that of the moralists of the previous century: ours is not only familiar and self-congratulatory, it is also titillating.

Chapter 5

1. Riis, *Out of Mulberry Street*, p. 143.
2. Riis, *The Battle with the Slum*, pp. 236, 239.
3. Riis, *The Children of the Poor*, p. 74.
4. Riis, *The Battle with the Slum*, pp. 233–234.
5. Riis's suggestion might be a manifesto for the settlement houses and the social work projects that were just beginning to pop up in the American metropolises. The imperative to go into the neighborhoods of the poor and remain there was something new. Previously, it had been enough to visit the slums and their people briefly; the friendly visitors of the Charity Organization Society stopped in long enough to dispense alms to the worthy poor

and suggestions to the unworthy. One did not have to do much policing, investigation, or long-term observation to tell the worthy poor from the pauper or to explain how to improve one's character; the friendly visitor was naturally endowed, by virtue of her class (most were women), with the moral vision to make such distinctions and to provide such advice. But now a much more thorough-going surveillance was called for. Sympathy and understanding demanded it. The new conception of subjectivity was more complicated and, of course, less familiar than the old one—character had been essentially binary, and the vices and virtues, though numerous, had long ago been catalogued; meanwhile, ways and aims and ambitions were not only potentially infinite; they were largely unknown. The poor would have to be studied; there would have to be field work, and new things about the poor would have to be discovered. It would no longer be enough to know, for instance, if they were temperate or intemperate; now it would also be necessary to know why they drank, with what ideas, and in what situations.

Jane Addams would summarize the new requirements in 1910: "I learned that life cannot be administered by definite rules and regulations; that wisdom to deal with a man's difficulties comes only through some *knowledge of his life and habits as a whole*" (Jane Addams, *Twenty Years at Hull House*, p. 123, my italics). In the second half of the nineteenth century, Agents of the Association for Improving the Conditions of the poor and friendly visitors of the Charity Organization Society tried to observe and ameliorate the *moral habits* of the poor. What Jane Addams succinctly suggests is a new object of knowledge and administration in regards to the slums: *life as a whole*.

The concepts that Riis, Crane, and others, such as Addams, were developing, in an unsystematic, more or less haphazard way, would, in fact, give a foothold to a new and organized type of authority. Respectable members of the middle class were natural experts on questions of the poor when poverty was essentially a matter of character, but as the matter altered, expertise would have to come from a source other than class. It would come from study, and the study would eventually be institutionalized and professionalized. An entire profession would grow up around ways and aims and qualities of ambition: social work.

Mary Richmond's *Social Diagnosis* (1917), the premier textbook for training caseworkers that went through more than a dozen reprintings, would rely on the new sort of ethnographic and psychological concepts that one finds in Riis's work. In aiding families in "social need," she explains to would-be social workers,

> We must not be so bent upon getting clues to outside information that we miss our way to the even more important inside truths of personality—to our client's hopes, fears, plans, and earlier story. In family work, we must have sooner or later a pretty clear idea not only of the main biographical outlines of the two heads of the house and of the older children, but some conception of their attitude toward life. This is far more important that any single item in their story. Families have their own plans and their own ideals—more definite ones than the social worker realizes. These must be understood and taken into account from the beginning. All our plans otherwise will surely come to grief.

"At the base of social work," Richmond declares, is "the theory of the wider self." Social work should "consider the whole man." Richmond explains her project: "Social diagnosis . . . may be described as the attempt to make as exact a definition as possible of the situation and personality of the human being in some social need—of his situation and personality, that is, in relation to the other human beings upon whom he in any way depends or who depend upon him." *Social Diagnosis* includes a list of queries for social workers undertaking studies of immigrant groups, queries that touch not only on moral habits, but on psychological characteristics and ethnographic customs. Questions include, "Are they thrifty and industrious?" but also, "Are the people stolid or excitable? Warlike or submissive? Jealous? Hot-tempered?" and, "What are the peculiar customs of dress, cooking, etc? . . . What is the customary age at marriage? . . . What are the dowry customs?" (Mary Richmond, *Social Diagnosis* [New York: Russell Sage Foundation, 1917], pp. 168, 368, 357, 383–384).

6. Brace, *Dangerous Classes*, pp. 56–57.

7. Riis, *The Children of the Poor*, p. 134.

8. Ibid., p. 4.

9. Dr. William T. Harris, "Philosophy of Crime and Punishment," quoted in ibid., p. 135.

10. Ibid., p. 84.

11. Riis, *The Battle with the Slum*, p. 237.

12. Ibid., p. 136.

13. Riis, *The Children of the Poor*, p. 82.

14. The commissioner doesn't specifically comment about the psychological state of the person once he has become a criminal (whether or not he gains the self-respect he was lacking in legal life) but implies that he still lacks it; Riis is unambiguous on this point: he believes thieves and toughs have individuality.

15. Walter Channing explains "the saddest feature of poverty," the real reason "to prevent pauperism," in his "Address on the Prevention of Pauperism," p. 42. "It is not in its physical or mental suffering"; it is "because of its hopelessness,—its helplessness,—its dependence."

16. Fawcett, *The Evil That Men Do*, p. 88.

17. Sullivan, *Tenement Tales of New York*, p. 17.

18. We will analyze Crane's different meaning for "soul" in the next chapter.

19. Crane, *Stephen Crane: Letters*, p. 14.

20. Riis, *How the Other Half Lives*, 182; see the beginning of this chapter.

21. Thomas Cogswell Upham, *Elements of Mental Philosophy*, vol. 2 (New York: Harper, 1845), pp. 23, 24–25.

22. Crane, *Stephen Crane: Letters*, p. 133.

23. "The Open Boat," in Crane, *The Red Badge of Courage and Other Writings*, p. 290.

24. Ibid.

25. Crane, *Stephen Crane: Letters*, p. 133.

26. Henry Fleming, the hero of Crane's *The Red Badge of Courage*, undergoes a similar struggle for self-esteem, only he wins the battle, and this psychological battle occupies more time and space in the novel than the actual war he is fighting in. Before Henry ever sees battle, he worries not about dying but about running away under fire. Like Maggie, he is susceptible to self-doubt. His contemplation of himself involves moments of doubt, self-hatred, self-assurance, self-pity, and more detached evaluation. He tries "to mathematically prove to himself that he would not run from a battle"; he finds himself to be "an unknown quantity"; he continually tries "to measure himself by his comrades," and this gives him "some assurance," but he also passes moments of "severe condemnation of himself" and others of "vast pity for himself." As with the men of his regiment who jeer a fellow soldier who is caught trying to pilfer a horse, he becomes "so engrossed in [his personal] affair that

[he] entirely ceased to remember [his] own large war" (Crane, *The Red Badge of Courage and Selected Stories* [New York: Signet, NAL, 1960], pp. 18–25).

27. From the Long Version of the manuscript, as Stallman called it in his 1960 edition, see ibid., p. 217.

28. "The Open Boat," p. 306.

29. "Legends," ii, in Crane, *Prose and Poetry* (New York: Literary Classics of the U.S., Viking, 1984), p. 1346.

30. For the use of the term "self-esteem," see, for instance, *George's Mother*, in Crane, *The Red Badge of Courage and other Writings*, p. 78. "Self-pride": see Crane, *The Red Badge of Courage and Selected Stories*, p. 89. "Selfishness": see ibid., p. 107. "Egotism": see ibid., p. 133. "Conceit": see note 31, this chapter.

31. "The Blue Hotel," in Crane, *The Red Badge of Courage and Other Writings*, p. 273.

32. Upham, *Elements of Mental Philosophy*, vol. 2, pp. vi, 140–141.

33. "Without doubt, Upham's *Elements of Mental Philosophy* was the classic text prior to James' great work" (Roback, *History of American Psychology*, p. 50).

34. William James, *Principles of Psychology* (New York: Holt, 1890), pp. 289, 293, 305, 328–330, 306n. My italics in the last quotation.

35. "The New Psychology" (as Roback calls it, in *History of American Psychology*, p. 121) does not insure an ethnographic perspective, and James is a case in point. Though some historians reckon the new era in psychology from the publication of his famous tome, James sometimes lets traditional moral imperatives intrude on his scientific findings. See Roback, *History of American Psychology*, p. 122. Also, see Hilary Putnam and Ruth Anna Putnam, "William James's Ideas," *Raritan* 8.3 (Winter 1989), pp. 27–44: "We shall proceed from the assumption that, early and late, James's motivation was ultimately ethical." And later, "more relevant to our account of James as, first and foremost, a *moral* philosopher is his motivation for rejecting traditional sense datum epistemology. . . . Even in pure epistemology and metaphysics, the concern with human beings as interdependent members of a community guides James's every move" (pp. 27, 43).

36. James, *Principles of Psychology*, p. 314.

37. Here "character" (as in "fictional character") is a literary term, not to be confused with the Protestant moral term (as in "moral character").

38. We will come to the important exceptions at the end of the chapter.

39. Some of Crane's characters are scrupulously moralistic, such as George's WCTU mother; others, like the street gang in the same novel, are conscientiously contemptuous of traditional morals; still others, like Maggie's mother and brother, exploit moralism as a weapon when they have the chance; but in all cases, for Crane, the ultimate stakes of moral posturing—as with all posturing—is self-respect. The dynamics of self-protection and self-assertion have superseded the moralistic reality of virtue and vice: for example, in one scene in *George's Mother*, a church (for George) is not at all a place of worship and moral brotherhood but simply a hostile territory full of harshly judging eyes. For Crane, as we have seen, moralism is just one form of self-assertion and one criterion for admiration and scorn—one among many.

40. Michael D. Warner, "Value, Agency, and 'The Monster,'" *Nineteenth-Century Fiction* 40. 1 (June 1985), p. 84.

41. Stallman, *Stephen Crane*, p. 77. On the subject of Crane's typological imagination, see also Halliburton, *The Color of the Sky*, pp. 3–7.

42. Stallman, *Stephen Crane*, pp. 68–69. At first the characters were simply referred to as "the girl," "the girl's mother," and so on.

43. Ibid., p. 77.

44. Similarly, but more broadly, Halliburton finds that Crane is writing not about individuals but about the human condition. "In each individual human being Crane . . . sees all other human beings collectively, so that anyone's experience is precisely everyone's experience" (*The Color of the Sky*, pp. 6–7).

45. The following examples are all taken from Crane's slum novels, *Maggie* and *George's Mother*. Much the same argument could be made for Crane's slum sketches, as well as his novels and stories that are not set in the slums; examples from a few of these texts will be provided in the following footnotes.

46. *George's Mother*, pp. 72–73, 103.
Henry Fleming displays bravado before his fellow soldiers the morning after his shame has gone undetected in *The Red Badge*. Henry Johnson conspicuously and sartorially saunters through town in *The Monster*; the boy Jimmie Trescott daringly approaches the monster in front of friends. The Swede loudly boasts about his fight in "The Blue Hotel."

47. Some of the people who are subjected to Henry Johnson's cakewalk try to pull him down a peg: somebody shouts, "Throw out your chest a little more" (*The Monster*, in Crane, *The Red Badge of Courage and other Writings*, pp. 328–329). And Henry Fleming eventually wishes that the men who have held tough will lose the battle and be brought down. Fleming's own mouthing off the next day is completely shot down by "a sarcastic man" who suggests, "Mebbe yeh think yeh fit th' hull battle yestirday, Fleming" (Crane, *The Red Badge of Courage and Selected Stories*, p. 95). In response to Jimmie Trescott's bravado, his friends are "awed and entranced, fearful and envious," and soon an older boy who "habitually oppressed [Jimmie] to a small degree" challenges his bravery. Jimmie, in turn, reacts "with deep scorn" (*The Monster*, p. 367). To the Swede's insistent arrogance, a gambler at the Romper saloon finally responds with a "tone of heroic patronage" ("The Blue Hotel," p. 276).

48. Whenever a soldier claims to have news about what the regiment plans in *The Red Badge*, some of his comrades vehemently declare him a liar. The first bearer of news in the novel "swelled with a tale" and, in telling it, "adopted the important air of a herald in red and gold." One of the listening privates "took the matter as an affront to him" and doubted the story. These two soldiers "came near to fighting over it." When the tall soldier gives an opinion in response to a question of Henry's, the loud soldier again takes it as an assault on his own worth. "'Oh, you think you know—' began the loud soldier with scorn" (Crane, *The Red Badge of Courage and Selected Stories*, pp. 11–12, 20). Likewise, in *The Monster*, when the barber momentarily turns from his lathered client to watch the well-dressed man come strutting down the street, the client feels undervalued, looks around for "a weapon," and attacks the barber: "Why, that's only Henry Johnson, you blamed idiots!" Also in *The Monster*, Dr. Trescott's self-destructive loyalty to the mutilated man is treated as "infernal pig-headedness" (pp. 329, 377).

49. *George's Mother*, p. 74.
After the last skirmish in *The Red Badge*, the youth and his friend, carrying the colors of the Union and the Rebel army respectively, "sat side by side and congratulated each other" (Crane, *The Red Badge of Courage and Selected Stories*, p. 129).

50. When the gambler's condescension fails to mortify the Swede in "The Blue Hotel," a mortal clash ensues.

51. The use, in this slum novel, of the word "tenderfoot," a word that is familiar to us from the lexicon of the Western, is an instance in Crane's oeuvre of the cross-pollination of the slum and Western genres. For a discussion of the affinity of these genres, see the Introduction.

52. *George's Mother*, p. 96.

Henry Fleming runs like a rabbit from the battle line in *The Red Badge*. The Swede in "The Blue Hotel" cowers fearfully in anticipation of Wild West violence.

53. Henry Fleming doubts himself when he hears about the regiment going into battle (and presumes that those around him will behave bravely), and he hates himself for his flight when he realizes that the other soldiers have held tough. Little Jimmie Trescott in *The Monster* respects his father, so when the latter scolds him, he has a "desire to efface himself." Likewise, Henry Johnson's friend Pete, at work in a potato patch, "responded [to Johnson's strutting] in a mixture of abasement and appreciation" (*The Monster*, p. 325).

54. Thus Henry Fleming's misery becomes a source of uniqueness: no one has ever suffered so much; "there was a dreadful unwritten martyrdom in his state" (Long Version of the manuscript in Crane, *The Red Badge of Courage and Selected Stories*, p. 217).

55. After Jimmie Trescott is scolded by his father, he seeks out the company of the negro hostler Henry Johnson: "Then these two would commune subtly and without words concerning their moon, holding themselves sympathetically as people who had committed similar treasons" (*The Monster*, p. 326).

56. *George's Mother*, pp. 79, 80.

At one point in *The Red Badge* when Henry is excoriating himself, he returns to his fantasies of Greek heroism and feels momentarily restored.

57. *George's Mother*, pp. 80, 78–79.

58. Both George and his mother entertain fantasies of rescue: George imagines rescuing Maggie Johnson (of *Maggie*) "from her hideous environment," and his mother, in turn, dreams of rescuing him from "a woman, wicked and fair," and also from "many wondrous influences that were swooping down like green dragons at him." These fantastical rescues, which ally them both with St. George the dragon-slayer, are visions of personal prowess and superiority. It is no coincidence that in Mrs. Kelcey's dream, she goes "bravely to the rescue": rescue necessarily involves overcoming an opposing force and proving one's superior powers. Rescue also implies rewards of admiration and dominance: the rescued party is grateful and indebted. Again, what is desired is not love so much as the combination of prowess and admiration. George initially dreams of being the "sublime king of a vague woman's heart" and enjoying the respect not only of this woman but also of the people before whom he intends to display her and his self-possession. Rescue is perhaps a more acceptable and realistic means of achieving the same ends and is akin to the typical male fantasy of female protection, which, in *Maggie*, Pete lives out and Maggie vicariously enjoys.

Henry Fleming, similarly, is drawn to enlisting in the war because of his romance with "Greeklike struggle": he imagines himself as a "Homeric" hero. "He had, of course, dreamed of battles all his life—of vague and bloody conflicts that had thrilled him with their sweep and fire. In visions he had seen himself in many struggles. He had imagined peoples secure in the shadow of his eagle-eyed prowess" (Crane, *The Red Badge of Courage and Selected Stories*, pp. 13, 14).

59. *George's Mother*, p. 66.

60. Likewise, Henry Fleming's temporary advantage over his friend the loud soldier makes him swell with superiority. The loud soldier had entrusted Henry with a packet of his belongings in a moment when the former was sure he was going to be killed, and now Henry can wield this packet as a "small weapon." Henry, who had previously worried about the cross-examination of his comrade, now "was master." He "felt immensely superior to his friend," but at first, like Pete, "he inclined to condescension." When the loud soldier nervously asks for the packet back, Henry tries "to invent a remarkable comment upon the affair." Only his inability to conjure up something "of sufficient point" keeps him from shooting "the shafts of derision" and allows his friend "to escape unmolested" (Crane, *The Red Badge of Courage and Selected Stories*, pp. 89–92).

61. *George's Mother*, p. 105.

The parent abuse of *George's Mother* is the mirror image of the child abuse of *Maggie*. Maggie's mother, like George, is "chieftainlike" (8), and her egotism is also ungoverned. She too imagines "that the world had treated [her] very badly" and feels free to take "a deep revenge upon such portions of it as came within her reach." This includes her children (as well as her furniture). They are the defenseless ones here, just as George's mother is the "impotent one" in the other slum novel (*George's Mother*, p. 105). Maggie's mother, like George, regularly restores her wounded self-esteem through a vengeful subjection of others. Mrs. Johnson and George are driven by the same egotistical engine that makes other of Crane's characters rationalize their situations or put others down; but they have an audience that is captive and powerless, and their unopposed self-assertion is able to expand to sadistic lengths.

62. And, more rarely, frenzy. There are rare instances when Crane's characters react unselfishly in the face of danger, but these are hardly moments of rational agency: just the opposite. Vanities are escaped in a "state of frenzy" or by a "sublime recklessness" that can accompany the heat of battle or the consciousness of impending death. In *The Red Badge*, Henry and the rest of the regiment all have brief, wild moments of unselfishness in the midst of battle. And the "tattered soldier," as Henry realizes after the fact, was selfless on the verge of death: "[G]ored by bullets and faint for blood, [he] had fretted concerning an imagined wound in another . . . [and] had loaned his last of strength and intellect for the tall soldier" (Crane, *The Red Badge of Courage and Selected Stories*, pp. 125–126, 132).

63. Before he goes into battle, Henry Fleming so tortures himself with his doubts that he finally decides to get himself "killed directly and end his troubles." But in the next instant the youth finally gets a good look at a battle, and he goes into a "trance of observation. . . . The youth, forgetting his neat plan of getting killed, gazed spellbound" (ibid., p. 35). Likewise, in "An Experiment in Luxury," "the famous millionaire . . . was deeply absorbed in the gambols of a kitten. . . . The old man chuckled in complete glee. There was never such a case of abstraction, of want of care" ("An Experiment in Luxury," in Crane, *The Complete Short Stories and Sketches of Stephen Crane*, p. 151).

64. In "The Men in the Storm," the situation of "forgetfulness" is a scene of mockery as well as self-forgetfulness. The spontaneous spectacle that furnishes the temporary relief is a "very well clothed" man, looking down at them with "a certain grandeur of manner" and "a supreme complacence." The men outside react to his tacit superiority with jeers, such as "carefully-worded advice concerning changes in his personal appearance." When the man flees, "the mob chuckled ferociously, like ogres who had just devoured something"

("The Men in the Storm," in Crane, *The Complete Short Stories and Sketches of Stephen Crane*, p. 179).

65. *George's Mother*, p. 80.

66. Ibid., p. 96.

67. Crane, *Stephen Crane: Letters*, p. 133.

68. James, *The Principles of Psychology*, vol. 1, pp. 310–311.

69. "The Open Boat," p. 295.

70. Crane, *The Red Badge of Courage and Selected Stories*, pp. 86–87.

Chapter 6

1. Upham, *Elements of Mental Philosophy*, vol. 2, pp. vi, 140–141.

2. The notion of "disciplinary" power and techniques is from Michel Foucault's *Discipline and Punish: The Birth of the Prison*. Again, a disciplinary technology involves surveillance, a strict regime of rules of conduct, and punishments for their smallest violation.

3. Riis, *The Battle with the Slum*, pp. 134–135.

4. Ibid.

5. Riis, *The Children of the Poor*, pp. 135, 174–186.

6. Ibid., pp. 277, 209.

7. Discipline is a specific politics of the body: it treats the body as a collection of movements and habits and trains it, so that it yields morally (in the form of proper habits) and economically (in the form of efficient production).

8. David J. Rothman, *Conscience and Convenience* (Boston: Little, Brown, 1980), pp. 30–32.

9. Brace, *The Dangerous Classes of New York*, p. 76.

10. Riis, *The Children of the Poor*, p. 284.

11. In recent literary criticism, for example, Mark Seltzer has found that the realist art of the novel involves both "an aesthetic resistance to the exercises of power [and] a discreet re-inscription of strategies of control. . . . Even as it speaks out against systems of coercion, the novel reinvents them and makes them acceptable in another form, in the form of the novel itself. . . . Put simply, the novel makes power acceptable in the form of the aesthetic representation itself" (Seltzer, *Henry James and the Art of Power*, pp. 148–149). Similarly, Malek Alloula has discovered that the colonial postcard is "a ventriloquial art . . . [which], even—and especially—when it pretends to mirror the exotic, is nothing but one of the forms of the aesthetic justification of colonial violence" (Malek Alloula, *The Colonial Harem*, trans. Myrna and Wlad Godzich [Minneapolis: U of Minnesota P, 1986], p. 120).

12. I am indebted to Walter Michaels for this phrase.

13. Riis has one concise anecdote that shows the strong desire in children for both looking and being looked at. Riis recounts that he got ready to take photographs at a Thanksgiving dinner line, only to find that the presence of his camera instantly disturbed the line as a mob swarmed about him. A policeman restored the line, but a couple of girls refused to budge from in front of the camera, and soon a fight broke out. Riis had the idea of organizing a dogfight around the corner to scatter the mob, but "fatal mistake! At the first suggestive bark the crowd broke and ran in a body. Not only the hangers-on, but the hungry line collapsed too in an instant, and the policeman and I were left alone. As an attraction the dog-fight outranked the dinner." On Thanksgiving, perhaps the most special day for food

in the whole year, hungry city children will still instantly give up their places in line, first to be photographed, and then to watch a common enough urban spectacle (Riis, *The Children of the Poor*, pp. 83–84).

14. Ibid., p. 84.

15. Levine, *Jane Addams and the Liberal Tradition*, p. 133.

16. See chapter 4.

17. Crane recognizes this power and is pessimistic about it; in his ethics, it is to be resisted.

The destructive power of looks is nowhere more evident than in his novella *The Monster*. In that story, no one—besides Dr. Trescott—is able to buck the strength of appearance in the case of Henry Johnson: though the town first labels Johnson a hero for his bravery in the fire, the people of every class, when they learn of his facial mutilation, come to see him as a monster who must be expelled from the community.

Maggie's misfortune is largely decided by looks as well. She is, as we have seen, initially attracted to Pete's elegant appearance. And the moment she admires him, she begins to worry about her own appearance and that of her family's apartment. "She began to see the bloom on her cheeks as something of value. . . . She wondered how long her youth would endure" (25). Her valuation and anxiety turns out to be justified: Pete abandons her for Nell, "a woman of brilliance." Maggie herself recognizes the perfection of Nell's looks: "Maggie took instant note of the woman. She perceived that her black dress fitted her to perfection. Her linen collar and cuffs were spotless. Tan gloves were stretched over her well-shaped hands. A hat of a prevailing fashion perched jauntily upon her dark hair. She wore no jewelry and was painted with no apparent paint" (43). Maggie may have "blossomed in a mud puddle" (16), but natural good looks can take one only so far. She is no match for a woman "of a prevailing fashion" (who knows, not incidentally, how to improve her appearance without letting the effort become "apparent"). The "mere boy" whom Nell abandons for Pete is brutally frank, in his drunkenness, about the comparative value of Maggie's looks. When he and Maggie are left alone, he says to her: "You ain't such bad-lookin' girl, y' know. Not half bad. Can't come up to Nell, though. No, can't do it! . . . Nell fine-lookin' girl. F-i-n-ine. You look damn bad longsider her, but by y'self ain't so bad" (46). It is perfectly fitting that Maggie should work in a "collar-and-cuff establishment" (25), a shirt factory, part of the burgeoning clothing industry that is making appearance a fantastically more powerful force in the world—at the same time that it is destroying the appearances of its lower-class female workers. Looking at "some of the grizzled women" in her workplace, Maggie "imagined herself, in an exasperating future, as a scrawny woman with an eternal grievance" (25). The narrator holds forth in "An Experiment in Luxury" on the same theme: "The youth wondered then why he had been sometimes surprised at seeing women fade, shrivel, their bosoms flatten, their shoulders crook forward, in the heavy swelter and wrench of their toil. It must be difficult, he thought, for a woman to remain serene and uncomplaining when she contemplated the wonder and strangeness of it." Rich girls, meanwhile, "had time and opportunity to create effects, to be beautiful" ("An Experiment in Luxury," in Crane, *The New York City Sketches of Stephen Crane and Related Pieces*, ed. R. W. Stallman and E. R. Hagemann [New York: New York UP, 1966], p. 50). Looks, in the end, are effects of a social and economic structure. Maggie—like the working woman in general—turns out to be the victim of an unjust politics of looks.

18. David F. Noble, *America by Design: Science, Technology and the Rise of Corporate Capitalism* (New York: Knopf, 1977), pp. 269, 271.

19. Benjamin Franklin formulated the weakness of reason rather succinctly before these institutions had been imagined. In his own attempts at self-government, he found that "while my care was employed in guarding against one fault, I was often surprised by another; habit took advantage of inattention; inclination was sometimes too strong for reason" (Benjamin Franklin, *Autobiography* [1868; New York: Holt, Rinehart, and Winston, 1959], p. 78).

20. Dewey, *Psychology*, p. 415.

21. Crane, *Stephen Crane's Love Letters to Nellie Crouse*, ed. Edwin H. Cady and Lester G. Wells (Syracuse, N.Y.: Syracuse UP, 1954), pp. 43–44.

22. Quoted in Crane, *Stephen Crane: An Omnibus*, pp. 605–606.

23. Jack Potter, it might be argued, likewise stands up against a town in "The Bride Comes to Yellow Sky" (1898): he neither abandons his unacceptable bride nor ultimately hides from the judgment of the town; he returns to Yellow Sky and ends up facing down its symbolic and violent emissary, Scratchy Wilson.

24. Quoted in Stallman, *Stephen Crane*, pp. 219–224.

25. "The Open Boat," pp. 290, 293.

26. Upham, *Elements of Moral Philosophy*, vol. 2, p. 138.

27. Ralph Waldo Emerson, "Self-Reliance," in *Ralph Waldo Emerson: Selected Essays*, ed. Larzer Ziff (New York: Viking Penguin, 1982), p. 178.

28. In the Art Students' League Building. The quote from Emerson, which Crane copied into his pocket notebook: "Congratulate yourselves if you have done something strange and extravagant and broken the monotony of a decorous age" (Stallman, *Stephen Crane*, p. 81).

29. Upham, *Elements of Mental Philosophy*, vol. 2, p. 145.

30. Emerson, "Nature," in *Ralph Waldo Emerson: Selected Essays*, p. 39. Vision or spectating is hardly a transcendental experience in Crane's fictions.

31. *The Monster*, p. 346.

32. For this insight, I am indebted to Michael Warner, who has pointed out that Trescott's action does not indicate moral choice or agency or "moral courage"; he is, rather, "trapped by debts of unaccountable gratitude" (Warner, "Value, Agency, and 'The Monster,'" p. 87).

33. *The Monster*, pp. 346–347, 363, 349.

34. Crane, *The Red Badge of Courage and Selected Stories*, pp. 98, 109, 111–112, my italics.

35. *The Monster*, p. 377.

36. "The Open Boat," p. 306.

37. Even when the opposition is inanimate, as in "The Open Boat," there is an argument with opposing values: here, nature's indifference to the lives of the men in the boat.

38. Letter to William Dean Howells, 27 Jan. 1896, quoted in Katz, Introduction, p. xiv.

39. *George's Mother*, p. 82.

40. Letter to William Dean Howells, 27 Jan. 1896, quoted in Katz, Introduction, p. xiv, my italics.

41. A premier adversary, for both Crane and the Bowery, is Protestant morality. The armor that clads Jimmie's soul is to a large degree a hostility to Protestant ethics; this becomes explicit a few paragraphs later when we are told: "Above all things he despised obvious Christians" (14). Nell's attack on Maggie's "virtue" is another example.

Afterword

1. The 1950s and 1960s brought a revolt against middle-class life that shared certain major themes, including an interest in the slums, with that of the 1890s, even if the postwar revolt was more dramatic. So it is not an accident that three of the five authors I will discuss here are from that period.

2. His one sustained effort was the romantic-comic novel *The Third Violet* (1897) in *The University of Virginia Edition of the Works of Stephen Crane*, vol. 3, ed. Fredson Bowers (Charlottesville: UP of Virginia, 1969).

3. Henry Miller, *Tropic of Cancer* (New York: Grove, 1961), pp. 241, 220, 278, 227.

4. Jack Kerouac, *On the Road* (1957; New York: Penguin, 1976), pp. 242–243, 194.

5. William S. Burroughs, *Junky* (1953; New York: Penguin, 1977), p. 106.

6. Norman Mailer, "The White Negro," in *Advertisements for Myself* (New York: Putnam, 1959), p. 354. Kathy Acker proclaims the need to "fight the dullness of shit society. Alienated robotized images. . . . No to anything but madness" (Acker, *Blood and Guts in High School*, in *Blood and Guts in High School, Plus Two* [London: Pan Books, 1984], p. 35).

7. Tom Wolfe, *The Electric Kool-Aid Acid Test* (Boston and New York: Houghton Mifflin, 1989), p. 116.

8. Miller, *Tropic of Cancer*, p. 228.

9. Burroughs, *Junky*, p. 106.

10. Kathy Acker, *My Death, My Life, by Pier Paulo Pasolini*, in *Blood and Guts in High School, Plus Two*, p. 336.

11. Miller, *Tropic of Cancer*, p. 60.

12. Ibid., p. 258.

13. Crane seems to want to indicate something akin to what Mailer is asserting here about "flipping": Jimmie and Pete cannot afford to do it too often. Interestingly, Pete "flips" again, in Mailer's terms, at the end of the Crane's book, when he gets drunk and pathetically implores Nell and her cohorts to tell him he is a good fellow. With this failure, his "Hip" standing among them seems pretty well demolished: they rob him when he passes out.

Meanwhile, Mailer is also aware of Maggie's brand of failure; he may as well be talking about her when he observes that "one can hardly afford to be put down too often, or one is beat, one has lost one's confidence" (Mailer, "The White Negro," pp. 340, 352, 351, 352).

14. Ibid., p. 351.

15. Miller, *Tropic of Cancer*, p. 228.

16. For Burroughs's use of this term, see *Junky*, p. 31.

17. Kerouac, *On the Road*, p. 180.

18. Mailer, "The White Negro," pp. 340, 348.

19. "The Negro has the simplest of alternatives," writes Mailer, "live a life of constant humility or ever-threatening danger." Mailer's "Negro" (who refuses to be humiliated) is attractive to the Hipsters because, living in a "partially totalitarian society," the postwar Hipsters find that the "black man's code . . . fit their facts" (ibid., pp. 339–341).

Mailer's essay and Kerouac's novel, with their romanticization of "the Negro," have inspired extensive criticism; one of the earlier attacks came from James Baldwin, "The Black Boy Looks at the White Boy," in his *Nobody Knows My Name: More Notes of a Native Son* (New York: Dell, 1961). Baldwin speaks of "that myth of the sexuality of Negroes which Norman, like so many others, refuses to give up," and goes on to say: "[M]y temperament and my experience in this country had led me to expect very little from most American whites . . . : so it did not seem worthwhile to challenge . . . Norman's views on life on the periphery, or to put him down for them. I was weary, to tell the truth. I had tried, in the States, to convey something of what it felt like to be a Negro and no one had been able to listen: they wanted their romance" (pp. 220–221). Much of Baldwin's antipathy "had to do with my resistance to [Mailer's] title ["The White Negro"], and with a kind of fury that so antique a vision of the blacks should, at this late hour, and in so many borrowed heirlooms, be stepping off the A train. But I was also baffled by the passion with which Norman appeared to be imitating so many people inferior to himself, i.e., Kerouac, and all the other Suzuki rhythm boys." Of Kerouac's passage quoted here, Baldwin wrote: "Now, this is absolute nonsense, of course, objectively considered, and offensive nonsense at that: I would hate to be in Kerouac's shoes if he should ever be mad enough to read this aloud from the stage of Harlem's Apollo Theater" (pp. 228–229, 231).

Baldwin characterized the notion of "hip" or "beat" as a "*mystique* [which] depended on a total rejection of life, and insisted on the fulfillment of an infantile dream of love, [and so] the *mystique* could only be extended into violence. No one is more dangerous than he who imagines himself pure in heart: for his purity, by definition, is unassailable." He went on to say, in response to Mailer's and Kerouac's reference to blacks, "But *why* should it be necessary to borrow the Depression language of deprived Negroes, which eventually evolved into jive and bop talk, in order to justify such a grim system of delusions? Why malign the sorely menaced sexuality of Negroes in order to justify the white man's own sexual panic?" (pp. 229–230).

Interestingly, Baldwin's attack on Mailer inspired a counterattack in Mailer's defense by Eldridge Cleaver in "Notes on a Native Son," in *Soul on Ice* (1968; New York: Dell, 1992). Cleaver wrote that a "racial death-wish is manifested as the driving force in James Baldwin. His hatred for blacks, even as he pleads what he conceives as their cause, makes him the apotheosis of the dilemma in the ethos of the black bourgeoisie who have completely rejected their African heritage, consider the loss irrevocable, and refuse to look again in that direction. This is the root of Baldwin's violent repudiation of Mailer's *The White Negro*" (p. 101).

20. Mailer, "The White Negro," p. 339.

21. Ibid., p. 340.

22. Ibid., p. 343.

23. The punk (music) movement, for example, might be mentioned in this context. It presented (and to some extent still presents) another, different style of bohemian and youth-culture flirtation with the slums.

24. Kerouac's yearnings in *On the Road* may have "unwittingly caricatured the proliferating, insatiable wants of consumer capitalism," as Jackson Lears argues (*No Place of Grace*, p. 306), but even if they were as racist and classist as those of teenagers today, Kerouac's yearnings were not satisfied by television, shopping, dressing up, and mimicking but involved a degree of defiance and personal risk that these teenagers are generally spared.

25. Mailer, "The White Negro," p. 351.

26. Mailer, *An American Dream* (New York: Holt, 1964), pp. 82, 100.

27. Ibid., p. 128. Miller's and Mailer's misogynistic attitudes have been much discussed. A seminal book is Kate Millet's *Sexual Politics* (Garden City, N.Y.: Ballantine, 1970). Millet writes of Miller: "Miller's ideal woman is a whore." She likewise suggests that Miller's sexual pose is a sort of revenge for perceived wounds: "To love is to lose. In his one honest

book, *Nexus*, Miller reveals that he lost very badly. His beloved Mara turned out to be a lesbian who inflicted her mistress upon him in a nightmarish menage-a-trois. . . . It would be fascinating to speculate on how much of Miller's arrogance toward 'cunt' in general is the product of this one lacerating experience" (pp. 301, 304). Millet calls Mailer "a prisoner of the virility cult." She finds the source for his misogyny in the army: "In Mailer's work the sexual animus behind reactionary attitude erupts into open hostility. It is hardly surprising that a man whose most formative adult experience took place in the men's-house culture of the army might tend to see sexual belligerence in the terms of actual warfare" (pp. 314–315). On Kerouac's sexual politics, see, for example, Carolyn Cassady's *Off the Road: My Years with Cassady, Kerouac, Ginsberg* (New York: Morrow, 1990). I would argue that in the cases of all three of these male writers, their misogyny (at the least) finds outlet and articulation in their flirtation with the slums.

28. Acker, *Blood and Guts in High School*, p. 99.

29. Ibid., p. 94.

30. Of course, rap music differs from bohemian literature in that the former originates in black urban street culture, and much rap music still issues from this culture. By my inclusion of rap music (and rap videos) in the discussion here, I do not mean to categorize it as a bohemian art form (though its packaging by record companies and music television stations that are outside black urban street culture should be considered part of its production, and though it has also been co-opted by performing artists from the middle class). I am including it here because of its misogynist affinities with bohemian literature—and because it is today the single most important window on urban street life for middle-class teenagers.

On rap and misogyny, see, for example, Venise T. Berry, "Female Images in Rap Music," in *Cecilia Reclaimed: Feminist Perspectives on Gender and Music*, ed. Susan C. Cook and Judy S. Tsou (Urbana: U of Illinois P, 1994):

> The negative images and messages concerning women in rap music have spawned tremendous publicity. . . . Born in the New York streets of Harlem and the South Bronx, rap evolved as part of the privileged black male urban street culture, popularizing black dialect, street fashion, style, attitude, and mannerisms. . . . Rap music . . . has defined the images of women from that limited perspective. Many male rap groups tend to view women with a common lack of respect, but controversial groups like the 2 Live Crew, The Ghetto Boys, Easy E, and Too Short perpetuate extreme negatives. In many male rap videos, the female body is presented as a product of male sexual pleasure; candid shots of breasts, crotches, and buttocks are the norm. Women in these raps are called "skeezers," "hoes," "sluts," "whores," and "bitches." They are described as objects to be sexually used, physically and verbally abused.

Berry does add: "In all fairness it should be noted there is a significant number of male rap groups that do not advocate misogyny toward women" (pp. 186–188).

For other views on rap and misogyny, see Lisa Lewis, "Female Address in Music Video," *Journal of Communication Inquiry* 11 (Winter 1987), p. 75; Reebee Garofalo, "Crossing Over: 1938–1989," in *Split-Image: African Americans in the Mass Media*, ed. Janette Dates and William Barlow (Washington: Howard UP, 1990); David Toop, *The Rap Attack* (Boston: South End, 1984).

31. Published posthumously.

32. Follet quoted in Crane, *Stephen Crane: An Omnibus*, p. 606.

33. Quoted in ibid., pp. 605–606.

34. John Dewey, "The Need for a Recovery of Philosophy" (1917), quoted in Morton White, *Social Thought in America* (Boston: Beacon P, 1959), pp. 129–130.

35. Christopher Lasch, *The New Radicalism in America, 1889–1963: The Intellectual as Social Type* (New York: Knopf, 1965), introduction.

36. Again, the legacy of the literature Riis epitomizes is our present mainstream discourse on social problems, as represented in part by the *Time* article with which we began, a discourse carried on in newspapers, in books, and on television, whose terms are articulated by social workers, sociologists, urban anthropologists, and psychologists.

37. This aesthetic is available for consumption in the forms of music, music videos, and clothes.

References

Books

Acker, Kathy. *Blood and Guts in High School*. In *Blood and Guts in High School, Plus Two*. London: Pan Books, 1984.

———. *My Death, My Life, by Pier Paolo Pasolini* in *Blood and Guts in High School, Plus Two*. London: Pan Books, 1984.

Addams, Jane. *Twenty Years at Hull-House*. New York: Macmillan, 1961.

Ahnebrink, Lars. *The Beginnings of Naturalism in American Fiction*. New York: Russell and Russell, 1961.

Alger, Horatio. *Ragged Dick; or, Street Life in New York*. New York: Collier, 1962.

Alland, Alexander, Sr. *Jacob A. Riis, Photographer and Citizen*. Millerton, N.Y.: Aperture, 1974.

Alloula, Malek. *The Colonial Harem*. Trans. Myrna and Wlad Godzich. Minneapolis: U of Minnesota P, 1986.

Baldwin, James M. *Mental Development in the Child and the Race*. 2nd ed. New York: Macmillan, 1895.

Barthes, Roland. *Mythologies*. New York: Hill and Wang, 1972.

Beecher, Catharine, and Harriet Beecher Stowe, *The American Woman's Home, or, Principles of Domestic Science*. New York: J. B. Ford, 1869.

Bellah, Robert. *Habits of the Heart*. Berkeley: U of California P, 1985.

Bellamy, Charles Joseph. *The Breton Mills: A Romance*. New York: G. P. Putnam and Sons, 1879.

Benfey, Christopher. *The Double Life of Stephen Crane*. New York: Knopf, 1992.

Bergon, Frank. *Stephen Crane's Artistry*. New York: Columbia UP, 1975.

Berryman, John. *Stephen Crane*. Cleveland: Meridian, 1950.

Berthoff, Warner. *The Ferment of Realism: American Literature, 1884–1919.* New York: Free Press, 1965.

Boorstin, Daniel J. *The Americans: The Democratic Experience.* New York: Vintage Books, 1974.

Boyer, Paul. *Urban Masses and Moral Order in America, 1820–1920.* Cambridge, Mass.: Harvard UP, 1978.

Boyesen, Hjalmer Hjorth. *Social Strugglers: A Novel.* New York: Scribner's, 1893.

Brace, Charles Loring. *The Dangerous Classes of New York, and Twenty Years' Work among Them.* New York: Wynkoop and Hallenbeck, 1872.

Brooks, Van Wyck. *The Confident Years, 1885–1915.* New York: Dutton, 1952.

Burroughs, William S. *Junky.* 1953. New York: Penguin, 1977.

Cady, Edwin H. *Stephen Crane.* New York: Twayne, 1962.

Cahan, Abraham. *Yekl and the Imported Bridegroom and Other Stories of the New York Ghetto.* New York: Dover, 1970.

Campbell, Helen. *Mrs. Herndon's Income: A Novel.* Boston: Roberts Brothers, 1886.

———. *Prisoners of Poverty: Women Wage-Workers, Their Trades and Their Lives.* Boston: Roberts, 1887.

Cassady, Carolyn. *Off the Road: My Years with Cassady, Kerouac, Ginsberg.* New York: Morrow, 1990.

Chapin, Reverend Edwin Hubbell. *Humanity in the City.* New York: DeWitt and Davenport, 1854.

Colvert, James. *Stephen Crane.* San Diego: Harcourt, 1984.

Corrigan, Robert S. *An Introduction to C. S. Peirce.* Lanham, Md.: Rowman and Littlefield, 1933.

Crane, Stephen. *The Complete Short Stories and Sketches of Stephen Crane.* Ed. Thomas Gullason. Garden City, N.Y.: Doubleday, 1963.

———. *Maggie: A Girl of the Streets.* Ed. Thomas Gullason. 1893. New York: Norton, 1979.

———. *The New York City Sketches of Stephen Crane and Related Pieces.* Ed. R. W. Stallman and E. R. Hagemann. New York: New York UP, 1966.

———. *Prose and Poetry.* New York: Literary Classics of the U.S., Viking, 1984.

———. *The Red Badge of Courage and Other Writings.* Ed. Richard Chase. Cambridge, Mass.: Houghton Mifflin, 1960.

———. *The Red Badge of Courage and Selected Stories.* Ed. Robert Wooster Stallman. New York: Signet, NAL, 1960.

———. *Stephen Crane: Letters.* Ed. Robert Wooster Stallman and Lillian Gilkes. New York: New York UP, 1960.

———. *Stephen Crane: An Omnibus.* Ed. Robert Wooster Stallman. New York: Knopf, 1961.

———. *Stephen Crane's Love Letters to Nellie Crouse.* Ed. Edwin H. Cady and Lester G. Wells. Syracuse, N.Y.: Syracuse UP, 1954.

———. *The Third Violet* in *The University of Virginia Edition of the Works of Stephen Crane.* 1897. Vol. 3. Ed. Fredson Bowers. Charlottesville: UP of Virginia, 1969.

Davis, Allen F. *American Heroine: The Life and Legend of Jane Addams.* New York: Oxford UP, 1973.

Davis, Rebecca Harding. *Life in the Iron Mills*. 1861. New York: Feminist, 1972.

Debord, Guy. *The Society of the Spectacle*. Detroit: Black and Red, 1970.

DeForest, Robert Weeks, and Lawrence Veiller, eds. *The Tenement House Problem, Including the Report of the New York State Tenement House Commission of 1900, by Various Writers*. New York: Macmillan, 1903.

Dewey, John. *Human Nature*. New York: Henry Holt, 1922.

———. *Psychology*. New York: Harper and Brothers, 1898.

Douglas, Ann. *The Feminization of American Culture*. New York: Knopf, 1977.

Dreiser, Theodore. *Sister Carrie*. Boston: Houghton Mifflin, 1959.

Fawcett, Edgar. *The Evil That Men Do*. New York: Belford, 1889.

Flynt, Josiah (pseud.). *Tramping with Tramps: Studies and Sketches of Vagabond Life*. New York: Century, 1899.

Foucault, Michel. *Discipline and Punish: The Birth of the Prison*. Trans. Alan Sheridan. New York: Vintage, 1977.

———. *The Use of Pleasure*. Trans. Robert Hurley. New York: Pantheon, 1985.

Franklin, Benjamin. *Autobiography*. 1868. New York: Holt, Rinehart, and Winston, 1959.

Freud, Sigmund. *Civilization and Its Discontents*. Trans. James Strachey. New York: Norton, 1961.

Fried, Michael. *Realism, Writing, Disfiguration*. Chicago: U of Chicago P, 1987.

Friedman, Isaac Kahn. *The Autobiography of a Beggar*. Boston: Small, Maynard, 1903.

———. *Poor People: A Novel*. Boston and New York: Houghton Mifflin, 1900.

Hales, Peter. *Silver Cities: The Photography of American Urbanization, 1839–1915*. Philadelphia: Temple UP, 1984.

Halliburton, David. *The Color of the Sky*. New York: Cambridge UP, 1989.

Hapgood, Hutchins. *Types of City Streets*. New York: Garrett Press, 1970.

Heath, William. *The Children Bob Moses Led*. Minneapolis: Milkweed, 1995.

Holland, Josiah Gilbert. *Nicholas Minturn*. New York: Scribner, Armstrong, 1877.

Holton, Milne. *Cylinder of Vision: The Fiction and Journalistic Writing of Stephen Crane*. Baton Rouge: Louisiana State UP, 1972.

Howells, William Dean. 1890. *A Hazard of New Fortunes*. New York: Dutton, 1952.

———. *The Rise of Silas Lapham*. 1885. New York: Signet NAL, 1980.

James, Henry. *The American Scene*. London: Harper, 1907.

James, William. *Principles of Psychology*. New York: Holt, 1890.

Kaplan, Amy. *The Social Construction of American Realism*. Chicago: U of Chicago P, 1988.

Kazin, Alfred. *On Native Grounds: An Interpretation of Modern American Prose Literature*. New York: Reynal and Hitchcock, 1942.

Kerouac, Jack. *On the Road*. 1957. New York: Penguin, 1976.

Kuhn, Thomas. *The Structure of Scientific Revolutions*. Chicago: U of Chicago P, 1962.

LaFrance, Marston. *A Reading of Stephen Crane*. Oxford: Clarendon, 1971.

Lane, James B. *Jacob A. Riis and the American City*. Port Washington, N.Y.: Kennikat, 1974.

Lasch, Christopher. *The Culture of Narcissism*. New York: Norton, 1978.

———. *Haven in a Heartless World: The Family Besieged*. New York: Basic Books, 1977.

———. *The New Radicalism in America, 1889–1963: The Intellectual as a Social Type*. New York: Knopf, 1965.

Lears, T. J. Jackson. *No Place of Grace: Antimodernism and the Transformation of American Culture, 1880–1920*. New York: Pantheon, 1981.

Leiby, James. *A History of Social Welfare and Social Work in the United States*. New York: Columbia UP, 1978.

Leonard, Thomas. *The Power of the Press: The Birth of American Political Reporting*. New York: Oxford UP, 1986.

Levine, Daniel. *Jane Addams and the Liberal Tradition*. Westport, Conn.: State Historical Society of Wisconsin, 1971.

Lippard, George. *The Quaker City or The Monks of Monk Hall*. 1844. New York: Odyssey P, 1970.

Lubove, Roy. *The Professional Altruist: The Emergence of Social Work as a Career, 1880–1930*. Cambridge, Mass.: Harvard UP, 1965.

Mailer, Norman. *An American Dream*. New York: Holt, 1964.

May, Henry. *The End of American Innocence: A Study of the First Years of Our Own Times, 1912–1917*. New York: Knopf, 1959.

May, Larry. *Screening out the Past*. New York: Oxford UP, 1980.

Mayhew, Henry. *London Labour and the London Poor*. 1851. New York: Dover, 1968.

Michaels, Walter. *The Gold Standard and the Logic of Naturalism*. Berkeley: U of California P, 1987.

Miller, Henry. *Tropic of Cancer*. New York: Grove, 1961.

Millet, Kate. *Sexual Politics*. Garden City, N.Y.: Ballantine, 1970.

Moore, Edward C. *American Pragmatism: Peirce, James, and Dewey*. New York: Columbia UP, 1961.

Nagel, James. *Stephen Crane and Literary Impressionism*. University Park: Pennsylvania State UP, 1980.

Noble, David F. *America by Design: Science, Technology and the Rise of Corporate Capitalism*. New York: Knopf, 1977.

Parry, Albert. *Garrets and Pretenders: A History of Bohemianism in America*. New York: Dover, 1960.

Richmond, Mary. *Social Diagnosis*. New York: Russell Sage Foundation, 1917.

Riis, Jacob. *The Battle with the Slum*. New York: Macmillan, 1902.

———. *The Children of the Poor*. New York: Scribner's, 1892.

———. *Children of the Tenements*. New York: Macmillan, 1903.

———. *Hero Tales of the Far North*. New York: Macmillan, 1913.

———. *How the Other Half Lives: Studies among the Tenements of New York*. 1890. New York: Hill and Wang, 1957.

———. *The Making of an American*. 1901. New York: Macmillan, 1935.

———. *Out of Mulberry Street, Stories of Tenement Life in New York City*. New York: Century, 1898.

———. *Theodore Roosevelt: The Citizen*. New York: Outlook, 1903.

Roback, Abraham Aaron. *History of American Psychology*. New York: Library Publishers, 1952.

Roosevelt, Theodore. *The Strenuous Life: Essays and Addresses*. New York: Century, 1901.

Ross, Edward Alsworth. *Social Control: A Survey of the Foundations of Order*. New York: Macmillan, 1901.

Rothman, David J. *Conscience and Convenience.* Boston: Little, Brown, 1980.

Sanborn, Alvan Francis. *Meg McIntyre's Raffle and Other Stories.* Boston: Copeland and Day, 1896.

————. *Moody's Lodging House and Other Tenement Sketches.* Boston: Copeland and Day, 1895.

Seligman, Martin E. *The Optimistic Child.* Boston: Houghton, Mifflin, 1995.

Seltzer, Mark. *Henry James and the Art of Power.* Ithaca: Cornell UP, 1984.

Sinclair, Upton. *The Jungle.* 1906. New York: Penguin, 1965.

Solomon, Eric. *Stephen Crane: From Parody to Realism.* Cambridge, Mass.: Harvard UP, 1966.

Sontag, Susan. *On Photography.* New York: Dell, 1977.

Stallman, Robert Wooster. *Stephen Crane: A Biography.* New York: G. Braziller, 1968.

Stange, Maren. *Symbols of Ideal Life.* New York: Cambridge UP, 1989.

Stewart, William R., ed. *The Philanthropic Work of Josephine Shaw Lowell.* New York: Macmillan, 1911.

Stocking, George. *Race, Culture, and Evolution: Essays in the History of Anthropology.* New York: Free Press, 1968.

Sullivan, James W. *Tenement Tales of New York.* New York: Holt, 1895.

Sumner, William Graham. *Folkways: A Study of the Sociological Importance of Usages, Manners, Customs, Mores, and Morals.* Boston: Ginn, 1906.

Susman, Warren. *Culture as History: The Transformation of the American Society in the Twentieth Century.* New York: Pantheon, 1984.

Talmage, Thomas De Witt. *The Abominations of Modern Society.* New York: Adams and Victor, 1872.

Taylor, Walter Fuller. *The Economic Novel in America.* Chapel Hill: U of North Carolina P, 1942.

Thomson, John. *Street Life in London.* London: Sampson Law, Marston Searle and Rovington, 1877.

Thomson, John, and Adolphe Smith. *Street Life in London.* New York: B. Blom, 1969.

Toll, Robert C. *On with the Show!: The First Century of Show Business in America.* New York: Oxford UP, 1976.

Tompkins, Jane. *Sensational Designs: The Cultural Work of American Fiction, 1790–1860.* New York: Oxford UP, 1985.

Toop, David. *The Rap Attack.* Boston: South End, 1984.

Townsend, Edward Waterman. *Chimmie Fadden.* New York: Lovell, Coryell, 1895.

————. *"Chimmie Fadden," Major Max, and Other Stories.* New York: Garrett, 1969.

————. *A Daughter of the Tenements.* New York: Coryell and Company, 1895.

Trachtenberg, Alan. *The Incorporation of America: Culture and Society in the Gilded Age.* New York: Hill and Wang, 1982.

Trattner, Walter I. *Crusade for the Children: A History of the National Child Labor Committee and Child Labor Reform in America.* Chicago: Quadrangle Books, 1970.

Tuckerman, Joseph. *On the Elevation of the Poor: A Selection from His Reports as Minister at Large in Boston.* Boston: Roberts Brothers, 1874.

Upham, Thomas Cogswell. *Elements of Mental Philosophy.* Vol. 2. New York: Harper, 1845.

Veiller, Lawrence. *Tenement House Reform in New York, 1834–1900*. New York: The Evening Post Job Printing House, 1900.

Wertheim, Stanley, and Paul M. Sorrentino. *The Crane Log: A Documentary Life of Stephen Crane*. New York: Maxwell Macmillan International, 1994.

White, Morton. *Social Thought in America*. Boston: Beacon P, 1959.

Wiebe, Robert. *The Search for Order, 1877–1920*. New York: Hill and Wang, 1967.

Wiggin, Kate Douglas. *Timothy's Quest: A Story for Anybody, Young or Old, Who Cares to Read It*. Boston: Houghton Mifflin, 1890.

Winslow, Charles Edward Armory. *Twenty Years of Mental Hygiene, 1901–1929*. New York: American Foundation for Mental Hygiene, Inc., 1929.

Wolfe, Tom. *The Electric Kool-Aid Acid Test*. 1968. Boston and New York: Houghton Mifflin, 1989.

Articles and Television Programs

Aaron, Daniel. "Howells' 'Maggie.'" *Maggie: A Girl of the Streets*. Ed. Thomas Gullason. New York: Norton, 1979. 112–115.

Adams, Ansel. Preface. *Jacob A. Riis, Photographer and Citizen*. By Alexander Alland. Millerton, N.Y.: Aperture, 1974.

Ahnebrink, Lars. "Zola as Literary Model for *Maggie*." *Maggie: A Girl of the Streets*. Ed. Thomas Gullason. New York: Norton, 1979. 92–94.

"The American Underclass." *Time*. 29 Aug. 1977: 14–27.

Baldwin, James. "The Black Boy Looks at the White Boy." *Nobody Knows My Name: More Notes of a Native Son*. New York: Dell, 1961.

Berry, Venise T. "Female Images in Rap Music." *Cecilia Reclaimed: Feminist Perspectives on Gender and Music*. Ed. Susan C. Cook and Judy S. Tsou. Urbana: U of Illinois P, 1994. 183–201.

"Black America Today." *San Francisco Chronicle*. 28 Mar. 1988: A6.

"Black Hard-Liners in the War on Drugs." *San Francisco Chronicle*. 28 Mar. 1988: A7.

Buitenhuis, Peter. "The Essentials of Life: 'The Open Boat' as Existentialist Fiction." *Modern Fiction Studies* 5 (Autumn 1959): 243–250.

Channing, Walter. "An Address on the Prevention of Pauperism." Boston: Office of the Christian World, 1843.

Cleaver, Eldridge. "Notes on a Native Son." *Soul on Ice*. 1968. New York: Dell, 1992.

Colvert, James. "Structure and Theme in Stephen Crane's Fiction." *Modern Fiction Studies* 5 (Autumn 1959): 199–208.

Cordasco, Francesco. Introduction. *The Children of the Poor*. By Jacob Riis. New York: Garrett, 1970.

Cox, James T. "The Imagery of 'The Red Badge of Courage.'" *Modern Fiction Studies* 5 (Autumn 1959): 209–219.

Cunliff, Marcus. "Stephen Crane and the American Background of *Maggie*." *Maggie: A Girl of the Streets*. Ed. Thomas A. Gullason. New York: Norton, 1979. 94–103.

Dewey, John. "The Need for a Recovery of Philosophy." 1917. *Social Thought in America*. By Morton White. Boston: Beacon P, 1963. 129–130.

Elsing, William T. "Life in New York Tenement Houses as Seen by a City Missionary."

The Poor in Great Cities: The Problems and What Is Doing to Solve Them. New York: Scribner's and Sons, 1895.

Emerson, Ralph Waldo. "Self-Reliance." *Ralph Waldo Emerson: Selected Essays.* Ed. Larzer Ziff. New York: Viking Penguin, 1982. 175–203.

Fitelson, David. "Stephen Crane's *Maggie* and Darwinism." *American Quarterly* 16 (Summer 1964): 182–186.

Fleming, Anne Taylor. "Will the Real Self-Esteem Please Stand Up?" *New York Times.* 9 Nov. 1988: C10.

Fried, Michael. "Realism, Writing, and Disfiguration in Thomas Eakins's Gross Clinic." *Representations* 9 (Winter 1985): 95.

Garland, Hamlin. "An Ambitious French Novel and a Modest American Story." *Maggie: A Girl of the Streets.* Ed. Thomas Gullason. New York: Norton, 1979. 144–145.

Garofalo, Reebee. "Crossing Over: 1938–1989." *Split-Image: African Americans in the Mass Media.* Ed. Janette Oates and William Barlow. Washington: Howard UP, 1990.

Gibson, Donald. "The Flawed *Maggie*." *Maggie: A Girl of the Streets.* Ed. Thomas Gullason. New York: Norton, 1979. 212–218.

Gullason, Thomas. "The Sources of Stephen Crane's *Maggie*." Ed. Thomas Gullason. New York: Norton, 1979. 103–108.

———. "Tragedy and Melodrama in *Maggie*." *Maggie: A Girl of the Streets.* Ed. Thomas Gullason. New York: Norton, 1979. 245–253.

Hamill, Pete. "Breaking the Silence." *Esquire.* Mar. 1988: 91–102.

Higham, John. "The Re-orientation of American Culture in the 1890s." *The Origins of Modern Consciousness.* Ed. John Weiss. Detroit: Wayne State UP, 1965. 25–48.

Howells, William Dean. "New York Streets." *Impressions and Experiences.* New York: Harper, 1909.

Katz, Joseph. Introduction. *Maggie: A Girl of the Streets: A Facsimile Reproduction of the First Edition of 1893.* By Stephen Crane. Gainesville, Fla.: Scholars' Facsimiles and Reprints, 1966.

Kolata, Gina. "Grim Seeds of Park Rampage Found in East Harlem Streets." *New York Times.* 2 May 1989: B5.

LaFrance, Marston. "*George's Mother* and the Other Half of *Maggie*." *Stephen Crane in Transition: Centenary Essays.* Ed. Joseph Katz. DeKalb: Northern Illinois UP, 1972. 35–53.

Leviatin, David. "Framing the Poor." Introduction to *How the Other Half Lives.* By Jacob Riis. Boston: Bedford Books, 1996.

Lewis, Lisa. "Female Address in Music Video." *Journal of Communication Inquiry* 11 (Winter 1987): 75.

Magnet, Myron. "America's Underclass: What to Do?" *Fortune.* 11 May 1987: 130.

Mailer, Norman. "The White Negro." *Advertisements for Myself.* New York: Putnam, 1959.

"New Ways to Battle Gang Violence." *San Francisco Chronicle.* 1 May 1989: A6.

Norris, Frank. "Stephen Crane's Stories of Life in the Slums: *Maggie and George's Mother*." *Maggie: A Girl of the Streets.* Ed. Thomas Gullason. New York: Norton, 1979. 151–152.

Parker, Hershel, and Brian Higgins. "Maggie's 'Last Night': Authorial Design and Editorial Patching." *Maggie: A Girl of the Streets.* Ed. Thomas Gullason. New York: Norton, 1979. 234–245.

Parrington, Vernon L. "The Beginnings of Critical Realism in America." *Main Currents in American Thought.* 3 vols. New York: Harcourt, Brace, 1930.

Pizer, Donald. "Stephen Crane's *Maggie* and American Naturalism." *Criticism, a Quarterly for Literature and the Arts* 7. (Spring 1965): 168–175.

"Psychology in American Colleges and Universities." *American Journal of Psychology.* 3 Apr. 1890: 275–286.

Putnam, Hilary, and Ruth Anna Putnam. "William James's Ideas." *Raritan* 8.3 (Winter 1989): 27–44.

Roosevelt, Theodore. "Jacob Riis." *The Outlook* 57 (June 1914): 284.

Seltzer, Mark. "Statistical Persons." *Diacritics* 17.3 (Fall 1987): 84–85.

Smith, Allan Gardner. "Stephen Crane, Impressionism and William James." *Revue Francaise d'Etudes Americaines* 17 (May 1983): 237–248.

Stallman, R. W. "Crane's 'Maggie': A Reassessment." *Modern Fiction Studies* 5 (Autumn 1959): 251–259.

"Street Gang Violence." *Nightline.* Narr. Ted Koppel. ABC. 11 Oct. 1988.

Trachtenberg, Alan. "Experiments in Another Country." *American Realism: New Essays.* Ed. Eric J. Sundquist. Baltimore: Johns Hopkins UP, 1982. 138–54.

"The Vanishing Family: Crisis in Black America." *CBS Reports.* Narr. Bill Moyers. CBS. 25 Jan. 1986.

Walker, Francis A. "Restriction of Immigration." *Atlantic Monthly* 77 (June 1896), 822–829.

Walcutt, Charles Child. "Stephen Crane: Naturalist and Impressionist." *American Literary Naturalism: A Divided Stream.* Minneapolis: U of Minnesota P, 1956. 67–72.

Warner, Michael D. "Value, Agency, and 'The Monster.'" *Nineteenth-Century Fiction* 40.1 (June 1985): 76–93.

Warner, Sam Bass. Editor's Introduction. *How the Other Half Lives.* By Jacob Riis. Cambridge, Mass.: Belknap P of Harvard UP, 1970.

Wexler, Laura. "Tender Violence: Literary Eavesdropping, Domestic Fiction, and Educational Reform." *The Culture of Sentiment.* Ed. Shirley Samuels. New York: Oxford UP, 1992.

Wilson, William Julius. "The American Underclass: Inner-City Ghettos and the Norms of Citizenship." *The Godkin Lecture*, John F. Kennedy School of Government, Harvard University. 26 Apr. 1988. 1–51.

———. "The Cost of Racial and Class Exclusion in the Inner City." *The Ghetto Underclass: Social Science Perspectives.* Special issue of *The Annals of the American Academy of Political and Social Science* 501 (January 1989): 9, 25.

Index

Acker, Kathy, 130, 131, 132, 134, 189n.6
Addams, Jane, 152n.69, 180n.5
adventure, search for, 10–14, 21, 152n.63. *See also*
    masculinity, crusade for
  and Crane, 11
  and rebel morality, 132–134
  and Riis, 12, 149n. 42, 151–152nn.58, 60–62
  and spectacle, 71
aesthetics, street, 133, 135, 138, 191n.30, 192n.37
  and Crane, 13, 74–75, 84, 85, 86
  and Riis, 13, 20–22, 74, 86
aesthetics of excitement, 5–6, 10, 17, 21, 22. *See also*
    spectacle of the poor
  and Crane, 78–81, 86
  and Riis, 20–21, 77–81, 82, 86
aesthetics of representing poverty, 5, 17, 33, 39–40.
    See also aesthetics of excitement; picturesque
    representation of poverty
aesthetics and social programs, 116–121
Alger, Horatio, 40, 42, 46, 48, 56
Americanization, 40, 72, 79, 118
antimodernism, 11, 13, 157n.112
architecture. *See* housing reform

Baldwin, James, 189–190n.19
Barthes, Roland, 72
beggar
  in bohemian literature, 164n.20, 166n.8
  in charity writing, 3, 31, 37, 163n.15
  and Crane, 18–19, 62, 64, 73, 98, 127, 172n.5
  in fiction of the slums, didactic, 40, 56, 166n.8
  and Riis, 61, 71, 91, 94–95, 147n.26
Benjamin, Walter, 70

Berryman, John, 81, 173n.5
bohemian literature, 130–136, 137, 138, 159n.112,
    164n.20, 189–191nn.2, 19, 24, 27, 30. *See also*
    rebel morality
bohemians, 13, 15–16, 23, 133–134, 159n.112, 190n.23
  and Crane, 13–15
Boorstin, Daniel J., 85–86
Boyeson, H. H., 39, 43, 154n.78, 165–166n.6
Brace, Charles Loring
  The Dangerous Classes of New York, 28–31, 34–36,
    38, 47, 49–50, 84, 93, 117, 162–163nn.11, 13,
    164n.20, 169n.36
Burroughs, William, 130, 131, 132–133

Channing, Walter, 31, 181n.15
Chapin, E. H., 30, 36–38, 84, 163n.15
charity work, 14, 16–17, 29–30, 35–36, 38, 84, 162n.3.
    See also friendly visiting
  of Charity Organization Society, 150–151n.57,
    179–180n.5
charity writing, 22, 27–38, 61, 93, 138
  as compared to ethnography of the poor, 31–34, 35,
    163–164n.20
  logic of, 30–31, 37–38
  major tropes of, 29–30, 36–38, 163nn.15–16, 181n.15
  Riis, as example of, 29–31, 33, 164n.20
  spectacle of the poor in, 34–38
chastity. *See* modesty, sexual, among the poor
class, 139–140n.5, 144n.19. *See also* middle class
cleanliness among the poor
  as aesthetic vice, 75, 78–79, 86, 87
  in charity writing, 28–30, 34–35, 36, 75–76, 93, 162n.3.
  and Crane, 49

cleanliness among the poor (*continued*)
   in fiction of the slums, didactic, 43
   and Riis, 9, 28–30, 33, 61, 66, 75, 78–79, 86, 87
Cleaver, Eldridge, 190n.19
colorism
   and Crane, 79–81
   and Riis, 79–80
conscience. *See* moral character
consumer culture, 10, 85–86, 143n.14
   and disciplinary society, 6, 17–22, 136,
      156–157n.101, 157–161n.112
   rebellion against, 135, 136
   and slums, 13, 133–134, 136, 138, 152n.65
countercultural rebellion. *See* rebel morality
Crane, Stephen, 7
   and animism, 81
   biographical information concerning, 11, 134
   The Black Riders, 79
   "The Blue Hotel," 79, 102, 150n.49, 183n.46,
      184nn.50, 52
   "The Bride Comes to Yellow Sky," 79, 150n.49,
      188n.23
   city sketches of, 53, 64
   criticism of, 147–48n.27, 153–154n.76, 170n.49,
      171n.54, 174n.5
   and Dora Clark affair, 123–124
   "Experiment in Luxury," 53, 135, 185n.64, 187n.17
   "Experiment in Misery," 14, 18, 19, 64, 73, 98–99
   fictional characters of, 97, 99, 105–106, 107, 108,
      110, 176n.32, 183nn.42, 44
   George's Mother, 53, 55, 83, 106–111, 128, 135,
      182n.30, 39, 184 n.58, 185 n.61
   irony of, 64, 72–73, 84, 147n.27, 171n.54, 172–174n.5
   legacy of, in regards to slums, 8, 130–136, 138,
      159n.112, 180n.5
   Maggie: A Girl of the Streets, 8, 14, 16, 22, 49–57,
      61–62, 72–73, 74–75, 80–85, 96–102, 104,
      105–114, 122–123, 124, 127, 132, 135,
      147–148n.27, 153–154n.76, 156n.100, 157n.109,
      170n.49, 171n.54, 172–173nn.3, 5, 176nn.31–32,
      176–177n.4, 184n.58, 185n.61, 187n.17, 188n.41,
      189n.13
   "Men in the Storm," 83, 185n.64
   The Monster, 105, 123–124, 125, 127, 135,
      183–184nn.46–48, 53, 55, 187n.17,
      188n.32
   "The Open Boat," 98, 101, 106, 113, 124, 127
   The O'Ruddy, 135
   use of profanity by, 74, 86, 176n.4
   and publishers, 21, 74, 155n.88, 172n.3, 173n.5,
      188n.37
   The Red Badge of Courage, 11, 79, 101, 104, 105,
      113, 125–126, 127, 128, 181–182nn.26, 30,
      183–185nn.46–49, 52–54, 56, 58, 60,
      62–63
   sources for slum writing of, 144–145n.21,
      153–154n.76
   and success, 11, 127–128
   The Third Violet, 135
   and war, 11, 81
   "When a Man Falls a Crowd Gathers," 83
   writing style of, 98–99, 111–112

crime in the slums
   in charity writing, 28–29, 30–31, 35–36, 37, 93,
      162n.3
   and Crane, 64, 172–173n.5
   in fiction of the slums, didactic, 41, 43
   reporting, 155n.80
   and Riis, 28, 31, 61, 77, 93, 95, 181n.14
customs of the poor
   and Crane, 22
   and Riis, 32–33, 34, 63, 72, 93, 154n.77, 164n.20
   in fiction of the slums, didactic, 50

Davis, Rebecca Harding, 40, 41, 44, 102
Debord, Guy, 70, 155–156n.93
Dewey, John, 33, 121, 136, 152n.74
Dickens, Charles, 151n.58, 155n.80
dime novels, 21, 74, 86, 152n.63
   of the slums, 41, 63
disciplinary institutions, 116–121, 156n.100
disciplinary society, 6, 17–22, 156n.100,
      157–161n.112
disciplinary techniques, 116–118, 120–121, 156n.100,
      186nn.2, 7, 188n.19
   and photography, 120–121
disease in the slums
   in charity writing, 3, 29–31, 93, 162n.3
   and Crane, 49
   in fiction of the slums, didactic, 43, 44
   and housing reform, 116
   and Riis, 29–30, 116
disorder in the slums, 29–30, 34–35, 36, 49,
      162–163n.13
domestic ideology, 66
Douglas, Ann, 11, 149n.41, 158n.112, 160n.112,
      170n.48
Dreiser, Theodore, 40, 166–167n.10

Emerson, Ralph Waldo, 124–125, 188n.28
Engels, Friedrich, 49
entertainment. *See* spectacle, culture of
entertainment, mass-culture, 84, 88, 112,
      161n.112
entertainment ethics. *See* spectatorship, ethics of
environmental causes of individual behavior. *See*
      social causes of individual behavior
ethnic jokes, 63–64, 70, 72, 174n.8
ethnic literature, 144n.19, 165n.2
ethnicity, 4, 30, 61, 63, 87, 154n.77. *See also* customs of
      the poor; ethnography of the poor; spectacle
      of the poor
ethnography, history of, 154n.77
ethnography of the poor, 3–6. *See also* values of the
      poor, separate
   in bohemian literature, 164n.20
   in charity writing, 163–164n.20
   contemporary, 3–6, 87–88, 138, 140–143n.9,
      178–179n.38
   and Crane, 8, 17, 22, 49–57, 97, 112, 154nn.76–77,
      156n.100
   in fiction of the slums, didactic, 39–40, 42, 43, 44,
      46, 48, 50, 154n.76, 165–167nn.3–12,
      169–170n.43

and Riis, 8, 17, 22, 27–28, 31–34, 36–38, 50, 63, 67, 69, 70, 93, 146n.24, 154n.77, 156n.100, 163–164n.20
and social work, 180–181n.5
exoticism. *See* spectacle of the poor

Fawcett, Edgar
The Evil That Men Do, 39, 41–42, 43–44, 47–48, 49–50, 96, 102, 165n.3, 168n.21
feminization of American life, 10, 20, 132, 134, 136, 138, 149n.41, 158n.112, 160n.112
fiction of the slums, didactic. *See* ethnography of the poor; Protestant moral account of the poor
Foucault, Michel
Discipline and Punish, 18, 155–156n.93
on morality, 7, 144n.18, 158n.112
Franklin, Benjamin, 188n.19
Freud, Sigmund, 5
Fried, Michael, 81, 145n.21, 161n.112
Friedman, I. K., 40, 41, 166nn.8–9, 168n.23, 169n.29
friendly visiting, 12, 13, 43, 84, 150–151n.57, 179–180n.5

gangmember. *See* tough
Griffith, D. W., 85

habits, 32–33, 34, 63, 72, 180–181n.5
spectacle of, 87–88
Hales, Peter B., 65, 145n.23, 174n.10, 175nn.14–15
Hemingway, Ernest, 132
Higham, John, 10, 152n.63, 160n.112
Hipsters. *See* bohemians
housing conditions in the slums
in charity writing, 28–29, 32, 34–35, 38, 93
and Crane, 156n.100
in fiction of the slums, didactic, 41, 42–45
and Riis, 28–30, 32, 65, 93, 156n.100
housing reform, 8, 9, 22, 136, 137, 148n.29
and aesthetic techniques, 22, 116–121
and disciplinary techniques, 116, 118
Howells, William Dean, 70–71, 82, 127, 128, 153n.76, 164n.20, 176n.27
A Hazard of New Fortunes, 39, 43, 165n.5
humor about the poor, 63–64, 70, 72

immigrants, tropes concerning, 30, 162n.3. *See also* customs of the poor; ethnography of the poor
immigration, 139n.5
new, 8, 16
policy, 69, 72, 147n.26
individuality, 5, 7, 138, 158–159n.112. *See also* self-esteem
and Crane, 129, 130–131
and moral character, 94–95, 102, 119
and rebel morality, 130–131, 159n.112
and Riis, 8, 94–95, 102, 116–121
industrialization, 6, 8, 10, 16, 79–81, 120, 158n.112, 187n.17
intemperance in the slums, 3, 29, 30, 31, 38, 41, 163n.16, 180n.5

James, Henry, 40, 45, 167n.12, 169n.31
James, William,
and Crane, 103–105, 112, 145n.21
and masculinity, crusade for, 20
Principles of Psychology, 103–105, 112, 152n.74, 182nn.33, 35
and self-esteem, 103–105, 112, 149n.33
juvenile asylum, 91, 116–119, 137

Kaplan, Amy, 17, 21
Kerouac, Jack, 130, 131, 133, 159n.112, 189–190nn.19, 24

Lasch, Christopher, 7, 137, 143n.14, 157–158n.112
Lears, Jackson, 6, 11, 13, 20, 149n.42, 157–160n.112, 190n.24
Leonard, Thomas, 54–65, 147n.26, 155n.80, 175n.14
Leviatin, David, 20–21, 151n.58
Levine, Daniel, 87, 88, 119–120, 147n.26
liberation, personal, 130–133, 136, 158–160n.112
literature and social practices, 18, 156n.100, 186n.11

Mailer, Norman, 130, 190–191n.27
An American Dream, 134
"The White Negro," 131, 132, 133, 134, 189–190nn.13, 19
masculinity, crusade for, 7, 10–13, 20, 117, 149n.42, 160n.112. *See also* adventure, search for
and Crane, 11, 13, 79, 136
and rebel morality, 132, 134, 136, 138
and Riis, 12–13, 79, 138
and Roosevelt, 12, 20, 151n.60
Mayhew, Henry, 145n.23, 174n.10
middle class
privilege of, 10, 20–21
self-doubt of, 10, 13, 20–21, 85, 130–136, 137–138, 189n.1
Miller, Henry, 130, 131, 132, 190–191n.27
misogyny, 134–136, 190–191nn.27, 30
and Crane, 11, 135–136
modesty, sexual, among the poor, 7, 170n.48
in charity writing, 29, 30, 35, 36, 162n.3, 163n.15, 169n.36
and Crane, 50, 51, 52–53, 136, 171n.54
in fiction of the slums, didactic, 41–42, 44, 45, 47–49
and housing reform, 116, 120
and Riis, 33, 76–78, 116, 120
moral character, 4, 5, 7, 10, 13, 149n.33, 160–161n.112, 180n.5. *See also* Protestant moral account of the poor
and Crane, 8, 9, 10, 22, 57, 96–98, 100, 102, 121–122, 124, 125, 128, 153n.76
and disciplinary techniques, 117–118, 120
and mental philosophy, 97–98, 115, 124, 126, 128
and privacy, 77–78
and Riis, 8, 10, 22, 77–78, 92–93, 94–95, 97, 102, 116, 117–120
and tough, 94–97
moral degradation in the slums, 3, 4, 30–31, 44. *See also* virtue and vice in the slums

morality. *See* Protestant moral account of the poor;
        Protestant morality, decline of; psychological
        morality; rebel morality
movies, 85–86, 161n.112, 178n.32
muckraking, 8, 16, 62, 155n.80
Mulberry Bend, 27–28, 40, 45–46, 62, 75, 76, 77,
        86–87, 88, 148n.29

naturalism, 9, 18, 143n.14, 147–148n.27, 149n.31,
        157n.112
newspaper reporting, 15, 70, 85–86, 161n.112
    and Crane, 15, 144n.21
    and crime, 16, 63, 119, 155n.80
    mass-market, 15, 16
    and photography, 16, 17, 64–65
    and Riis, 15, 16
    and slums, 8, 16–17, 19, 140n.31, 161n.112, 192n.36
    and war, 16, 155n.81
Norris, Frank, 49

observation of the poor, 13–17, 18–19, 156n.100,
        179–181n.5
    and bohemians, 14
    and photography, 14
overcivilization, 10–11, 130, 160n.112
overcrowding. *See* privacy among the poor

panopticism, 17–19
passions. *See* moral character
penitentiary, 17–18, 116–117, 121, 137
photography of the slums, 4, 5–6, 161n.112
    history of, 64–65, 145n.23, 174n.10, 175n.14
    in newspapers, 16, 17, 64–65, 175n.14
    and Riis, 8, 14, 17, 19, 20, 22, 61, 64–73, 86, 87, 91,
        118, 119, 145n.23, 152n.70, 174n.10,
        175nn.14–15, 177n.6, 186–187n.13
    and social reform, 65, 67, 146n.24, 174n.10,
        177n.6
picturesque representation of poverty, 16, 20, 39, 40,
        154–155n.80
    as obsolete, 87
    and Riis, 9, 16, 30, 33, 38, 61, 70, 75, 78, 81, 118,
        148n.29, 154–155n.80
Pierce, C. S., 33
poverty, culture of. *See* values of the poor, separate
Pragmatists, 33, 143n.14
pride, 5. *See also* self-esteem
    and Crane, 57, 98, 111, 126–127
    in Protestant mental philosophy, 103
    and Riis, 9, 95, 102, 115
privacy among the poor
    in charity writing, 31, 93
    and housing reform, 116
    as obstacle to spectacle, 78–79, 86, 87
    and Riis, 9, 33, 76–79, 86, 87, 116
Progressive Era, 23
    and Crane, 8, 97, 137
    and habits, 33
    and masculinity, crusade for, 149n.42
    moralities of, 137–138
    political corruption, 10

and Riis, 8, 33, 93–94, 137, 138
and social causes of individual behavior, 8, 33,
        93–94, 136–137
social reform, 10–11, 137, 149n.42
Protestant mental philosophy, 5, 7
    and Crane, 10, 97–100, 102–103, 104, 105, 106,
        124–125, 128–129
    and fiction of the slums, didactic, 42, 49
    and Riis, 10, 92–94
Protestant moral account of the poor, 3–6, 17, 137,
        139nn.1–2, 5. *See also* virtue and vice in the
        slums
    challenges to, 8, 9, 10, 14–15, 18, 20, 22, 137,
        176n.32
    by ethnography of the poor, 32–33, 39, 53,
        55–56, 93, 97
    by psychological account of the poor, 22,
        91–100, 101–102, 105, 115, 120, 124–126, 137,
        156n.100, 161n.112, 180n.5, 182n.39
    by spectacle of the poor, 62, 71–73, 75–76, 79,
        86, 120
    in charity writing, 27–38, 84, 93, 159n.112, 162nn.3,
        6, 169n.29, 181n.15
    contemporary, 4–6, 137–138, 178–179n.38
    and Crane, 8–9, 10, 14, 49, 51–53, 55–56, 57, 62–63,
        72–73, 96–102, 105, 172–174n.5, 176n.32
    in fiction of the slums, didactic, 40–49, 55–56, 96,
        99, 102, 153–154n.76, 168n.21
    and moral drama, representation of, 40–42, 48–49,
        55–56, 168nn.21, 23
    and Riis, 8–9, 14, 27–33, 62–63, 71, 72, 75–76, 77,
        81–82, 92–97, 137, 147n.26, 164n.20
Protestant morality, decline of, 6–7, 10, 15, 86,
        137–138, 143n.14, 157–161n.112
psychological account of the poor, 3–6, 150–151n.57.
        See also self-esteem
    as challenging Protestant moral account, 22,
        91–100, 101–102, 105, 115, 120, 124–126, 137,
        156n.100, 161n.112, 180n.5, 182n.39
    contemporary, 4–6, 138, 178–179n.38
    and Crane, 8, 9, 10, 22, 96–102, 105–106, 110–112,
        115–116, 121–125, 156n.100
    and mental philosophy, 5, 92–94, 97–105, 106. *See
        also* psychological morality, mental philoso-
        phy of
    and Riis, 8, 9, 22, 91–95, 102, 115–121, 137,
        156n.100, 192n.36
    and social reform, 115–121, 137, 156n.100,
        180–181n.5
    and tough, 91–97, 123–124
psychological morality. *See also* rebel morality
    contemporary, 5–7, 130–138, 157–161n.112
    and Crane, 9, 10, 22, 23, 113–114, 115–116, 121–129,
        188nn.23, 32, 37, 41
    mental philosophy of, 124–129, 188n.32
    nature of, 5, 115
    origin of, 13
    and Riis, 10, 22, 23, 115–121
    and social reform, 115–121
    and tension with Protestant morality, 6, 10, 120,
        128–129, 137–138, 188n.41

psychology, history of, 152–153n.74, 182nn.33, 35
Pulitzer, Joseph, 16

race, 4, 30, 32–33, 87, 139–140n.5. *See also* Riis, Jacob,
    and racism
rap music, 133, 135, 191n.30
realism, 143n.14. *See also* naturalism
    and aesthetics, street, 21–22
    and consumer culture, 17–22
    and Crane, 9, 143n.14, 149n.31, 153–154n.76,
        156–157n.101, 161n.112
    and disciplinary society, 17–22
    and fiction of the slums, didactic, 45
    and Protestant morality, decline of, 143n.14
rebel morality, 130. *See also* masculinity, crusade for;
    misogyny; sexual revolt
    and anger, 125–129, 188n.41
    and asceticism, 128–129, 131, 132, 189n.13
    and blacks, 130, 160n.112, 189–190n.19
    and cool, 131, 132, 133–134
    and Crane, 22–23, 121–129, 130–131, 132, 133,
        135–136, 137, 188n.23, 32, 37, 41, 189n.13
    and frontier ethics, 132, 133
    and Protestant morality, 124–129, 130–132, 134, 136,
        137
    and slums as moral inspiration, 13, 130, 132–134,
        137–138, 189–190n.19
    and vitality, 131–134, 189n.6
rich, compared to poor
    in charity writing, 37–38, 163nn.15–16
    and Riis, 37
Riis, Jacob, 7
    antecedents of, 145–146nn.23–24, 154–155n.80. *See*
        also charity writing; newspaper reporting
    The Battle with the Slum, 12, 155n.80
    biographical information concerning, 12, 151n.58
    The Children of the Poor, 66, 70, 74, 91, 95, 116, 117
    Children of the Tenements, 164n.20
    criticism of 9, 146–147n.26, 177n.6, 178n.36
    Hero Tales of the Far North, 12, 151–152nn.61–62
    How the Other Half Lives, 8, 19, 27–38, 61–73,
        75–80, 81–82, 86–88, 91–95, 115–121, 144n.21,
        146n.24, 155n.80, 156n.100, 163–164n.20,
        174–175nn.10, 14–15
    legacy of, in regards to slums, 8, 87–88, 130,
        137–138, 159n.112, 178–179n.38, 180–181n.5,
        192n.36
    The Making of an American, 12
    Out of Mulberry Street, 91, 146n.24, 164n.20
    and police reporting, 11–12, 16–17, 155n.80
    and political reform, 12, 155n.80
    prose style of, 65, 155n.80, 175n.15
    and racism, 9, 30, 63–64, 148n.29, 154n.77
    and slum clearance, 9, 40, 87, 93, 136, 148n.29
Roosevelt, Theodore
    and masculinity, 10, 20, 150n.49, 151n.60
    and Riis, 12, 146n.26, 148n.29, 151n.60

Sanborn, Alvan Francis, 40, 164n.20, 166n.7
self-discovery, 130–131, 133, 158–160n.112
self-esteem, 4–7, 10, 138, 140–143nn.9, 11–14, 160n.112

and Crane, 8, 9–10, 22, 96, 100–102, 103, 105–114,
    115–116, 121–123, 126–128, 181–182nn.26, 30,
    39, 183–185nn. 46–64, 189n.13
history of concept of, 102–105, 115, 149n.33
    in Protestant mental philosophy, 102–103, 104, 115
    and Riis, 8, 9–10, 22, 95, 102, 115–121, 159n.112
    and social reform, 4–5, 9, 116–121, 143n.9, 159n.112
    and spectacle, 110–113, 119–121, 187n.17
    and tough, 13, 22, 95–96, 115, 137, 138
Seltzer, Mark, 18–19, 145n.21, 156–157nn.100–101
sensationalism, 15, 16, 87–88. *See also* spectacle of the
    poor
sentimentalism, 10, 17, 21, 117, 137, 158n.112
    and Crane, 11, 49, 50, 73, 75, 136, 138
    and fiction of the slums, didactic, 47
    and rebel morality, 132, 134, 136
    and Riis, 62
settlement houses, 84, 152n.69, 156n.100, 179–180n.5
sexual revolt, 7, 129, 131, 132, 134–135, 136, 137,
    189–191nn.19, 27, 30
sight-seeing of the slums, 16–17, 22, 27, 34, 61, 65,
    69–71, 164n.20, 177n.6. *See also* spectacle of
    the poor
Sinclair, Upton, 40, 56, 155n.80, 167n.11, 168n.21
slang of the slums, 4, 5, 15
    and Crane, 8, 17, 74, 84, 85, 86
    and spectacle, 84
slumming parties, 15, 39, 87, 154n.78
social causes of individual behavior, 8, 140n.6
    and Crane, 8, 49, 96–97, 122, 129, 137, 156n.100
    and Progressive Era, 8, 93–94, 97, 136–137
    Protestant moral theory of, 93–94, 96–97, 136–137
    psychological theory of, 93–97, 136–137
    and Riis, 8, 32–33, 93–95, 97, 137, 156n.100
social order, theme of, 17, 31
    and Crane, 62–63, 72–73, 172–174n.5
    and Riis, 31, 62–63, 67, 68–69, 71–72, 147n.26
social protest, theme of, 17. *See also* housing condi-
    tions in the slums; working conditions in the
    slums
    and Crane, 8, 49, 62–63, 72–73, 172–174n.5
    and Riis, 8–9, 28, 40, 62–63, 67, 69, 71, 72, 91–92,
        146–147n.26, 164n.20, 177n.6, 178n.36
    and tough, 71, 91–92
social reform, 12. *See also* housing reform
    and Crane, 8, 11, 72, 172n.3
    and psychological account of the poor, 4–5, 22,
        115–121, 179n.38, 180–181n.5
    and Riis, 8–9, 11, 12, 16–17, 22, 40, 61, 75, 76, 77,
        86–88, 115–121, 137, 146–147n.26, 148n.29,
        177n.6, 178n.36
    and spectacle, 17, 87–88, 116–121, 160n.112, 179n.39
social thinking. *See* social causes of individual behavior
social welfare. *See* social reform; social work
social work, 156n.100, 179–181n.5, 192n.36
    and ethnography of the poor, 180–181n.5
    and psychological account of the poor,
        180–181n.5
    and psychological morality, 118, 137, 159n.112
soul, Crane's conception of, 9, 96, 121–123, 126–127,
    128, 130

spectacle, culture of, 17–18, 155–156n.93, 157–161n.112
  and social reform, 116–121, 160n.112
spectacle, the poor's interest in,
  and Crane, 82–85, 176–177n.4, 185n.64
  and Riis, 81–82, 83, 85, 119–120, 138, 186–187n.13
spectacle, theory of, 70–71, 176n.27
spectacle of the poor, 5–6, 8, 13, 16–17. *See also*
      ethnography of the poor
  in charity writing, 34–38
  contemporary, 5–6, 87–88, 138, 140–143nn.9, 11–13,
      178–179n.38
  and Crane, 22, 62–64, 72–73, 82–85
  critique of, 179n.38
  in nonfiction of the slums, 164n.20
  and photography, 65–72
  and Riis, 21, 22, 27, 34, 36–38, 61–72, 74–79, 81,
      86–87, 88, 119–120, 144n.20
  and traditional relationships to the poor, 20–22,
      62–63, 72–73, 74–79, 85–87, 120, 138
spectatorship, ethics of,
  and Crane, 84, 120, 188n.30
  among the middle class, 85–86, 88, 138, 160n.112
  among the poor, 82–85, 110
  and Riis, 76, 78–79
  and self-esteem, 110–113, 119–121
Stallman, R. W., 105–106, 135, 148n.27, 173n.5
Stange, Maren, 19–20, 145n.21, 150–151n.57, 161n.112
street Arabs, 37, 65, 66, 91
streets, versus home, 76, 77
Sullivan, James W., 39–40, 42, 47, 56, 96, 168n.23
surveillence. *See* disciplinary society
Susman, Warren 10, 149n.33, 160–161n.112
sweatshops. *See* working conditions in the slums
sympathy for the poor, 17. *See also* social protest,
      theme of
  and Crane, 62–63, 72–73, 172–174n.5, 176n.32
  and rebel morality, 132
  and Riis, 62–63, 67, 69, 70–72, 81–82, 86, 120,
      146–147n.26

Talmage, Thomas de Witt, 49–50, 144n.21
tenements. *See* housing reform; Riis, Jacob, and slum
      clearance
therapeutic culture. *See* consumer culture
Thomson, John, 145n.23, 174n.10
tough, 13, 117, 142n.9
  and beggar, 71, 91, 94–95
  and Crane, 13, 22, 51, 53–55, 62, 96–97, 123–124,
      127, 132, 135–136, 137
  and fiction of the slums, didactic, 40, 43, 56
  genesis of, 91–96
  and individuality, 94, 118, 119, 181n.14
  and photography, 19, 70, 91, 119
  and Riis, 9, 13, 19, 20, 22, 61, 70, 71, 91–95, 118, 119,
      137, 138, 147n.26, 181n.14
  and self-esteem, 95–96, 137, 138

tourism of the slums. *See* sight-seeing of the slums;
      spectacle of the poor
Townsend, Edward
  Chimmie Fadden, 46–47, 155n.88
  and Crane, 49, 170n.44
  A Daughter of the Tenements, 40, 43, 45–47, 48, 49,
      50, 56
Trachtenberg, Alan, 20, 66, 70, 143n.14, 145n.21,
      147n.26, 160n.112
Tuckerman, Joseph, 3, 4–5, 139nn.1–2, 5, 140n.6

underclass, 3–4, 139n.3, 140–143n.9, 178n.37, 179n.38
Upham, Thomas, 97, 102–103, 105, 115, 124–125,
      182n.33
urbanization, 6, 8, 16, 79–80

values of the poor, separate, 4, 8, 17, 88, 140–143nn.9,
      12–13, 179n.38
  in bohemian literature, 130, 132–134, 137–138,
      164n.20
  and Crane, 22, 50–57, 84–8 5, 97, 99, 127, 171n.54
  in fiction of the slums, didactic, 45–46
  and Riis, 85
Van Doren, Mark, 80–81
virtue and vice in the slums, 3, 4, 13, 14, 17. *See also*
      Protestant moral account of the poor
  in charity writing, 28–30, 35–37, 84, 93, 140n.6,
      159n.112, 162–163n.13
  and Crane, 49–52, 56, 64, 182n.39
  in fiction of the slums, didactic, 40–49, 56
  questioning of categories of, 32–33, 81–82, 91–97,
      168n.21, 180n.5, 182n.39
  and Riis, 28–30, 32, 33, 77
vulgarity, 21, 74–75, 86

war writing
  and Crane, 11, 13, 105. *See also* Crane, Stephen, *The
      Red Badge of Courage*
  and Riis, 12–13, 151–152nn.60–62
Warner, Michael, 105, 188n.32
western writing, 152n.63
  and Crane, 11, 105, 150n.49, 184n.51
  and Riis, 12–13, 151–152nn.60–62
Wiggin, Kate Douglas, 39, 46, 48, 165n.4
Wilson, William Julius, 178–179n.38
Wolfe, Tom, 131
working conditions in the slums
  in charity writing, 28–30, 162n.3
  and child labor, 66, 76, 175n.19
  and Crane, 49, 172n.5, 187n.17
  in fiction of the slums, didactic, 43–45, 168–
      169n.24
  and Riis, 28–30, 66, 67, 77

youth culture and the slums, 23, 133–136, 138,
      190nn.23–24